A Guide to Funding from

Government Departments & Agencies

SUSAN FORRESTER
RUTH PILCH

Supported by the
HOME OFFICE

DIRECTORY OF SOCIAL CHANGE

Published by
The Directory of Social Change
24 Stephenson Way
London NW1 2DP
Tel: 0171 209 5151, fax: 0171 209 5049
e-mail: info@d-s-c.demon.co.uk
from whom further copies and a full publications list are available.

The Directory of Social Change is a Registered Charity no. 800517

First published 1998

ISBN 1 900360 42 X

British Library Cataloguing in Publication Data
A catalogue record for this book is available from the British Library

Cover design by Kate Bass
Designed and typeset by Linda Parker
Printed and bound by Anthony Rowe

Other Directory of Social Change departments in London:
Courses and Conferences tel: 0171 209 4949
Charityfair tel: 0171 209 1015
Charity Centre tel: 0171 209 1015
Research tel: 0171 209 4422

Directory of Social Change Northern Office:
3rd Floor, Federation House, Hope Street, Liverpool L1 9BW
Courses and Conferences tel: 0151 708 0117
Research tel: 0151 708 0136

Contents

Acknowledgements

Particular thanks need to be given to the Voluntary and Community Unit of the Home Office for their financial support to this guide.

We would also like to give warm thanks to all those people who have helped in providing information for this guide. They are too many to name individually, but we would especially like to thank Ruth Hill and Janet Novak of the Voluntary and Community Unit.

Foreword

Paul Boateng, Minister of State at the Home Office

Welcome to this new and much needed guide. As the Minister responsible for volunteering and the voluntary and community sector, I am very pleased to see such a comprehensive and authoritative source of information on government grants. It is an important development which, in the spirit of the recently launched Compact between government and the sector, makes grant information more accessible and the application process more transparent.

The guide is a unique breakdown of some £2 billion of government support for the voluntary and community sector across the United Kingdom. The diversity of programmes and funding initiatives covered is a testament to the vitality of the sector and its importance to the delivery of key aspects of government policy. I am sure it will be valuable tool not only for voluntary and community organisations but also for government departments and their agencies when the scope and direction of funding is being considered. It should also assist the drive for more joined up thinking between departments and more joint initiatives in overlapping areas of concern — as shown for example by the work of the Social Exclusion Unit.

The Home Office is working at the heart of this government's social policy agenda. In dealing with some of society's greatest problems partnership is crucial to our work. It is at the heart of our policy for building a safe, fair and prosperous society. Grant aid is one of the most tangible ways that government departments demonstrate their commitment to this approach.

I am very grateful to Susan Forrester and her colleagues at the Directory of Social Change for all their hard work in producing this guide. It is a publication that I am sure will help voluntary and community organisations to work more effectively and develop their relationship with government.

Scope of this guide

This guide describes the funding to the voluntary sector during 1998/99 from central government departments and their agencies. These agencies include the 'arms length' governmental bodies known as NDPBs (Non-Departmental Public Bodies) and voluntary organisations administering delegated funds for government departments.

The book serves a number of roles, as a basic guide for fundraisers (particularly newcomers), as a comparative resource to other government departments, and as a broad survey of tranches of finance to which the voluntary sector has access.

Our definition of 'voluntary organisation' is inclusive, from major national bodies to local community groups. The common factors are that they are independent and self-governing, non-profit making (any profits are ploughed back), and voluntary ie. having considerable voluntary help – whether from donations, public support or unpaid trustees though many have a mainly salaried workforce.

We have aimed to outline the range of ways in which the voluntary sector receives financial support covering:

- funding programmes, directed specifically at voluntary organisations;
- funding programmes, often from NDPBs, covering a wider constituency than the voluntary sector alone;
- grants to individual voluntary organisations on an annual review basis;
- special departmental initiatives to tackle a problem and to test and pilot new approaches/methods;
- service contracts.

Service contracts occur most extensively at local authority level.

The guide does NOT cover
- the National Lottery;
- European Funding;
- local authority funding (although some time-limited exploratory programmes with a central government dimension are included).

It only lightly touches upon the arts and regional programmes. The regional tier of governmental operations is growing in strength and the focus of much funding is shifting to this level. At the time of writing many proposed structural changes were still under consultation. A brief section outlines some of the key areas.

The Landscape of Change

We have been working through 'interesting times', including devolution, regionalisation, departmental reorganisation, and the Comprehensive Spending Review. The New Deal is introducing many new measures which are relevant to this guide but which are still in preparation and undergoing consultation.

A changing landscape, though it has been particularly pronounced during 1998, is a continuous feature of government. The fact that the one of the key reference guides to government, *Vacher's Parliamentary Companion,* is reprinted every four months underlines this point.

Organisation of the Guide

The guide aims to map out the main funding sources and show them clearly within their administrative structures. Our division into departments within countries, followed by the agencies linked to these departments, obscures some funding responsibilities which are multi-country. Obviously Defence, the Foreign Office, International Development are departments with UK-wide remits. On the other hand Social Security covers mainland Britain and not Northern Ireland (and will continue to do so after devolution). But the Home Office and a few other agencies have responsiblity for certain functions which span two or sometimes three countries. These variations in remit have been shown by a symbol beside the relevant entry and also noted in the index.

For example ⓔ or (E) = England, ⓢ or (S) = Scotland, ⓦ or (W) = Wales, ⓝ or (NI) = Northern Ireland, and ⓤ or (UK) = United Kingdom.

The Entries

The names of the directorates, divisions and units etc. within departments have been given in full to clarify the shorthand acronyms. We have, for instance, spelt out SCG, CPD and CRU fully as Social Care Group, Criminal Policy Directorate and Community Relations Unit, to help newcomers develop a 'feel' for the department and its internal structure. An awareness of this kind can help trace potential contacts and other sources of funding. (A couple of amusing 'misfits' occur – in the Home Office the Voluntary and Community Unit falls within the Criminal Policy Directorate, and the Fire Safety Unit gives a water safety grant.)

Contact Names and Telephone Numbers

Readers must not be surprised if these prove to be out-of-date. Personnel changes are frequent and have occurred within the course of this research. Despite this they provide a trail to be pursued.

Seeking Information

Be clear about the questions you want to have answered. Civil servants reply helpfully to the questions asked, but rarely offer information. The replies you get depend on the questions you ask. Sometimes their understanding of their own department, let alone their division, may be limited. If the person you are talking to can't help, for whatever reason, and you want more clarification, ask for an officer with a wider brief. (See note on staff levels.) As a general rule it is more satisfactory to start higher than lower (but not too high).

Administration/Assessment

Be always aware of the autonomy of government departments and agencies. Each operates individually and the arrrangements with grant programmes vary also.

There are considerable administrative differences in the processing of applications. Many departments have a central grant unit but each will function according to the scope, size and purpose of its grant programmes. For instance the General Grant Programmes of the Voluntary and Community Unit (some 45-50 grants totalling £11.4 million in 1998/99) is serviced by a grant unit of four staff backed up by three specialist advisers with experience in the voluntary sector. In contrast the Department of Health's major programme of Section 64 funding (624 grants totalling £21.17 million 1998/99) has a grant unit of five staff and applications are farmed out to the relevant policy divisions of the department for assessment (about 120-130 grant applications to each).

Many NDPBs eg. the Rural Development Commission and the Countryside Commission (shortly to merge into a new countryside agency) and English Nature devolve grant work to their regional offices where staff members can develop closer working partnerships with local applicants.

Treasury Rules

The strictures for public accountability under Treasury Rules are common to all departments: the annual round of the financial year (April to March); accounting requirements: financial monitoring; payment in arrears; annual clawback of funding. *The Regulation Taskforce* in July 1998 pointed out areas where some common approaches and useful modifications could be made. Its recommendations are reproduced in Appendix 2. It seems that many departments are quite responsive to the Taskforce proposals but that Treasury resolve to maintain its contact is firm. It appears that the recent budget, which announced funding over a three year period is unlikely, at this stage, to lead to any relaxation of the financial reins held by the Treasury.

The annual funding cycle

Many grant programmes run to this timetable:

Sept/Autumn	Closing date for applications
Jan	Notification of awards to applicants
Feb/Mar	Programme of work agreed with applicants

Chart (1) *Annual application deadlines for grant schemes* covers those schemes where deadlines were clear at the time of editing. It shows that whilst deadlines vary, in general they are in early autumn.

New Programmes and Opportunities

Most of the administrators of grant making programmes inform their own constituency of voluntary organisations about new application rounds and new arrangements. For example the Environmental Action Fund mailed nearly 2,000 organisations with its new policies and an application pack after the ministerial announcement of its review was delayed until September 1998. However, such assistance is not common to all programmes.

Organisations new to certain fields of work must be sure to get on the mailing lists relevant to them. In addition, organisations should also be alert to check for announcements about other opportunities to work with departments on matters of mutual concern to them. These announcements are made in the specialist press and also sometimes in the national press. For example in late July 1998 the *New Deal for Lone Parents* jointly run by the DfEE and the DSS called for "proposals for pilots from organisations in the private, public and voluntary sectors including those representing ethnic minorities to test new and innovative ways to build on existing provision".

On occasions a respected voluntary organisation with a good track record is able to negotiate a special funding arrangement with the policy division of a department. Such an arrangement occurs when the voluntary organisation wishes to explore particular approaches which are in line with, and particularly important to, aspects of government policy which are in the developmental stage.

(1) Annual application deadlines for grant schemes (as at late summer 1998)

(months of the year January to December)

England / UK	J	F	M	A	M	J	J	A	S	O	N	D
Culture, Media & Sport												
The Heritage Grant Fund									■			
Education												
Adult & Community Learning Fund	■				■				■			
Pupil Motivation, Community & Business Links					■				■			
Environment												
Darwin Initiative											■	
Environmental Action Fund									■	■	■	
Single Homelessness									■	■		■
Special Grants Programme									■			
Health												
Section 64 Grants										■		
Shared Training Grant Programme										■		
Home												
Probation Unit Grants											■	
Voluntary & Community Unit									■			
International Development												
Charity Know How		■		■			■			■		
Development Awareness Fund											■	
Non-Governmental Organisations Unit											■	
Youth												
Commonwealth Youth Exchange Council										■		
National Youth Agency										■		

Annual application deadlines for grant schemes (as at late summer 1998)

(months of the year January to December)

Scotland	J	F	M	A	M	J	J	A	S	O	N	D
Agriculture												
Scottish Rural Partnership Fund, RCF											■	
Development												
Historic Scotland, archaeology									■			
Housing & Homelessness Grants									■			
Scottish Homes, Homepoint Grant											■	
Education												
Cultural Organisations Grants									■			
Health												
Health Grants										■		
Home												
Ethnic Minority Grant											■	
Social Welfare, Section 10 Grants										■		
Social Welfare, Training Grants									■			
Unemployed Voluntary Action Fund							■					

Annual application deadlines for grant schemes (as at late summer 1998)

(months of the year January to December)

Wales	J	F	M	A	M	J	J	A	S	O	N	D
Education												
National Voluntary Youth Organisations										■		
Welsh Language Board										■		
Local Government: Housing												
Home Improvement Agencies										■		
Social												
Combating Drugs & Alcohol Misuse										■		
Mental Handicap Strategy											■	
Mental Illness Strategy											■	
Older People or People with Physical/ Sensory Disabilities & their carers											■	
Support for Child & Family Services	■											
Support for Voluntary Intermediary Services									■			
Local Mental Health Grants Scheme										■		
Local Voluntary Services Scheme										■		

Annual application deadlines for grant schemes (as at late summer 1998)

(months of the year January to December)

Northern Ireland	J	F	M	A	M	J	J	A	S	O	N	D
Agriculture												
Forest Service												■
Economic												
Equal Opportunities Commission, research		■								■		
Education												
Community Relations Branch, core funding		■			■							
Youth Service Branch, minor grants			■									
Finance												
NI Community Relations Council:												
• Core funding												■
• Media grants										■		
Health												
Health grants											■	
Community Volunteering Scheme											■	

What Makes a Good Application?

Advice from an Adviser and a Grant Recipient

Readers will note the similar points made by the both adviser and the grant recipient. The importance of these points apparently cannot be stressed enough, as too many applicants appear to disregard them.

Making the best case

Common mistakes and tips on how to avoid them

from Janet Novak, Adviser at the Voluntary and Community Unit at the Home Office

Getting a grant from any funding source is difficult. Knowing the funder's ways of doing things is a key factor in surviving the agony of waiting and in winning through. I have been an adviser at the Voluntary and Community Unit at the Home Office for a number of years and during that time I have advised on and seen hundreds of applications. Large grants, small grants, for three years or for one, core, project and capital grants, even applications to run conferences – whatever you can think of they have crossed my desk.

So what are my top tips, and what might tip the balance in your favour in the competition for limited funds?

Top tips

Get to know as much as you can about the funder's priorities. Most government funders have written criteria for their grants, VCU certainly does. But these are often broadly drawn. In a given year there may be particular things which are nearer the top of the agenda. Use whatever opportunity you can to find out, *not* guess what these might be. Contact others who have got grants, use the advisers at VCU, or ask the civil servants. Be intelligent about what you read in the paper, hear on the radio or see in consultation documents. What are they telling you about the Government's priorities?

Not understanding the criteria and priorities or just plain ignoring them will not help you. Most of the applications we received in one year did not meet our criteria. That was a waste of time for everyone concerned.

The VCU is a bit different because it has advisers who can help you think about your application. Not seeking advice is a real mistake. One year I saw an application which came fresh to us. No-one had talked to us about it. As I read about this organisation I became more and more interested. It looked like a new way of tackling some of the issues we are concerned with. Finally I got to what they wanted. They wanted funding for one member of staff to carry out a very specific function. Had they discussed their application with me I would have said 'Don't apply for this.

It won't meet our criteria. It's not a priority for us, but, on the other hand, your organisation might have a lot to teach us and the rest of the voluntary sector. Let's see what I can advise you.' Perhaps they and VCU lost an opportunity there.

Listen very, very hard to the advice you are given. The language of the civil service is careful. People often want to help but they are constrained by the nature of their work.

Assume little knowledge. Explain. Describe. You live with the issues for your work all the time. We don't. Even if we have funded you before or for a long time, the people in the Unit might be new. Every applicant believes in themselves. Every applicant believes that their work is vital. Many then forget to explain why their work is needed because it seems so obvious. It isn't.

Demonstrate you know your field. Of course you know the work of your organisation but do you know who else is doing the same or similar work? How is your work different from theirs? Are you prepared to work with them? Remember innovation for you or your town or region may not be innovation to a funder with a national perspective.

Don't try it on. It's obvious when an applicant is pretending that theirs is a fresh proposal from nowhere, when actually it desperately needs match funding. We might want to match it if it fits our criteria. We might not as well. If the criteria include active partnerships don't pretend that your other funders are partners if they are not really. We can spot it and it doesn't help. Don't pretend you are about one thing when you are about another. An application for work with older people which includes child rearing classes might seem a bit obvious but it has been done. Simply mentioning the buzz words from the information we send won't do either.

Don't make assumptions about your contacts. Memories of the very senior, very slight quiet female civil servant come to my mind. People would ignore her and talk to the tall noticeable man by her side – never checking who the quiet lady was. On the other hand the quiet junior official may have a key role to play in advising on interpretation of criteria. The key is to find out who does what and what role they play.

Fill the form in properly. To some it even has to be said, don't assume you don't have to fill in the application form at all just because, say, you have had an advisory meeting. Be sure to give yourself enough time to fill it in. Rushing through this work at the last minute shows. If the need within your proposal is great, then answer that need by giving the time necessary to try and get the money to do the work. Remember everyone says the same to a funder – no time/ no money /great need.

Take it from me, big or small – no organisation is safe from failing to pay attention to criteria, priorities, application forms and advice, misunderstanding the process, forgetting deadlines, making assumptions about knowledge and trying it on!

What makes the difference?

When all is said and done there are usually too many applications which make the grade. What helps in the final assessment that draws the lucky few to the top of the list?

For VCU, the balance of our portfolio of grants is often important both in itself and in relation to the significance of our priorities. What do I mean by this? Our main grants cover a range of areas focusing primarily on infrastructure support for voluntary organisations, the promotion and support of volunteering and community development. Within these broad areas we try and ensure there is no duplication, that funded organisations are playing distinctive roles and complement each other. We also try and make sure that the balance between the three areas matches our priorities. In a way there is nothing you can do about this. We can't tell you in advance either because applications are unsolicited. It just boils down to the fact that the policy area you are applying within is a key factor to your chances of success in getting a grant (assuming everything in your application is on course).

That being said, applications which are thought through stand out. As do applicants who know where they are going during the funding period, cost their work effectively, know the field they are working in and have thought about the consequences of the grant coming to an end.

Particularly attractive are real partnerships and coalitions which bring the strengths of several organisations together. It is also really helpful when applicants can offer us honest choices. So for example we can choose to fund a whole programme or an equally valid 'stand alone' part, or we can choose to fund a stage in the process envisaged. This means that limited money can be used effectively with real benefit to all concerned. Often applicants who can suggest this approach also demonstrate that they have thought things through. They have planned what they want to do and it shows.

It's hard to give readers fail-safe advice. Fundamentally you need to know where your proposed funder is coming from, what has been funded in the past, what's new in the policy and practice field for the funder, what sorts of money are likely to be available. Getting that right is demanding for the applicant and entails much more than simply filling in a form neatly.

So you get the grant...

Anything to say about this phase? Yes. Treat your funder with respect. Return the reports and information asked for on time. Read the grant conditions. I am constantly surprised by how many organisations clearly do not do this. Not surprised – shocked. If you get the reporting relationship right you can then move on to the relationship that counts for your work – a relationship that influences the thinking and policies of the funder.

Advice from a grant recipient

The following advice accompanied a call by the Department of Health to applicants for funding during 1999/00 under Section 64 of the Health Services and Public Health Act 1968.

This major funding programme of some £21 million a year invites voluntary organisations in England which operate on a national scale to apply for these grants. Its aims are to award grants which take forward the department's objectives by drawing on the expertise and initiative of voluntary organisations, and in doing so help to sustain and develop a healthy voluntary sector (see entry for full details).

DIAL UK, the national organisation for the DIAL network of disability advice centres, has received a number of Section 64 grants over recent years. Grants under the scheme have enabled the organisation to develop a 'tool kit' for DIAL advice centres, and to spread their support around the network in the form of telephone helplines, on-site consultancies, and training courses. Most recent grants will help with the setting up of new DIAL advice centres and with developing quality standards.

DIAL UK puts their success with Section 64 down to four things.

Firstly, they place emphasis on demonstrating in their applications a good fit between the purpose of the grant and the department's objectives. DIAL UK shows clearly how its work furthers the department's key objectives relating to disabled people and independent living.

Secondly, they realise the department is looking for value for money when choosing between grant applications. 'We understand the department receives many more good quality applications than it is able to fund. So we are always careful to show that DoH money goes much further with an organisation like ours which attracts volunteer help and non-statutory funding from charitable trusts and companies.'

Thirdly, because section 64 funding is targeted at work of national significance, it is important that the results of grant awards will have widespread effect. 'For DIAL UK this is fairly easy to demonstrate as there are over 100 DIAL advice centres, serving 200,000 people a year.'

Finally, DIAL UK puts some of its success down to building up confidence within the department in their ability to deliver. 'Track records are built slowly by showing that you've done what you said you would do – and making clear the knock-on benefits of your work. Delivering progress reports on time is important but it also helps to send an occasional letter between reports, especially if something good – or bad – has happened. It pays to be honest about failures, so that you will be believed when things have gone really well.'

A Short Introduction to Civil Service Job Titles

A Civil Servant Writes

There was a time (around the late 80s) when there were standard grades or levels that applied right across the Civil Service, so you could know whom you were dealing with. The Permanent Secretary (the top civil servant in any major department) was a Grade 1; a Deputy Secretary was a Grade 2; an Under Secretary (who, just to make it easy, was known in some historic departments as a Permanent, or Deputy, or Assistant Under-Secretary of State) was a Grade 3. And then there was Grade 5, previously called Assistant Secretary, Grade 7 (previously Principal); followed by, in descending order, Senior Executive Office (SEO); Higher Executive Officer (HEO); Executive Officer (EO) and Administrative Assistant.

Since 1996 departments have been free to make their own grades and job titles, though the old terminology persists in some places. The idea is to help each department create a management structure that makes sense for its particular business, instead of being locked into an old-fashioned, rigid, military-style hierarchy. The trouble is that it does make it difficult to know your way around – even for insiders.

The result is that departments are moving to a rather more varied grading structure, and confusingly different use of apparently standard titles such as 'Director'. To make it worse, many of the guide books, even the department's own) still use some of the old titles or grade numbers (see Table). (For the curious: Grades 4 and 6 were reserved for certain specialist areas; Grade 4 has now been entirely delayered, though some specialists with relatively small scale management responsibilities, such as economists, statisticians and lawyers may still be referred to as 'Grade 6s'.)

The only fixed points are the Permanent Secretary, and the line draw below the former G5: above the line everyone is in the Senior Civil Service (SCS) – a top cadre of about 3,000 across the Civil Service (now about 460,000 strong).

Since there is no longer any simple answer, you really have to use your wits to guide you, though the table below may help. Anyone wanting to plug into the government machine will have to research each department. The best way to look up the department concerned is in the *Civil Service Yearbook*, published by the Stationery Office, and CD-ROM (and also available on the Internet at www.civil-service.co.uk). This shows that each division or unit in a department, with a brief description of its work and managers within it.

If in doubt about whom to contact, go up a level first – but don't try going to the very top because they probably won't know! Usually if you explain who you are, and what you need you will find people will try to be helpful, provided you don't imply that they are all tea-drinkers or idiots (serious guidance from an affronted idiot!). Explain what you need to know and why you want the information and be as specific as you can. If first attempts don't work, see if there is an enquiry point. The switch board may suggest a place to start, or the library may be able to provide the information you want or, in some cases, you may be able to approach the press office, because you are writing a report, and so on. But please remember that government departments are big, complicated organisations, who need to be helped to be helpful.

Civil Service Job Titles

The following table gives an approximate guide.

Old Title	Grade Number	Present equivalent
Permanent Secretary (or Permanent Under-Secretary of State)	G1	Still called Permanent Secretary
Deputy Secretary (or Deputy Under-Secretary of State)	G2	In some cases Director-General Others still Deputy Secretary
Under Secretary (or Under Secretary of State)	G3	In some cases Director
Assistant Secretary	G5	Elsewhere Deputy Director In some, Deputy Director or Director; Elsewhere Team Leader or Head of Group

All of the above are members of the Senior Civil Service.

Senior Principal	G6	All these have almost infinite variations
Principal	G7	of title. In some departments the old
Senior Executive Officer	SEO	grade numbers persist. In others they
Higher Executive Office	HEO	will be Band, or Range A, B C. In other
Executive Officer	EO	places they will have job titles such as
Administrative Officer	AO	Policy Adviser, Manager of Unit, Team
Administrative Assistant	AA	Member, Support Staff.

Analysis of funding

Background

The guide covers the funding to the voluntary sector from 16 government departments, including the Scottish, Welsh and Northern Ireland Offices, and of over 50 agencies related to them.

Unfortunately we did not have the advantage of being able to work using the results of an up-to-date Parliamentary Question (PQ). This is the annual survey of funding to the voluntary sector usually carried out by the Voluntary and Community Unit, or its equivalent. The most recent survey covered 1994/95. The PQ is resuming in 1998 after a three year gap and will cover all the three financial years up to 1997/98. PQ survey contacts with individual departments started in July 1998, close to the completion of our main work on this guide. As a result we have been unable to compare our findings with the PQ.

A recent PQ survey would have been an interesting source of statistical comparison and would, maybe, have made for more useful and helpful responses from some sections of some departments. Occasionally we met a distinct lack of helpfulness (in marked contrast to the great majority of respondents who have been most cooperative).

We have had the opportunity to look at the funding we have identified and to make some observations to give the voluntary sector some ideas about the relative scale of funding to different areas of work.

Funding by grant programmes targeted specifically at the voluntary sector

Only the funding programmes administered by government departments and agencies and *targeted specifically at voluntary organisations alone* could be quantified with certainty. The grant officers in many NDPBs, where funding programmes are open to a wider constituency than the voluntary sector, were unwilling, or unable, to give estimates of the proportion of their funding which reached the voluntary sector.

Funding programmes targeted at the voluntary sector throughout the UK totalled over £2.1 billion in 1998/99. The pie-chart (2) splits this total funding into three sectors. This shows the huge predominance of funding for housing, with the funding to the four national arts councils similar in size to the funding

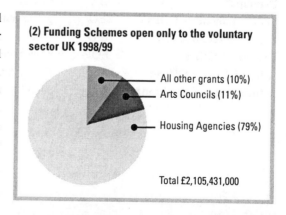

(2) Funding Schemes open only to the voluntary sector UK 1998/99

All other grants (10%)
Arts Councils (11%)
Housing Agencies (79%)

Total £2,105,431,000

to 'All other grants' ie. all other funding programmes open only to voluntary organisations.

The following table gives the breakdown of the £2 billion showing the proportions which derive specifically from the Welsh, Scottish and Northern Ireland Offices. Departments with UK-wide and multi country remits are grouped with those covering England. These handle the lion's share of funding specifically open to the voluntary sector totalling £1.67 billion.

Total Funding – 1998/99
by country remit of departments

	£'000	%
UK-wide remit + England	1,676,469	80
Scotland	212,989	10
Wales	135,536	6
N I	80,437	4
TOTAL UK	**2,105,431**	**100**

(Further analysis and information about the funding programmes from the Scottish, Welsh and Northern Ireland Offices is placed in the introduction to the sections devoted to funding in Scotland, Wales and Northern Ireland.)

The total funding UK-wide and England is also split into three broad sectors. Pie-chart (3) shows how funding from the Housing Corporation accounts for well over three quarters of the total funding for England/UK. It also shows that the size of funding to the Arts Council of England (and thereby

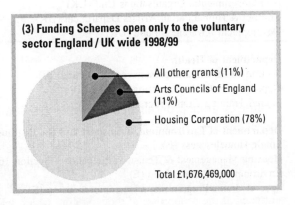

(3) Funding Schemes open only to the voluntary sector England / UK wide 1998/99

All other grants (11%)
Arts Councils of England (11%)
Housing Corporation (78%)

Total £1,676,469,000

also to the 10 Regional Arts Boards) is similar to the funding for 'All other grants' ie. programmes open only the voluntary sector (11% each).

Chart (4) breaks down 'All other grants' (totalling £168.5 million) in the pie-chart. It shows the different contributing departments and the relative proportions of the funding which they made available in programmes aimed exclusively at the voluntary sector in 1998/99.

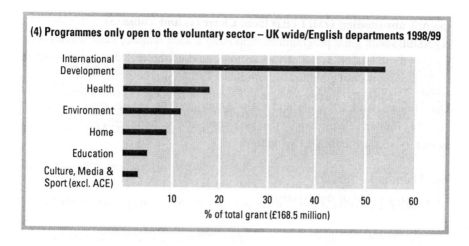

(4) Programmes only open to the voluntary sector – UK wide/English departments 1998/99

% of total grant (£168.5 million)

The detailed figures are as follows:

Table (5)

UK wide and England

Departmental grant programmes specifically for voluntary organisations – 1998/99

(agency administered schemes excluded)

	£'000	%
Department for International Development		
Non-Governmental Organisations Unit (UK)	63,919	
Conflict & Humanitarian Affairs Department (UK)	25,800	
Development Awareness Fund (UK)	1,500	
	91,219	**54**
Department of Health		
Section 64 (health and personal social service) (E)	21,173	
Opportunities for Volunteering Scheme (E)	9,100	
Shared Training Grant Programme (E)	150	
	30,423	**18**
Department of Environment, Transport and the Regions		
Single Homelessness (E)	8,100	
Housing Management & Tenant Participation – Section 16 (E)	5,175	
Environmental Action Fund (E)	4,190	
Special Grants Programme, regeneration/housing (E)	1,287	
	18,752	**11**
Home Office		
Voluntary and Community Unit:		
General Grants (UK, but mainly E)	11,400	
Volunteering Section (E)	2,759	
	14,159	**9**
Department of Education		
Section 64 – Early Years Division (E)	760	
Adult and Community Learning Fund (E)	5,000	
National Voluntary Youth Organisations (E)	3,250	
	9,010	**5**
Culture, Media and Sport		
Heritage Grant Fund (E)	546	
Pairing Scheme, ABSA (E,S,W)	4,450	
	4,996	**3**
TOTAL	**168,500**	

Significant funding OMITTED from Chart (4) and Table (5)

1) NDPBs with grant programmes supporting a wide range of beneficiaries often in the public as well as the private sectors could not be included in this analysis as their proportion of grant-aid to the voluntary sector was not consistently supplied. (This is a particular instance where the results of a recent PQ could have assisted our review.) Such major NDPBs/agencies include: English Heritage; British Council; Countryside Commission; English Nature; Forest Authority; Rural Development Commission.

2) Annual grant-in-aid to certain key voluntary sector organisations, many originally set up via governmental initiatives (see list and graph below).

3) Major regional/local programmes such as the Single Regeneration Budget.

Annual grants-in-aid to voluntary organisations outside competitive programmes

It is also of interest to look at those grants to voluntary organisations made on a regular, annual review basis outside the competitive arrangements for funding programmes. These totalled **over £218 million** in 1998/99, £50 million more than the competitive funding programmes listed above.

These are generally referred to as grants-in-aid. The distinction between grants and grants-in-aid is not always clear even within the Civil Service. **Grants-in-aid** tend to be on a continuing basis to bodies towards their operational costs. These organisations are closely linked to particular government policies and interests and many have owed their genesis as voluntary organisations to joint initiatives arising between government departments and/or their agencies and voluntary sector interests.

Chart (6) shows this by department and Table (7) gives a detailed breakdown showing the grant recipients. Over half the total amount (53%) was given as grant-in-aid to the Independent Living Funds by the Department of Social Security. Three

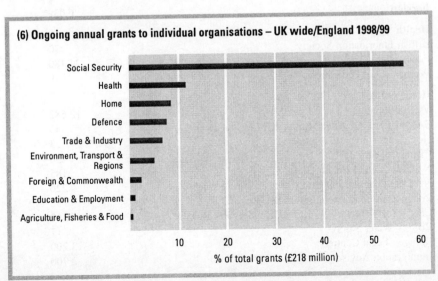

(6) Ongoing annual grants to individual organisations – UK wide/England 1998/99

% of total grants (£218 million)

grants of over £10 million each were awarded to: the Family Fund Trust by the Department of Health, Victim Support by the Home Office and the National Association of CABx by the Department of Trade and Industry.

Most of this funding is given to the work of organisations which are themselves funding bodies, providing financial and other support to people and young children with physical problems, such as Independent Living Funds, Motability and the Family Fund Trust.

Table (7)

Grant-in-aid outside Funding Programmes and Special Initiatives – 1998/99

Department	£'000
MAFF	
Farming and Wildlife Advisory Group	259
National Federation of Young Farmers' Clubs	36
Defence	16,443*
DfEE	
Lifelong learning (7 organisations including National Institute for Adult Continuing Education (NIACE) – 400)	559
Pre-Retirement Association	85
Further Education for disabled people:	
SKILL: National Bureau for Students with Disabilities	86
View	4
DETR	
Encams (Keep Britain Tidy/Going for Green)	3,697
Groundwork	6,675
Community Transport Association	70
Mobility Roadshows	70
Royal Society for the Prevention of Accidents (RoSPA)	260
Medical Commission on Accident Prevention	8
Foreign	6,039*
Health	
British Fluoridation Society	70
Family Fund Trust	24,180
Women's Aid Federation	49
Home Office	
Victim Support	12,682
SAMM (Support After Murder & Manslaughter)	43
Homestart – juvenile offenders	23
Crime Concern	750
NACRO Mental Health Unit	185
NACRO Prisons Link Unit (from Prison Service)	226
Prisoners Abroad (from Prison Service)	85
CSV – for Voluntary Work by Offenders Pre-Release	150
RoSPA Water Safety	17
Refugee Legal Centre	3,200
Immigration Advisory Service	2,700

Social Security

Independent Living Funds	115,500
Motability (2 grants)	7,690
BLESMA	10

Trade & Industry

RoSPA (home safety)	170
National Association of CABx	14,416
Citizens' Advice Scotland	1,455

* The breakdown for the grant totals from the Department of Defence and the Foreign Office is given in the entries. Many of their large grants are made on a regular annual basis whilst others are contractual arrangements. However, in the case of these departments funding programmes as such are not set up and most grants appear to be made as a result of individual approaches.

UK-WIDE, ENGLAND & REGIONAL

Contents

The indented entries relate to annual grant-in-aid made outside grant programmes and other contract initiatives.

(E) MINISTRY OF AGRICULTURE, FISHERIES AND FOOD (MAFF)

Nobel House, 17 Smith Square
London SW1P 3JR

Tel: 0171-238 3000; Fax: 0171-238 6241
E-mail: helpline@inf.maff.gov.uk

The Ministry of Agriculture, Fisheries and Food (MAFF) supports a small number of national voluntary bodies with concerns close to its own objectives.

Grants to Voluntary Bodies – 1997/98

Conservation and Rural Development Division

Farming and Wildlife Advisory Group (FWAG). A number of FWAG's farm conservation advisers are supported with services in kind including professional advice, and free office accommodation in addition to core funding grant-aid and an annual subscription (£259,000).
Budget officer: Frances Radcliffe, Room 111
Tel: 0171-238 5668; Fax: 0171-238 6126

Agricultural Resources and Better Regulation Division

National Federation of Young Farmers' Clubs, towards its agricultural education activities (£36,000).
Budget officer: Geoff Webdale, Room 718
Tel: 0171-238 5755; Fax: 0171-238 6553

Applications: Voluntary bodies should contact the MAFF division relevant to their work about potential funding where there is mutual benefit. This should be done at least nine months in advance of the time when a grant is required.

Conservation Grant Schemes

> **Grant total:**   £71,068,000 (1998/99 estimate)
>   £58,396,207 (1997/98)

These substantial schemes are directed mainly, but not always exclusively, at farmers. Charities and voluntary bodies which own and maintain farmland are eligible to apply.

Relative Size of Grant Schemes - 1997/98

	£'000	% of total
Environmentally Sensitive Areas	32,982	56
Countryside Stewardship	14,652	25
Nitrate Sensitive Areas (NSAs)	4,600	8
Farm Woodland Premium	3,177	5.4
Habitat Scheme: Water Fringe and Saltmarsh	1,790	3
Organic Aid Scheme	850	1.4
Moorland Scheme	170	0.3
Farm Waste Grant Scheme	100	0.1
Countryside Access Scheme	80	0.1

Environmentally Sensitive Areas Scheme (£32,982,000 1997/98)
To help conserve areas of high landscape, historic or wildlife value which are vulnerable to changing farming practices via voluntary management agreements.

Countryside Stewardship (£14,652,000 1997/98)
For conservation and enhancement of some key English landscapes, features and habitats, and where appropriate, public access to them. Targets include the countryside around towns including community forests, traditional field boundaries, traditional orchards, historic landscapes, old meadows and pastures, coasts, uplands, watersides, lowland heath and chalk and limestone grassland.

Farm Woodland Premium Scheme (£3,177,000 1997/98)
Operates throughout the UK and encourages the planting of new woods on currently productive agricultural land. These grants are additional to the Forestry Authority's Woodland Grant Scheme (see separate entry). A single application can be made for both. Packs are available from the Forestry Authority Conservancy offices.

Nitrate Sensitive Areas (NSAs) (£4,600,000 1997/98)
For farmers in NSAs who reduce nitrate leaching and in doing so help protect drinking water.

Farm Waste Grant Scheme (£100,000 1997/98)
To help farmers in Nitrate Vulnerable Zones improve their farm waste facilities.

Habitat Scheme: Water Fringe Areas and Saltmarsh (£1,790,000 1997/98)
Incentives to manage land to create or improve wildlife habitats.

Organic Aid Scheme (£850,000 1997/98)
For farmers wishing to convert in accordance with the rules of the UK Register of Organic Food Standards. *These grants are to double in size – announcement July 1998.*

Moorland Scheme (£170,000 1997/98)
For upland farmers outside ESAs who want to reduce stocking density and manage their land to improve the upland moorland environment, especially heather moorland.

Countryside Access Scheme (£80,000 1997/98)
Aims to increase opportunities for public access on land which is in the guaranteed set-aside option of the Arable Area Payments Scheme (AAPS) for a period of 5 years and is additional to those payments.

In 1998, MAFF launched a pilot *Arable Stewardship* scheme in East Anglia and the West Midlands to address the decline of wildlife on arable land. Farmers will be able to apply for aid in return for following specific land management options designed to benefit wildlife.

Free conservation advice is available and a farm visit will be made on request by a conservation adviser either from ADAS or FWAG (funded by MAFF or part funded by MAFF and DETR, respectively). Free visits are not available to farmers who have received free advice on the same subjects from either ADAS or FWAG within the previous three years.

For more information on these schemes or to apply for a free conservation visit contact your local MAFF Regional Service Centre.

Anglia - Beds, Cambs, Essex, Herts, Norfolk, Suffolk
Tel: 01223-462727; Fax: 01223-455652

Carlisle - Cumbria, Lancs, Northumberland, Tyne & Wear
Tel: 01228-523400; Fax: 01228-640205

Nottingham - Derby, Leics, Lincs, Northamptonshire, Notts, Rutland
Tel: 0115-9291191; Fax: 0115-9294886

Reading - Berks, Bucks, E & W Sussex, Hampshire, Isle of Wight, Kent, Gtr London, Oxfordshire, Surrey
Tel: 0118-9581222; Fax: 0118-9392198

Bristol - Bath, Dorset, Somerset, Wilts
Tel: 0117-9591000; Fax: 0117-9505392

Crewe - Cheshire, Gtr Manchester, Merseyside, Shrops, Staffs
Tel: 01270-654000; Fax: 01270-669494

Exeter - Devon, Cornwall, Isles of Scilly
Tel: 01392-447400; Fax: 01392-410936

Northallerton - Cleveland, Durham, Humberside, Yorks
Tel: 01609-773751; Fax: 01609-780179

Worcester - Glos, Hereford, Worcester, Warwickshire, W Midlands
Tel: 01905-763355; Fax: 01905-763180

DEPARTMENT FOR CULTURE, MEDIA AND SPORT

> **2-4 Cockspur Street, London SW1Y 5DH**
>
> **Tel: 0171-211 6000; Fax: 0171-211 6032**

The department is responsible for government policy on the arts, sport, the National Lottery, libraries, museums and galleries, broadcasting, film, the music industry, press freedom and regulation, the historic environment and tourism.

Contents

Culture, Media & Sport
Heritage Grant Fund

Related Agencies
English Heritage
National Heritage Memorial Fund
Arts Council of England
Pairing Scheme, ABSA
British Council Arts Division (see International)
Visiting Arts (see International)
Regional Arts Boards (see under regional)
English Sports Council
Sportsmatch

The department publishes a useful guide to its organisation and the contact points within its group structure. It also includes a list of all the public bodies it funds. The following note highlights the structural links with organisations of particular interest to this guide (as at summer 1998). Consultations were taking place in late summer/early autumn 1998 about proposals for considerable administrative changes to and amalgamations of related bodies which are financially dependent on the department.

Arts, Buildings and Creative Industries Group

- **Arts Division** responsibilities include: support to the Arts Council of England, the Crafts Council, regional arts boards; arts development including the Pairing Scheme.
- **Buildings, Monuments and Sites Division** responsibilities include: support to the Heritage Grant Fund, the National Heritage Memorial Fund and the Churches Conservation Trust.
- **Creative Industries Unit** responsibilities include: the establishment of National Endowment for Science, Technology and the Arts (NESTA).

Libraries, Galleries and Museums Group

Responsibilities include sponsorship of:
- British Library;
- other major national institutions, eg. the British Museum, Tate Gallery, National Gallery, National Portrait Gallery;
- Museums and Galleries Commission;
- education matters including Area Museums Councils;
- independent and university museums and volunteering.

Broadcasting and Media Group

Responsibilities include grant-in-aid to the British Film Institute and the National Film and Television School, funding for British Screen and European Co-Production Fund.

Sport, Tourism, Millennium & NLCB/NOF Groups Group

Responsibilities include:
- funding of UK and English Sports Councils and Sportsmatch;
- sponsorship of and policy on the National Lotteries Charities Board and the establishment of the New Opportunities Fund Unit.

Proposed Structural changes

Consultations during summer/autumn 1998 re grant-aided bodies

Along with the announcement of increased funding for three years (1999 - 2002) resulting from the Comprehensive Spending Review, the department produced a series of consultation papers on proposals to "streamline quangos and cut bureaucracy". These included proposals to create three new bodies which would:
- amalgamate the work of the Arts Council of England and the Crafts Council;
- incorporate the Museums & Galleries Commission and the Library and Information Commission;
- undertake all aspects of film development from education to commercial production.

Another major proposed change was an increased emphasis on regional bodies and the development of *regional cultural bodies*, covering the arts, the built heritage, modern architecture, museums and libraries. "The expectation is that these new bodies would in time exercise executive functions for grant-in-aid and lottery money and might be – for the cultural field – the equivalent of Regional Development Agencies, working alongside RDAs and Regional Chambers."

Ⓔ Heritage Grant Fund

3rd Floor, 2-4 Cockspur Street
London SW1Y 5DH

> **Grant total: £546,000 (1996/97 also in 1997/98 and 1998/99)**

The Heritage Grant Fund (HGF) of the Department of Culture, Media and Sport assists voluntary organisations in *England* whose activities further its own policy objectives for the historic environment, including landscape. Normally only organisations providing national coverage are considered for grant although "local projects providing an exemplar of good practice with potential for wider application" are also considered.

The HGF does not support activities covered by other DNH funding, including grants for capital projects such as repairs to historic buildings and monuments from English Heritage, and the museums and galleries funding available from the Museum and Galleries Commission and the Museums and Galleries Improvement Fund.

Two main types of grant are given:
- project grants for innovatory or experimental projects;
- management grants to help meet administrative or start up costs.

Grants for 1998/99 were offered for one year, with those for future years dependent on the department's Spending Review. The priorities for funding in 1998/99 were for projects:
- identifying and recording neglected aspects of the historic environment;
- promoting high standards in conservation practice;
- promoting understanding and enjoyment of the historic environment and widening access for all;
- promoting good maintenance for buildings at risk;
- promoting conservation through the planning system.

Grants have ranged between £2,400 and £62,000. They are intended to provide support towards revenue costs. Grants are normally limited to 50% of costs, but may be tapered to reduce the percentage of the costs met by grant in later years. A total of 31 awards were made in 1998/99 to voluntary sector organisations including:

Civic Trust, for a programme of free public access to heritage properties over a weekend in September 1998 (£62,000);

Architectural Heritage Fund, towards the work of a development officer to help assist building preservation trusts (£30,000);

Association of Small Towns and Villages, to help set up a network of local societies to share information about historic buildings (£10,000).

Applications: Application forms and full grant guidelines are available. Closing date for applications is the end of October. Approach the contacts for more detailed advice.

Contacts: Margaret Prythergch, Tel: 0171-211 2097; Linda Godfrey, Tel: 0171-211 2103; Tania Field, Tel: 0171-211 2102

The Heritage Grant Fund is to transfer to English Heritage in time for the funding round beginning April 2000 (applications solicited autumn 1999).

English Heritage

23 Savile Row, London W1X 2HE

Tel: 0171-973 3000; Fax: 0171-973 3001
E-mail: www.english-heritage.org.uk

> Grant schemes: £36.5 million (1997/98)
> £40.8 million (1996/97)

These figures contrast with £99.1 million in 1993/94.

English Heritage (EH) is the national body created by Parliament in 1984 and charged with the protection of the country's historic environment and with promoting the public's access to, and enjoyment and understanding of it. It is the government's official adviser on all matters concerning heritage conservation and is funded by the Department for Culture, Media and Sport (DCMS) to run its grant programmes.

It is known that EH will assume responsibility for the Heritage Grant Fund (see separate entry) in time for the funding round beginning 1st April 2000.

English Heritage has a number of grant giving programmes.

Historic Buildings and Monuments Grants

These grants help with repairs to the most significant of England's historic sites and buildings. Applications are welcome from domestic, agricultural and industrial structures and archaeological sites, as well as from grander and more famous places. Assessment will take into account the architectural and historic importance of the property/site, the urgency and nature of the work, and the need for financial help. Priority is given to buildings at risk and emergency repair work. In general, only properties which are legally protected as scheduled monuments or listed buildings will qualify.

In addition, a special grant scheme operates in London concentrating on Grade 11 listed buildings at risk. During 1998 new 'fast track' and emergency works grant schemes will be introduced. These will target resources at smaller historic buildings needing strategic repairs and those that have suffered from disasters such as fire and flood.

Grants are made for major structural repairs to an agreed standard of materials and workmanship. Grants are occasionally offered for repairs to interior features including the conservation of objects, such as sculpture. Grants are not available for routine maintenance, alterations, conversions, improvements or demolition.

The demand for grant exceeds the funds available. Each application is carefully assessed and the grant rate varies to suit particular circumstances. Recipients are expected to ensure an acceptable level of public access and that the public investment in the property is properly protected.

Management agreements can be offered to occupiers of monuments in farmland and these usually include small grants. The amount paid is based on the monument's acreage, but capital costs can also be met.

Joint Church Grants Scheme

This scheme, started in autumn 1995, is run jointly with the Heritage Lottery Fund to help with repair to historic religious buildings used for public worship by any denomination. Where a church has moral objections to receiving Lottery Funds a 'traditional' English Heritage Church grant may be possible.

The criteria for funding again rely on historic importance, urgency and financial need. Some 'improvements' such as lighting, heating and toilets may be eligible in certain circumstances. Where funding is sought for other than structural works, some benefit to the wider public normally has to be shown. Repairs to bells and pipe organs have their own special assessment arrangements.

In addition to the Joint Churches Scheme, English Heritage gives grants to cathedrals each year.

Survey Grants

Grants are offered towards the cost of archaeological investigation and recording before the unavoidable destruction of important ancient monuments and sites.

Projects are selected for assistance according to the criteria used to define a monument as being of national importance and thematic strategies are discussed with the period societies and other specialist groups.

Applications: From January 1999 grants will operate through the nine regional offices. Information on grants and application forms can be obtained by calling the relevant regional office telephone number listed below. There are no specific deadlines; proposals are reviewed throughout the year. The annual report, other literature and information on national programmes are available from the English Heritage head office.

All numbers start with 0845-3010 then are followed by the three numbers below:
North East - 001;
North West and Merseyside - 002;
Yorkshire and The Humber - 003;
West Midlands - 004;

East Midlands - 005;
Eastern Region - 006;
South West - 007;
South East - 008;
London - 009.

The National Heritage Memorial Fund

7 Holbein Place, London SW1W 8NR

Tel: 0171-591-6000; Fax: 0171-591 6001

Grant total:	£4 million (2000/01)
	£3 million (1999/00)
	£2 million (1998/99)
	£5 million (1997/98)

The National Heritage Memorial Fund (NHMF), funded annually by the Department of Culture, Media and Sport, was initially funded by the sale of land compulsorily purchased for military reasons in wartime. The fund's role is to protect land, buildings, objects and collections which are of outstanding interest and are important to the national heritage.

The NHMF became the national distributor of the Heritage Lottery Fund which transformed this small organisation in terms of its size, powers and responsibilities. Now the two operations are more clearly divided. The NHMF still carries out its original functions and is able in an emergency to move with great rapidity. The government's grant-in-aid has reduced considerably over the past years (from £12 million for most years before 1996/97, down to £5 million for 1997/98).

Grants and loans are provided for buying items which:
■ are at risk of being sold abroad, developed, damaged or lost;
■ have a clear memorial link.

Funding has been provided for land, buildings, works of art, museum collections, manuscripts and items of transport and industrial history. It also provides grants and loans to maintain and preserve most of these items.

Applications should *only be made as a last resort*, after all other possible sources of funding have been tried. The fund will only pay for the total cost of a project in exceptional cases.

Projects, whether large or small, will only be considered if *all* the following points apply.

- projects to buy, maintain or preserve land, buildings, objects or collections of outstanding interest and importance to the national heritage;
- projects based in the UK;
- projects which have already received financial help from other sources of funding but which need more money to be finished off or projects for which no other funding is available;
- projects to which the public will have access, unless public access might reduce the value of the item;
- projects which will be financially secure in the long-term;
- projects where there is a genuine worry that the item is otherwise going to be lost or damaged.

Examples of projects supported in 1997/98 included:
Dulwich Picture Gallery (£1 million towards endowment);
Launde Abbey Woods, Leicestershire and Rutland Wildlife Trust (£57,000);
Auckinleck House, Scottish Historic Buildings Trust (£50,000);
Upper Square, Hynish, Isle of Tiree, Hebridean Trust (49,500).

Exclusions: Private individuals and businesses. Grants to repair or restore buildings. For such assistance contact: English Heritage, Cadw, Historic Scotland, the Department of the Environment Northern Ireland, or the relevant local authority.

Applications: These should be made in writing and sent to the head of the fund, signed by the chairman, director or chief executive, and with a full justification of the need for help from the fund including: the reason for the grant; a full description of the project; photographs of the item and, for land and buildings, a map showing exactly where the property is and a site plan; full financial details, including an account of the money already raised or promised from other sources; formal valuation of the item, where appropriate; a description of the body applying for assistance, its finances; and plans to care for/manage the project in the future.

Applications are usually acknowledged within three working days. If the proposal meets all the conditions for applying for grants or loans, the applicant will be informed of the date when the trustees meet.

The Arts Council of England

14 Great Peter Street, London SW1P 3NQ

Tel: 0171-333 0100; Fax: 0171-973 6590
E-mail: information.ace@artsfb.org.uk
Web site: www.artscouncil.org.uk

> **Grant-in-aid: £184.6 million (1998/99); £186.1 million (1997/98) from Department for Culture, Media and Sport (+ additional £5 million allocated during 1998 for the *New Audiences Fund*)**

The Arts Council of England (ACE) is the national funding body for the arts in England. It is responsible for fostering the arts across the nation through the distribution of public money from central government and revenue generated by the National Lottery (some £250 million in 1998/99). It receives annual grant-in-aid from the Department for Culture, Media and Sport.

ACE has the following objectives:
- to develop and improve the knowledge, understanding and practice of the arts;
- to make the arts more accessible to the public;
- to advise and co-operate with central government departments, local authorities, the Arts Councils of Scotland, Wales and Northern Ireland and other bodies on any relevant matters.

ACE distributes part of its annual grant-in-aid directly through the ten Regional Arts Boards (RABs) with which it works closely and which receive about a third of its funding (£63.3 million in 1998/99). The RABs are independent organisations responsible for developing the arts in their area. Together ACE and the RABs make up the integrated system for arts funding and development in England.

Excluding the funding to the RABs, the major part of the council's grant-in-aid (some 90%) is devoted to a group of organisations funded on a *regular or fixed-term* basis.

Development funds are also available to support the production, distribution and development of specific projects, and research. A general leaflet about these programmes is available from the Library and Information Service.

ACE administers arrangements for the Arts Lottery (see appendix).

Museums & Galleries Commission

16 Queen Anne's Gate, London SW1H 9AA

Tel: 0171-233 4200; Fax: 0171-233 3686

Contact: Ruth Selman, Grants and Lottery Officer

Grant-in-aid from DCMS:	**£8.9 million (1998/99)**
	£9 million (1997/98)

The Museums & Galleries Commission is a registered charity incorporated under Royal Charter funded by the Department of Culture, Media and Sport. It supports the development of museums and galleries *in the UK*.

MGC grants fund many non-national museums. Some grants are administered directly, others at 'arm's length' through the English Area Museum Councils, the Science Museum and the Victoria & Albert Museum. The commission provides revenue funding for the seven Area Museum Councils in England. (Those in Scotland, Northern Ireland and Wales receive money from the Scottish, Northern Ireland and Welsh Offices, respectively.)

MGC/V & A Purchase Grant Fund
Grant total: £1 million (1998/99 and in 1997/98)

This fund, administered by the Victoria and Albert Museum on behalf of the MGC, helps with the purchase of objects relating to the arts, literature and history by non-national museums, art galleries, libraries and record offices in England and Wales. In Scotland a similar scheme is administered by the National Museums of Scotland.

Applications: Contact MGC/V&A Purchase Grant Fund, V & A Museum, London SW7 2RL (Tel: 0171-938 9641).

Preservation of Industrial and Scientific Material (PRISM)
Grant total: £250,000 (1998/99 and in 1997/98)

This fund, administered by the Science Museum on behalf of the MGC, aims to further the preservation in the public domain of items or collections important for the history and development of technology and science in all their branches.

Fully or provisionally registered English and Welsh non-national museums and galleries are eligible to apply. In Scotland a similar scheme is administered by the National Museums of Scotland.

Applications: Contact the Manager, PRISM Grant Fund, The Science Museum, South Kensington, London SW7 2DD (Tel: 0171-938 8005; Fax: 0171-938 9736).

Conservation Unit Grants

Grant total: £80,000 (1998/99)
£91,000 (1997/98)

This programme promotes and encourages high standards of conservation and collection care by fostering the expertise and skills of conservation professionals in the public and independent sectors in England, Wales and Northern Ireland.

Grants are available under three headings:
- Partnership projects;
- Continuing Professional Development;
- New Professionals.

Applications: Contact the Grants and Lottery Assistant for full details, guidelines and application forms. There was one June deadline in 1998.

Jerwood/MGC Cataloguing Grants

Grant total: £40,000 (1998/99 and in 1997/88)

This scheme funded by the Jerwood Foundation and DCMS ran for three years from 1997.

International Travel Grants

Grant total: £25,000 (1998/99)
£20,000 (1997/98)

Grants are available to promote longer term contacts and mutual cooperation between UK and overseas museums and to enable museum and conservation professionals to maintain and develop their skills and knowledge.

Applications: Contact the Grants and Lottery Officer for full details of these programmes. Application deadlines vary for different kinds of proposal.

● Area Museum Councils

(see Regional Section)

● The Pairing Scheme –
● ● Association for Business Sponsorship of the Arts (ABSA)

Nutmeg House, 60 Gainsford Street, Butlers Wharf, London SE1 2NY

Tel: 0171-378 8143; Fax: 0171-407 7527
E-mail: pairing.scheme@absa.org.uk
Web site: www.absa.org.uk

ABSA is an independent membership organisation set up and funded by companies already involved in arts sponsorship. It exists to promote arts sponsorship and advises both businesses and arts organisations on good practice in sponsorship and how to go about it.

The Pairing Scheme

> **Grant-in-aid: £5.05 million (1998/99)**

ABSA administers the government's arts sponsorship initiative (formerly called the Business Sponsorship Incentive Scheme) funded by the Department for Culture, Media and Sport. (**This funding is likely to be routed via the Arts Council of England in future.**) The scheme started in 1984. It has three main objectives:
- to encourage businesses to sponsor the arts for the first time;
- to foster strong, lasting partnerships between business and the arts;
- to develop wider access to the arts through business sponsorship.

Sponsorship is part of the general promotional expenditure of a business. Its payment from a business to an arts organisation is for the purpose of promoting the business, its products or services. The scheme is an incentive scheme for business sponsors, not simply another source of public subsidy for the arts. It helps both businesses and the arts get the most from their partnership by providing additional money. This is given on the basis that it is used by arts organisations to supply extra benefits to their sponsors that would not otherwise be available. The awards are discretionary and calculated as a percentage of the sponsors' investment. The percentage match can be 25%, 50% or 100% and is dependent on the length of time a business has been an active sponsor of the arts and the nature of their sponsorship project and agreement.

During 1998/99 the pairing scheme worked on three levels designated as: First Time Sponsors; New Sponsors; Established Sponsors. There were detailed criteria for eligibility of business sponsorship within each of these categories. Alterations and refinements have been made during the course of the scheme's history and interested organisations should be sure to obtain full information from ABSA and that they understand the current arrangements.

Financial levels

During 1998/99 the following levels applied.

- The total amount of Pairing Scheme money available to an arts organisation in one financial year is £50,000. This is always paid to the arts organisation.
- The minimum amount of eligible sponsorship is £1,000.
- The minimum single award is £500 and the maximum £25,000.
- Arts organisations can apply to the Pairing Scheme for as many awards as they want up to a maximum value of £50,000.
- Businesses may apply to the scheme as many times as they wish.
- The maximum sponsorship in-kind which can be matched is £5,000.

Applications: ABSA is not itself a 'dating agency' between companies and organisations. The arts organisation and a business sponsor agree all terms of the sponsorship, then both parties complete their respective sections of the application form. The arts organisation submits the form to ABSA. Deadlines for receipt of applications and the dates of panel meetings are available from ABSA. The application is discussed with both parties by a member of the ABSA staff team who oversees its progress to the panel meeting.

Information should be obtained from the relevant ABSA offices, either the head office, noted above, or the regional offices listed below. Contact should be maintained with the respective office.

ABSA Head Office (see address above)
London & Eastern Arts Boards

ABSA Southern
Southern Arts Board
The Point Dance and Arts Centre, Leigh Road, Eastleigh, Hampshire SO50 9DE
Tel: 01703-619172; Fax: 01703-619173

ABSA South East
South East Arts Board
21-22 Old Steine, Brighton BN1 1EL
Tel: 01273-683604; Fax: 01273-572022

ABSA Midlands
East & West Midlands Arts Boards
Suite 16-18, 21 Bennetts Hill, Birmingham B2 5QP
Tel: 0121-248 1200; Fax: 0121-248 1202

ABSA North (main office)
Yorkshire & Humberside Arts Boards
Dean Clough, Halifax, West Yorkshire HX3 5AX
Tel: 01422-367 860; Fax: 01422-363 254

ABSA North
North West Arts Board
Room 413, 4th Floor, St James's Buildings, Oxford Street, Manchester MI 6FQ
Tel: 0161-236 2058; Fax: 0161-236 2068

ABSA North
Northern Arts Board
9-10 Osborne Terrace, Jesmond, Newcastle-Upon-Tyne NE2 1NZ
Tel: 0191-281 3921; Fax: 0191-281 3276

ABSA Wales and South West
Arts Council of Wales and South West Arts Board
16 Museum Place, Cardiff CF1 3BH
Tel: 01222-303 023; Fax: 01222-303 024

ABSA Scotland
Scottish Arts Council
100 Wellington Street, Glasgow G2 6PB
Tel: 0141-204 3864; Fax: 0141-204 3897

ABSA Northern Ireland
(see separate entry)

British Council Arts Division

(see International)

Visiting Arts

(see International)

English Regional Arts Boards

(see Regional)

English Sports Council

16 Upper Woburn Place, London WC1H OQP

Tel: 0171-273 1500; Fax: 0171-383 5740
Web site: www.sports.gov.uk

Contact: The Information Centre

Governing Bodies of Sport and National Bodies

> Total grant: £10.5 million (1997/98)

The staff at the London headquarters and 10 regional offices of the English Sports Council work closely with governing bodies of sport, local authorities and other national and regional organisations to develop and maintain the infrastructure for sports development in England. The council aims to increase participation in sport and improve standards of sports performance throughout the country.

The English Sports Council is one of five independent sports councils created in 1997 – one in each of the countries of the UK, plus another representing the UK as a whole. The four national sports councils are responsible for distributing National Lottery proceeds for the development of sport. Each receive a share of the Sports Lottery revenue based on their population. Accordingly applications from voluntary organisations are welcomed and approaches should be made to the *Lottery Sports Fund*.

Exchequer grant-in-aid is given to key voluntary sports organisations such as the Central Council for Physical Recreation as well as national governing bodies of sport. Application guidelines are issued which set out eligibility criteria. Activities must firstly be recognised as a sport by the council. Only one governing body will then be recognised for each sport and therefore be eligible to receive advice and funding support.

Sportsmatch Scheme

Institute of Sports Sponsorship, Warwick House,
25-27 Buckingham Palace Road, London SW1W OPP

Tel: 0171-233 7747; Fax: 0171-828 7099
E-mail: info@sportsmatch.co.uk
Web site: www.sportsmatch.co.uk

Contact: Mike Reynolds, Director

Total funding for projects: £2.8 million (1998/99)

Sportsmatch is the business sponsorship incentive scheme for *amateur* sport managed by the Institute of Sports Sponsorship and funded with £3.2 million in 1998/99 by the Department for Culture, Media and Sport. Schemes in Scotland and Wales are funded by the Scottish and Welsh Offices and managed by their Sports Councils – see separate entries.

Sportsmatch gives sports organisers a better 'selling position' with potential sponsors. It matches a sponsor's investment in *grass roots sports* on a £ for £ basis from a minimum of £1,000 to a maximum of £50,000. For schools the minimum award is £500. The sponsorship must represent *new* money, either as first item sponsorship or increased sponsorship. Sports organisers and potential sponsors are expected to work together to develop a joint proposal. National schemes can qualify provided they benefit sport at grass roots level.

Events and programmes should:
■ increase participation and improve standards;
■ target young people, schools, disabled sports people or areas of recreational deprivation in rural or urban communities.

Support covers revenue activities or essential capital equipment directly related to the activities eg. nets, bats, balls, canoes. A capital project is only permitted a *total* budget of less than £5,000.

The scheme assists a wide range of organisations and the proportion of funding which reaches the voluntary sector organisations as such is not easy to estimate. All projects have to be local. A successful proposal relevant to this guide has been Manchester Salvation Army which was sponsored by British Nuclear Fuels and Granada Television to offer coaching in football, netball, judo and aerobics in the inner city area. A female coach was specially recruited to encourage women from the large Asian community to take part.

Exclusions: Individuals and professional sporting events, though professional coaching services for amateurs are eligible.

Applications: Full information and a newsletter are available from the above address. Applications have to be made jointly by the organisers and the sponsors. Scheme managers are on call at the institute to give advice and help frame applications. The awards panel meets every six weeks.

ⓊⓀ THE MINISTRY OF DEFENCE

Main Building, Whitehall, London SW1A 2HB
Tel: 0171-218 9000

Grants to voluntary organisations

> **Total funding: £16,443,178 (1997/98)**

Funding to voluntary organisations derives from as many as eight differing areas of the Ministry of Defence and the Armed Services. There is no general fund to which voluntary organisations may apply and in most cases an initial approach will be made by the Ministry.

In 1997/98 a large proportion of the funding (over £7 million – 44%) was paid to five voluntary organisations for 'services rendered' for welfare work for servicemen and their families. These were:
   SSAFA-FH Soldiers, Sailors, Airmen and Families Association – Forces Help (£3,943,777);
   Women's Royal Voluntary Service (£1,918,943);
   Service Hospitals Welfare Department, managed by the Joint Committee of the British Red Cross and the Order of St John of Jerusalem (£914,000);
   Pre-School Learning Alliance (£164,569);
   Relate (£110,158).

Other grants were given to:
   Army Cadet Corps (£3,700,000);
   Sea Cadet Corps (£1,987,653);
   Combined Cadet Force (£1,167,000);
   Air Training Corps (£513,971);
   Officers' Association (£314,000);

Royal British Legion, for relief of Polish Ex-servicemen & Women (£191,500) and for war widows' pilgrimages (£147,000);
Army Cadet Force Association (£106,000);
Council for Cadet Rifle Shooting (£72,600);
Victoria Cross & George Cross Association (£30,000);
Council for Voluntary Welfare Work, a consortium furthering HM Forces Christian work (£29,000);
Voluntary Cadet Corps (£28,665);
Combined Cadet Force Association (£7,000);
Missions to Seamen, British & International Sailors Society, Apostleship of the Sea, Royal Sailors Rests, Handicapped Children's Pilgrimage Trust (£1,000 each).

Many grants are recurrent.

Contact: Howard G Reynolds, SP (Pol) 2B-1, Room 5/68, Metropole Building Northumberland Avenue, London WC2N 5BL
Tel: 0171-218 9618; Fax: 0171-218 9626

ⓔ DEPARTMENT FOR EDUCATION AND EMPLOYMENT

Main Offices

Sanctuary Buildings (S B)
Great Smith Street, London SW1P 3BT

Caxton House (C H)
Tothill Street, London SW1H 9NF

Moorfoot (M)
Sheffield S1 4PQ

Main Switchboard: 0171-925 5000
Information Office: 0171-925 5189

Web site: www.dfee.gov.uk

Other offices are situated in Darlington and Runcorn but they do not feature in this guide.

Contents

National Childcare Strategy Division (C H)

Childcare Unit (C H Room 400, Level 4)

The Childcare Unit is concerned with all aspects relevant to childcare such as child development, education, labour market needs and equal opportunities. (See also the Under Fives Division in the Schools Directorate.) The consultations on the Green Paper *Meeting the Childcare Challenge* were drawing to a close in July 1998 and their outcome may well influence spending decisions. The bulk of the budget for 1998/99 is delegated to local bodies – TECs and local authorities (see below). These bodies may make grants to voluntary groups locally.

The budget allocation for future years is likely to take a very different form from that shown below though most of the funding will continue to be allocated to key organisations locally.

From April 1999 a significant amount of funding for *out of school* childcare will be provided through the Lottery's independent awarding body, the **New Opportunities Fund (NOF)** (see separate entry), created as a sixth good cause from the Wednesday Lottery. The Green Paper proposed a first tranche of £170 million NOF funding becoming available from April 1999.

National Childcare Strategy

> **Total funding: £34.5 million (1998/99)**

Allocated as follows:

Out of School Childcare Initiative (OSCI): £22 million

Contracted to Training and Enterprise Councils (TECs) which make grants to pump prime provision and carry out development work.

Training/business support for childcare workers & providers: £4 million

Contracted to TECs.

Childcare grant to Local Education Authorities: £6 million

For childcare for children aged 0-3 years and out of school care for 4 year olds. Some LEAs may provide grants to the voluntary sector.

Miscellaneous projects: £2 million

Support towards the development of the National Childcare Strategy, ie. research, training and development, promotional. Grants have been allocated centrally.

National Development Budget - Out of School Childcare Initiative (OSCI): £500,000

The objectives of the National Development Budget are:

- to provide value for money services to TECs which are more effectively carried out at national, rather than local level;
- to encourage the development and spread of good practice in TEC activities;
- to pilot innovative approaches to out of school childcare;
- to develop support materials and resources for TECs and schemes.

Support has been awarded to voluntary agencies such as Education Extra, National Council for Playwork Education and Kids Club Network. Initiatives are open to tender. The Childcare Unit keeps a register of suppliers, many of which are from voluntary sector.

Contacts: Shirley Trundle, Divisional Manager;
Carole Stanley, Tel: 0171-273 6265; Yvonne Hunt, Tel: 0171-273 6267;
Fax: 0171-273 5501; E-mail: childcare.unit@dfee.gov.uk

Schools Directorate

Early Years Division (C H)

> **Grant total to voluntary organisations: £3.4 million (1998/99)**

The Early Years Division (formerly known as the Under Fives Division) "provides grant aid to a number of national organisations in the voluntary sector which help promote the government's policies for young children". The only further information provided, apart from the total grant shown above, is as follows: "The criteria for funding are under review, but it is expected that where grants are made available, they will continue to be to national rather than local organisations".

It is believed that the above figure includes £500,000, a special one-off payment announced in June 1998 to the Pre-School Learning Alliance to help counterbalance some of the effects of the removal of nursery vouchers. It certainly includes the grant making taken over from the Department of Health during 1998.

Section 64 grants

Grant total: £760,000 (1998/99)

The division assumed responsibility for the Section 64 grants to under 5s from the Department of Health (see separate entry). Nine grants were transferred to this division in 1998/99:

  Pre-School Learning Alliance;
  National Children's Bureau Early Childhood Unit;
  National Childminding Association;
  National Playbus Association;
  National Early Years Network;
  The Daycare Trust;
  Kids Club Network;
  Choices in Childcare;
  Highscope.

Applications: Criteria, guidance notes and application forms were being reviewed at the time of writing August 1998. It is expected that grants starting the following April should be notified as usual around February / March.

Contact: Duncan Towner, Tel: 0171-925 5416

The above grants account for only 37% of the total figure given above. The greater part of the funding in 1998/99 was probably in the form of contracts for services, pilot schemes and research projects which may also be open to bids from the private as well as the voluntary sector.

It is not known if the total grant figure provided by the division is a useful indication of its likely funding to the voluntary sector in future years.

Contact: Mike Hipkins, Divisional Manager; Cathy Jones, Tel: 0171-925 6306

Sure Start (S B)

Total funding: £220 million (2001/02)
£220 million (2000/01)
£100 million (1999/00)

This new programme announced in July 1998 is part of the government's drive to tackle social exclusion. It is aimed at the most vulnerable young people and their families and arose from a major cross-departmental review led by the Treasury which examined the services currently provided for young children.

The programme will "build on and extend existing services but provide help to children and their families in a more coordinated way".

A range of services will be available including:
- primary health care including advice on breast feeding and childcare;
- childcare including stimulating and enjoyable play facilities for children and scope to involve parents;
- support for children with learning difficulties and emotional and behavioural difficulties;
- a range of support for families including educational opportunities depending on their needs and wishes.

The programme will focus on pre-school children and the families who face the greatest problems and live in areas of disadvantage.

Sure Start is to be funded through a **Children's Fund** which will be administered through new inter-departmental arrangements. It will be targeted on areas of greatest need, and aims to reach up to 5% of 0-3 year olds over time (125,000 infants in 250 deprived areas).

The programme may be coordinated via the Early Years Division of the DfEE. For the time being, until the new inter-departmental arrangements are in place, the main contact is:
Sally Burlington, HM Treasury, Tel: 0171-270 4482; Fax: 0171-270 5807.

Pupil Motivation and Community and Business Links Division (S B)

> **Total funding:** £1,561,500 (1998/99)

Divisional Manager: Susan Johnson

Out of School Hours Learning Activities (1)

> **Total funding:** £738,000 (1998/99)
> £105,897 (1997/98)
> £ nil (1996/97)

The government has set challenging targets for raising standards in schools. If these are to be met there needs to be effective learning opportunities outside school hours – involving schools and other agencies – to complement and support the work of teachers in the classroom. Study support activities help motivate young people and give them extra confidence to learn during their school days and beyond. The government is investing £200 million from the New Opportunities Fund/Lottery money to help expand study support and is also seeking the active involvement of business and voluntary sector partners.

Funding assistance is given to organisations which help the government meet the target of promoting and helping to improve the quality and quantity of out of school hours learning activities available to young people.

All the following organisations themselves approached the department for funding to develop work on study support. Initially, in 1997/98, funding was given to the Prince's Trust and the National Foundation for Educational Research (NFER).

In 1998/99 six organisations were funded:

   Prince's Trust, to support their network of study support centres, their publications (including Code of Practice) and longitudinal evaluation of study support (£250,000);
   NFER, for schools survey report, evaluation and report of Lottery Pilot projects, and LEA survey and report (£101,000);
   Education Extra (3 grants) for teacher training research and development (£125,000); to produce guidance for special schools setting up and running study support centres (£60,000); to develop a database of study support activities (£34,000);
   Children's Express, to set up 2 pilot satellite bureaux (£64,000);
   Resource Unit for Supplementary and Mother Tongue, to set up resource library, produce good practice guide and directory (£50,000);
   African Caribbean Network, to set up 4 Ishango Science and Technology Clubs (£54,000).

Contact: Bhavena Patel, Executive Officer, Tel: 0171-925 5957; Fax: 0171-925 5629; E-mail: bhavena.patel@dfee.gov.uk

Education-Community Links (2)

Total funding: £250,000 (1998/99)

This new funding allocation is available to projects which focus on forging and developing school-community links in order to motivate pupils and raise standards of achievement. The department is both proactive and responsive in its selection of initiatives, but all are expected to have a national relevance. Organisations which had received funding by July in 1998/99 included:

Community Service Volunteers for evaluation of the Reading Together Initiative (£8,825);

The Total Learning Challenge, strategic response to youth disturbance in North Tyneside (£5,000);

Community Education Development Centre, production of tool-kit to advise schools on how to develop effective community schools (£4,050).

Contact: Paul Jackson, Grade 7/Team Leader, Tel: 0171-925 6034; Fax: 0171-925 5629

Education Business Links and Parent / Family Learning (3)

Total funding:	£544,000 (1998/99)
	£326,200 (1997/98)
	£348,000 (1996/97)

Funding follows the government's priorities as set out in the White Paper *Excellence in Schools*. The division assumed responsibility for promotion of parenting skills and some aspects of family learning in 1998. During 1998/99 over half (55%) of the total funding (shown above) was allocated in this area but no information about these grants was available in July 1998.

The following five grants totalling over £200,000 had been awarded to voluntary sector organisations in 1997/98. (Other grants were awarded to consultancy firms, etc.)

Business in the Community (£94,000);

Association of Schools Science Engineering and Technology (ASSET) (£48,000);

Understanding Industry (£25,000);

Science & Engineering Technology Mathematics Network (SETNET) (£20,000);

Age Concern England, towards feasibility study to test extension to secondary schools (£15,000).

Contact: Sakina Jetha, Team Leader (0171-925 6303); Belinda Knowles, Executive Officer, Tel: 0171-925 5736; Fax: 0171-925 5629

Work Experience (4)

A single grant (£29,500 in 1998/99) is also awarded annually to **Trident**, which introduces school children to the world of work through quality work experience. This funding supports the development and training of its staff, most of whom are seconded from industry.

Contact: Stephen Haxton (Sheffield office), Tel: 0114-259 4164;
Fax: 0114-259 3847

Applications: Organisations seeking support in the areas listed above should contact the appropriate officer to discuss their proposals. Funds will normally only be allocated to national organisations or projects with a national, or potential national, relevance. For (2) and (3) obtain full criteria along with an application form in June of the financial year in which funding is sought. These proposals should contribute to the motivation and development of young people by raising their educational standards and improving their attainments and/or tackling disaffection.

Special Schools and Schools Governance Division (S B)

School Government Team

Certain organisations representing school governors have been supported. No information was given in summer 1998. However, it is believed that such organisations have been contracted for project work and that some core funding has been given.

Contact: June Nisbet, Team Leader, Tel: 0171-925 5606

Youth Service Unit (S B)

National Voluntary Youth Organisations (NVYOs)

> **Grant total: £9.5 million (for the three years, 1996-1999)**

These grants to the headquarters of NVYOs promote the *personal and social education* of young people in England. They support *planned* programmes of informal and experiential education providing opportunities for young people which help them cope with the transition from childhood to adult life.

A new three-year scheme, effective from April 1999 to March 2002, was announced in April 1998.

Priorities for funding

The two main objectives of the 1999-2002 scheme are:

- to combat social exclusion and inequality through targeting priority groups such as the disadvantaged (especially in inner cities, on run-down housing estates or in rural areas); the disaffected or at risk of drifting into crime; minority ethnic communities; young people with disabilities;
- to raise the standard and quality of youth work by, for instance, training programmes for youth workers and volunteers, increasing young peoples' participation in management and decision-making.

Programmes for young people aged between 11 and 25 are eligible, but 13-19 year olds are prioritised. Joint working and partnership among NVYOs are particularly encouraged and resources were earmarked specifically for such work.

Grants have normally ranged between £10,000 and £100,000 a year and do not exceed 50% of the total cost. Funding is given for core activities but such bids must accompany a bid based on at least one of the two objectives given above, and should not normally exceed 30% of the total grant sought.

Examples of organisations supported in the 1996-1999 programme included:
    Scout Association (£125,000 x 3);
    Duke of Edinburgh's Award (£106,000-£112,000 each year);
    Fairbridge (£100,000 x 3);
    Ocean Youth Club (£85,000-£90,000 each year);
    UK Federation of Jazz Bands (£52,000 x 3);
    St John Ambulance Youth (£28,000-£40,000 each year);
    National Association of Youth Theatres (around £36,000 x 3);
    National Federation of City Farms (£20,000-£23,000 each year);
    Young Muslim Organisation (£20,000 x 3).

An example of a joint programme was:
    Youth Hostels/RSPB/Youth Clubs UK (£19,000-£27,000 each year).

Exclusions: Youth exchanges, holiday playschemes, vocational preparation or volunteering for its own sake.

Applications: Advice and full guidance notes can be obtained directly from the Youth Service Unit.

All organisations applying for grant have to be *registered* with the department as a NVYO. The 1996-1999 scheme had some 60 registrants. This register was reviewed in summer 1998.

Applications for a grant under the 1999-2002 scheme were called for by 12th October 1998. Successful applicants are offered grant for the financial year 1999-2000, together, if appropriate, with indicative levels of grant for the following two years. Grant in these years depends on the outcome of monitoring and evaluation.

Contact: Geoff Doe, Tel: 0171-925 5266; Fax: 0171-925 6954;
E-mail: geoff.doe@dfee.gov.uk

Individual Learning Division (M, East 8d)

Adult and Community Learning Fund (ACLF)

Total funding: £5 million (each year, starting 1998/99, till March 2001)

This fund has been created to sustain and encourage new schemes locally that help men and women gain access to education, including literacy and numeracy. Support is available to community-based organisations, working in partnership with others, combining learning opportunities with other activities relevant to local people eg. environmental projects, tenants' associations, childcare, crime prevention, arts, health. The aim is to draw in new and non-traditional learners, especially people who are disadvantaged and isolated. The fund seeks to make a lasting impact on individuals and communities by equipping people to improve their own lives, progress to further learning, engage with others and make a greater contribution to their neighbourhood.

Some £5 million is expected to be allocated in each financial year till March 2001. It is intended that this funding be matched £ for £ with contributions from trusts, charities and other donors which share the fund's aims. In early July 1998 these arrangements had still to be settled.

Applications: A prospectus was issued in summer 1998 describing the parameters of the fund in more detail and providing guidance on the content of bids. Copies are available from the two organisations – the Basic Skills Agency (BSA) and the National Institute for Adult Continuing Education (NIACE) – managing the ACLF on DfEE's behalf. These should be the first point of contact for enquiries and applications:

Basic Skills Agency
7th Floor, Commonwealth House, 1-19 New Oxford Street, London WC1A 1NU
Tel: 0171-405 4017; Fax: 0171-404 5038; E-mail:charlotte@basic-skills.co.uk
Contact: Charlotte Pearson

National Institute for Adult Continuing Education (NIACE)
21 De Montfort Street, Leicester LE1 7GE
Tel: 0116-204 4200; Fax: 0116-285 4515; E-mail: suec@niace.org.uk
Contact: Sue Cara

The prospectus will be revised periodically though the life of the fund. In 1998 the plan was to hold *three rounds of applications* per year at the beginning of October, the end of November and the beginning of March. From 1999 these will change to deadlines in May, September and January.

Departmental contact: Kate McGimpsey, Tel: 0114-259 4199; Fax: 0114-259 3236; E-mail kate.mcgimpsey@dfee.gov.uk

Information will also appear on the DfEE Web site: www.lifelonglearning.co.uk

Basic Skills and Adult Further Education Policy Team (CH)

Lifelong Learning

Total grant:	£558,950 (1998/99)

Grants are awarded annually to seven national associations whose purposes include education. They each submit a work programme of educational activities for grant. Grants in 1998/99 were:

  National Institute of Adult Continuing Education (£400,000);
  Pre-Retirement Association (£85,000);
  National Association of Women's Clubs (£25,550);
  National Federation of Women's Institutes (£19.900);
  Townswomen's Guilds (£14,000);
  Educational Centres Association (£7,500);
  National Women's Register (£7,000).

Contact: Susan O'Dwyer, Tel: 0171-273 5160; Fax: 0171-273 5124

Powers: Regulation 11 of the Education (Grant) Regulations 1990

Further Education Division (SB)

The division makes two annual grants:

Skill, the National Bureau for Students with Disabilities, for its work in developing opportunities for students with disabilities and learning difficulties in post-16 education, training and the transition to work (£86,000 p.a.);

VIEW, the Association for the Education and Welfare of the Visually Handicapped, to support the Piano Tuners' Diploma of the Piano Tuners' Examination Board (£4,000).

Contact: Peter Clough, Tel: 0171-925 5245; Fax: 0171-925 6985

Resources & Budget Management Division (M)

Training for unemployed adults with special needs

In 1998 the department contracted with NACRO, Rathbone Community Industry and CSV for project based work. Under this contract, which will last for three to four years, the DfEE will fund a number of projects that will further its policies – particularly in relation to tackling the problems of social exclusion.

One of the first pieces of work on which the organisations will report is the impact of TEC funding mechanisms for the support of special needs provision.

Contact: John Thompson, Tel: 0114-259 3584; Fax: 0114-259 3902

National Training Organisation Division (M)

National Training Organisations (NTOs) are voluntary associations of employers and employment interests who have come together to represent their sectors and establish sectoral strategies for education and training. Most are established as limited companies and many are applying for charitable status. The sectors themselves fund the running of their NTO, but the department provides funding for particular initiatives or activities such as workforce analysis, developing training pathways, monitoring skill needs and shortages and representing the views of employers to government.

NTO funding is specifically earmarked for NTOs which have gone through a recognition process and NTOs are recognised by the Secretary of State for a period of three years. By mid 1998 a total of 59 NTOs had been recognised and approximately 20 others were in the process of making bids.

The Voluntary Sector National Training Organisation (VSNTO)

Funding: about £200,000 during 1998/99

The VSNTO is run by the National Council for Voluntary Organisations with the Scottish Council for Voluntary Organisations and the Welsh Council for Voluntary Action. It has been awarded three year funding for its strategic role in Britain, raising the profile of the voluntary sector, at skills needs and training routes in the sector.

Contact: Chris Loveland, National Council for Voluntary Organisations, Regent's Wharf, 8 All Saints Street, London N1 9RL; Tel: 0171-713 6161; Fax: 0171-713 6300

Departmental contact: Fiona Jordan, NTO 4, Room E4C, Tel: 0114-259 3646; Fax: 0114- 259 4482

Millennium Volunteers Team (M)

Start up funding: £12.7 million from the Windfall Tax

The Millennium Volunteers programme is the national programme of citizens' service for young people as proposed in the Labour Manifesto. Its delivery is contracted out to partner organisations. In England partner organisations were undecided at the time of going to press, with applications invited from September 1998. Eight demonstration projects started in summer 1998.

It is an entirely voluntary programme with no benefit sanctions, open to young people aged 16-25 in work, in full or part-time education or training and unemployed young people. They are supported and encouraged to make a sustained commitment to volunteering. Participants will have their achievements recorded and recognised by a national certificate. It is entirely separate from the New Deal although participants can take part in both schemes.

The framework of the programme was launched in late June 1998 following wide consultation. It set out nine key principles: community benefit; inclusiveness; ownership by young people; partnership; quality; recognition; sustained personal commitment through a Volunteer Plan; variety; voluntary participation.

Detailed funding and contracting arrangements and how organisations can apply for funding is published in the *Millennium Volunteers Guide* available from autumn 1998. Funding support is available where delivery partners can demonstrate a need to cover additional costs in the following areas:

■ supervision and support to volunteers;

- travel expenses for young people;
- publicity, promotion and recruitment;
- equipment and materials for use in activities;
- additional administrative and running costs.

The different delivery arrangements for Scotland, Wales and Northern Ireland were established at an earlier stage than in England, although the framework for the programme is consistent across the United Kingdom (see separate entries in other countries).

Contact: Brian Holmes, Team Leader, Tel: 0114-259 4792; Fax: 0114 259 4510; Vivienne Andrews, Line Manager, Tel: 0114-259 4541; Fax: 0114 259 3847

New Deal for 18-24 year olds (M)

Total Funding: £580 million (1998/99)
£100 million (1997/98)

The New Deal is not a grant making programme.

The total funding budgeted for 1997-2002 is £2.62 billion. All the costs of the New Deal for 18-24 year olds will need to be found from within these totals.

The New Deal for 18-24 year olds aims to help young people who have been unemployed and claiming Jobseeker's Allowance for six months or more to find work and improve their prospects of remaining in sustained employment. It begins with an initial period of up to four months individual help – the Gateway – which aims to get young people into work, or to prepare them for one of four New Deal options designed to improve their employability. The four options are:
- a subsidised job with an employer;
- full-time education or training;
- work on the Environment Task Force (ETF);
- work with the voluntary sector.

These options aim to improve the employability of young people through a combination of high quality work placements and training towards an approved qualification. Each option also aims to enable young people to move on from the option into work.

The total budget for New Deal cannot be broken down to identify how much will be allocated for the voluntary sector and ETF option. The amount to be spent on each option will depend on the number of young people who choose it.

Voluntary organisations have the opportunity to become involved in the New Deal by providing placements which offer valuable work experience opportunities to young people, and which at the same time benefit the organisations by supporting their work.

The voluntary sector and ETF options are being delivered by a range of organisations under contract with local New Deal partnerships. Organisations which wish to contribute to the delivery of these New Deal options should contact their local Employment Service.

Voluntary sector organisations involved in the New Deal by summer 1998 included: Prince's Trust Volunteers; the National Association for the Care and Resettlement of Offenders (NACRO); Groundwork; British Trust for Conservation Volunteers (BTCV).

New Deal Information Line: 0845-606 2626
Web site: www.newdeal.gov.uk

Employment Service

Level 6, Caxton House, Tothill Street, London SW1H 9NA

Tel: 0171-273 3000; Fax: 0171-273 6082

The Employment Service was launched as an Executive Agency by the Department for Education and Employment in 1990 and this status confirmed in 1996. It aims to provide a competitive, efficient and flexible labour market by helping unemployed people into work, while ensuring they understand and fulfil the conditions for receipt of the Jobseeker's Allowance.

Its main offices are in Caxton House (see address above) and in Sheffield. It has nine regional directors, two of which are in Scotland and Wales.

National Disability Development Initiative

Funding allocated: £470,000 (1998/99)

This initiative, first advertised nationally in July 1997, arose from a review that recommended a more coordinated and national approach across the whole of Great Britain by the Employment Service's Disability Service. The initiative enables new approaches to be tested and developed and for the Disability Service to promote these and put them into practice. In doing so, Head Office, the Employment Service regions and external partners work together to improve the service provided to both disabled people and employers. This initiative is 'permanent', with no fixed duration.

A total of nine projects were supported during the first round of tendering which began in August 1997 with projects of various durations, running from June 1998 to December 1999. Six of these were led by the following charitable organisations:

Association of Disabled Professionals, production of booklets by and for disabled people on entering and remaining in particular lines of employment;

Arthritis Care, providing a model for determining best employment rehabilitation strategies for disabled people (particularly those with arthritis);

Royal National Institute for the Blind, producing guidance on good practice in psychometric testing for visually impaired people;

Royal National Institute for the Deaf and the Western Training and Enterprise Council, development of careers guidance through mentoring schemes;

ENABLE, a Scottish charity working with Glasgow University on new approaches for people with learning disabilities referred to Employment Rehabilitation Services;

START – MIND Ealing, developing work preparation models for people recovering from mental illness.

New tendering rounds will seek additional ideas on how to develop an effective and relevant approach that enhances or extends current ES services for disabled job seekers and employers within available resources. The specific areas for prioritisation will be decided by the NDDI Board depending on the current perceived need.

The 1998/99 and 1999/2000 bidding rounds will be based on findings from a consultative exercise and the specification for the first of these is expected to be produced towards the end of 1998.

Organisations wishing to be on the NDDI mailing list should approach the given contact.

Contact: Annette Hughes, Employment Service, Unit 19, Eagleswood Business Park, Woodlands Lane, Bradley Stoke, Bristol BS32 4EU; Tel: 01454-848573; Fax: 01454-848540

ⓔ *National Youth Agency*

17-23 Albion Street, Leicester LE1 6GD

Tel: 0116-285 6789; Fax: 0116-247 1043
E-mail: nya@nya.org.uk
Web site: http://www.nya.org.uk

Contact: Terry Cane, Projects Manager

The National Youth Agency provides information, support and training to those involved in the informal and social education of young people. It changed from a non-departmental public body into a charitable company in 1996. It receives funding from three governmental sources, Department for Education and Employment, the Home Office, Voluntary & Community Unit and the Local Government Association.

In 1998/99 it administered the following grant schemes:

Youth Work Development Grants

> **Total funding: £400,000 annually**

The agency administers these grants for the Local Government Association. Revenue grants are given for three years to innovative projects by local or regionally based voluntary organisations, although projects by branches of national organisations can be assisted. Priority areas are: training of staff and volunteers; organisational development; partnership development; inner-city work; work with 13 to 19 year olds.

A total of 11 grants, ranging from £4,000 to £45,000 a year, were made in 1997 which included:

Jigsaw Youth Theatre, Dudley (£45,000);

Manchester Lesbian & Gay Switchboard (£40,000);

Devon Youth Association – Racism in rural areas (£36,000).

Applications: Application forms and guidance notes are available from the agency. The deadline was 30th October 1998 for the three year cycle.

Youth Volunteer Development Grants

> **£3 million allocated over the 2 years, 1997/98 and 1998/99**

These grants, administered on behalf of the Voluntary & Community Unit of the Home Office, have been made to appoint Youth Work Volunteer Facilitators to develop and implement local strategic plans for volunteering opportunities by 15 to 25 year olds. Funding has been given for 41 projects including:

Cambridge Youth Volunteer Project;

Merseyside Make A Difference;

Tower Hamlets Youth Volunteer Development Project.

Funding beyond the present cycle, which ends in March 1999, is not expected.

ⓔ *Further Education Funding Council*

Cheylesmore House, Quinton Road, Coventry CV1 2W

Tel: 01203-863000; Fax: 01203-863100
Web site: www.fefc.ac.uk

The council mainly funds general further education and tertiary colleges. It also supports sixth form colleges, some universities, local authority adult education centres and other independent organisations providing education and training.

The council funds some 800 institutions in total and a small number relevant to this guide receive support. They are listed within the 250+ 'External Institutions' supported. However, this sector receives only a very small proportion (2.5%) of the council's total funding and an even smaller number of these fall within the scope of this guide.

Funding allocations relevant to this guide in 1997/98 included:
Pre-school Learning Alliance, divided between its regions as follows:
Eastern – 52%; North West – 22%; South West – 18%; West Midlands – 5%; Greater London – 3% (£122,232);
Cambridge Women's Resource Centre (£93,799);
One Love Community Organisation, Greater London (£76,781);
Elfrida Rathbone, Camden (£64,142);
Sheffield Environmental Training (£59,205);
The Elfrida Society (£34,096);
Heeley City Farm (£30,428);
Shalom Employment Action Centre (£182,883).

Applications: Approach the nearest of the 10 regional offices for basic advice. Applications from voluntary agencies outside the formal Further Education colleges and LEA adult education can only be made if sponsorship arrangements have been made with the local FE college. The voluntary sector agency must be able to fill an identifiable gap in provision.

Powers: Section 6(5), Further and Higher Education Act 1992

(UK) *Equal Opportunities Commission*

Employment Policy Unit
Overseas House, Quay Street, Manchester M3 3HN

Tel: 0161-833 9244; Fax: 0161-835 1657
E-mail: info@eoc.org.uk
Web site: www.eoc.org.uk

Contact: Pauline Donegan

Grant total:	**£10,000 (1998/99)**
	£25,000 (1997/98)

Equality grants

Grants are offered to the voluntary sector for seminars, conferences and small projects which:

- eliminate discrimination on the grounds of sex;
- promote equality of opportunity between men and women especially in the fields of employment; economics; balance between work and family life; the law; facilities/services; education and training.

Exclusions: Academic institutions; general appeals; capital expenditure; re-applications within 12 months; retrospective grants; political organisations; individual grants; multiple applications; overseas projects/conferences and subsidies to public authorities carrying out their normal statutory duties.

Applications: Considered at monthly meetings during the year. A standard form from the above address must be used. It should be received no less than ten weeks before the start date of the event or project.

Powers: Section 54 of the Sex Discrimination Act

National Family and Parenting Institute

In summer 1998 it was announced that this new institute would be set up as an independent charity to raise the profile of family and parenting issues for professionals working in the field and to promote the development of parenting education and support programmes. It will work closely with existing bodies and public bodies and may also advise the Children's Fund (see Sure Start programme).

It arose from discussions within the Ministerial Group on the Family (including Education, Health, Social Security, Lord Chancellor's and Home Office) and will receive start up interdepartmental funding of £2 million.

Contact: Katharine Bramwell, Team Leader, or Marianne Lister, Family Policy & Community Development, Voluntary & Community Unit, Home Office, Tel: 0171-217 8453

E DEPARTMENT OF ENVIRONMENT, TRANSPORT & THE REGIONS

Ashdown House (A H)
123 Victoria Street
London SW1E 6DE

Eland House (E H)
Bressenden Place
London SW1E 5DU

Great Minster House (G M H)
76 Marsham Street
London SW1P 4DR

Tel: 0171-890 3000 (general line)

Contents

Environmental & Energy Awareness Division

Environmental Action Fund (A H, 7/F8)

Grant total:	**£4,190,000 in 115 grants (1998/99)**
	£3,673 million in nearly 100 grants (1997/98)

The Environmental Action Fund helps English voluntary groups to advance the government's environmental policies, supporting work which does not qualify for grant under other programmes.

New priorities for the fund were announced in September 1998 following a ministerial review. It will have one prime priority "to promote living more sustainably. (Sustainable living means lifestyles which achieve economic growth while protecting and, where possible enhancing, the environment, making sure that these benefits are available as widely as possible)".

It will continue to fund the core areas which were prioritised for 1998/99:
- education of the general public, or specific groups within it, about the importance of sustainable development, and the promotion of sustainable behaviour;
- encouragement of waste minimisation, recycling, re-use of materials and efficient energy use;
- improvement of local environments and their biodiversity.

Groups are also invited to consider how their proposals fit with the government's Millennium Celebration.

Types of funding:

Regional grants from £10,000 to £75,000 a year for up to two years (for both core and /or project activities) for regional and local groups.

National grants from £10,000 upwards per year for up to two years for national groups (covering core and/or project activities);

The Local Projects Fund, previously administered for the department by the Civic Trust, no longer operates.

The following information refers to grants made under the different arrangements for 1998/99.

Examples of core grants, each given on a one year basis, were:
    Council for Environmental Education (£125,000);
    National Society for Clean Air and Environmental Protection (£20,000);
    Young People's Trust for the Environment & Nature Conservation (£19,000).

Examples of project grants included:
    Birmingham Settlement (Asian Community Energy Awareness Training (£20,325, 1st of 2);
    Earthworks Trust – The Eco-Classroom (£12,695);
    RSPB – Action for Biodiversity – looking forward in Purbeck (£19,425, 1st of 2);
    SAFE Alliance – Food Facts, How Green is Your Food? (£33,375, 1st of 2);
    Warwickshire Wildlife Trust – GLOBE Programme (£39,450, 1st of 3).

Applications: Funding applications are usually invited each summer, and application papers are usually posted on the Web site. Grants are awarded from the start of the following financial year for a period of up to two years.

For the 1999/2000 round a grant panel will short list regional grants. In subsequent years Government Offices for the Regions will receive and short list applications in their areas. National grants will be considered by policy divisions within DETR.

Assessment criteria:
- the proposal has well-defined and achievable objectives and performance measures;
- the organisation will develop its own longer term capacity by carrying out the work;
- the proposal could not find adequate funding other than through the EAF;
- the organisation is likely to obtain all its matching funding;
- the proposal is innovative (either wholly or in the region) and does not duplicate the work of other bodies;
- the proposal represents good value for money.

Free publications are available to support projects: a six-monthly newsletter, *Activate*; a listing *Sources of Grant for Environmental Projects*; an annual report of grants made.

Contact: Andy Kirby, Environmental Action Manager, Tel: 0171-890 6693; Fax: 0171-890 6659; Web site: http://www.regeneration.detr.gov.uk

Powers: Section 153, Environmental Protection Act, 1990

Awareness and Action Programmes Team (A H,7/F8)

Environmental Campaigns Ltd (Encams)

Grant-in-aid: £3,697,000 (1998/99)

Encams was set up in January 1998 in Wigan as a 'parent' organisation encompassing the activities of both the **Tidy Britain Group (TBG)** and **Growing for Green (GfG)**, both of which continue as charitable companies. Nearly £1.2 million of the above grant-in-aid was conditional on matching funding from the private sector and non-grant income.

This single grant to Encams replaces the two grants previously paid totalling £3,997,000 in 1997/98 to TGB (£2,497,000) and to GfG (£1,500,000). The funding of the TBG, based in Wigan, is a long-standing arrangement over more than three decades. GfG, based in Manchester, was set up in 1996 as a government awareness campaign for environment action at a local level, and shares the same chairman as the TBG (Professor Maurice Ashworth).

Contact: Ray Shrimpton, Sponsorship Manager, Tel: 0171-890 6695; Fax: 0171-890 6659

Powers: Section 153, Environmental Protection Act 1990

Environment Protection International Division (AH)

Darwin Initiative for the Survival of Species (A H, 4/A2)

> **Grant total: £3 million (1997/98, and in 1998/99)**

The Darwin Initiative was set up after the Rio Earth Summit in 1992 to assist "countries rich in biodiversity but poor in resources". The funding helps *UK* biodiversity institutions carry out research and/or training with a partner in a developing country, thereby helping them to meet their obligations under the Biodiversity Convention.

Five principal areas of project work are targeted:
- institutional capacity building;
- training;
- research;
- work to implement the Biodiversity Convention of 1992;
- environmental education and awareness.

Each project is under the direction of a UK educational or scientific institution which includes many universities and other organisations. In 1996/97 a total of 32 projects were assisted (out of 175 applications). Most were in South East Asia, Africa and Central and South America. Examples of organisations receiving support were:

Botanic Gardens Conservation International, to set up institutional capacity for sustainable use of plant resources in Tam Dao National Park, Vietnam (£121,000);

Durrell Institute of Conservation and Ecology, to devise plans to resolve the conflict between wildlife and people in Masai Mara, Kenya (£123,000);

Earthwatch Europe, training on biodiversity projects for 45 students, Southern Africa (£120,000);

Fauna and Flora International, production and implementation of management plans in protected areas of Andaman Islands, India (£146,000);

Foundation for International Law and Development, to develop capacity to implement Biodiversity Convention by practical measures and policies, South Pacific (£110,000);

WWF-UK for study on fiscal incentives for biodiversity conservations with recommendations to policy makers, Brazil (£67,000).

Although grants may be up to 100%, encouragement is given for matching funding. Grants are typically around £40,000 each year for three years.

Applications: Full details and application forms are available from the above address. Applications are usually requested in September and close in late November for projects commencing the following April.

Contact: Maria Stevens, Darwin Initiative Secretariat, Tel: 0171-890 6205; Fax: 0171-890 6239; E-mail: mstevens@demon.uk.co

Environmental Know How Fund

(see Know How Fund – Department for International Development)

Regeneration Division 1

Special Grants Programme (E H, Zone 4/H10)

> **Grant total: £1.287 million (1997/98 and in 1998/99)**

In July 1998 a small increase in the resources to the programme for the first time for several years was announced (£1.4 million – 1999/00; £1.44 million – 2000/01; £1.5 million – 2001/02).

The Special Grants Programme (SGP) supports projects in England in the areas of regeneration and housing that fall within the department's policy interests. The following rules apply to both regeneration and housing projects.

Only national projects can be supported, but these may incorporate local pilot projects. Grants are intended to provide help with revenue costs, such as salaries and office running costs. They are usually offered for three years, renewable annually, but may be offered for shorter periods. They are normally limited to a maximum of 50% of costs and usually tapered in future years to reduce the percentage of the costs met by grant. Balancing income must come either from non-public sources, eg. private sector funding, subscriptions, donations, fees, or from the National Lottery.

SGP Regeneration Programme

The *regeneration* element provides support to establish or develop *national* voluntary organisations whose main activities complement the department's regeneration policy interests:

- improving the effectiveness and efficiency of organisations involved in local regeneration;
- improving the level and effectiveness of community involvement in local regeneration;
- fostering partnerships between the voluntary, private and public sectors in local regeneration;
- promoting good practice in urban management and in the creation, improvement, use and management of green and other open spaces in urban areas;
- developing long-term partnerships between the voluntary, private and public sectors and the local community to initiate and carry forward regeneration;
- providing high quality work placements for young people through the Environmental Task force;
- promoting good practice on ways in which high quality design can be secured in local regeneration;
- encouraging the involvement of volunteers in local regeneration.

In 1998/99 grants under the **regeneration** heading of the SGP included:

Association of Town Centre Management, four grants: capacity building as an umbrella organisation (£7,000); European links (£39,000); bench marking (£34,000); national accreditation scheme (£23,000);

Planning Exchange, pilot of an independent information service for community groups, with tailor-made info sheets on local topics, enquiry service, meetings, seminars, etc. (£17,840);

British Urban Regeneration Association, to set up regional urban regeneration networks as focus for contact with government and English Partnerships (£25,000);

Civic Trust: Enterprising Communities, training, etc. on strategic planning, capital project management, fundraising, sustainability (£45,000);

Improving level and effectiveness of community involvement in local regeneration
Free Form Design and Technical Aid Services, research on the attainment of realistic levels of community involvement in public and private infrastructure developments (£36,600);

Civic Trust: Winning Partnerships Phase 11, improving skills of community representatives, staff and partners, to increase effectiveness and accountability (£31,000);

Fostering partnerships between voluntary, private and public sectors involved in local regeneration
Business in the Community*, volunteer business support groups in 30 focus areas (£32,000) and for Best Practice Guide (£15,000);

Promoting good practice in urban management and in the creation, improvement and use of open spaces in urban areas
British Business Parks*, to establish an organisation and develop a national accreditation scheme (£103,000);

Urban Villages Forum, a national promotional campaign of seminars, technical advice and support, and creation and development of demonstration projects (£15,000);

Civic Trust – Realising the Vision, demonstration projects developing new town management partnerships (£40,000);

Developing long-term partnerships between the voluntary, private and public sectors and the community
Civic Trust: Market Towns, regeneration of selected market towns affected by industrial and other decline; development of best practice for national replication (£50,000);

Alternative sources of finance
Charities Aid Foundation, to improve voluntary organisations' access to private finance (£6,140).

Cross-cutting bids
Improving effectiveness and efficiency of voluntary organisations involved
British Association of Settlements and Social Action Centres (BASSAC)* for
information, training and consultancy services outside London (£15,091);
Civic Trust: Bridging the Gap, advising lead partners on how to involve the third
sector, working with them on developing these skills, promoting good partnership
practice – dissemination via national conference and report (£43,000).

SGP Housing programme

The department's *housing* policy interests include:
■ sustaining a healthy private rented sector;
■ developing policies on access to and management of, social housing;
■ developing policy on special needs housing and gypsy sites;
■ encouraging the involvement of volunteers in the housing area;
■ encouraging the wider provision of social housing in rural areas.

In 1998/99 grants under the **housing** part of the SGP awarded included:

Access to, and management of, social housing
Chartered Institute of Housing, tenants training programme (£24,000);
Crisis, for research into the development of rent guarantee schemes and to set up
pilots, raise funds and disseminate good practice among LAs (£40,430);
Churches National Housing Coalition, to establish an advice agency to promote the
use of church land and property for affordable housing (£13,878);
Habitat for Humanity GB* to establish a national office and set up and support local
groups (£79,000);

Special needs housing and gypsy sites
ACERT (Advisory Council for the Education of Romany and Other Travellers) to
improve the potential for private gypsy site provision and to encourage good
practice (£14,869);
SITRA to provide training and policy advice in the special needs housing field
(£41,050);
Women's Aid Federation of England*, training, resources and facilities (£44,221);

Encouraging wider provision of social housing in rural areas
Health and Housing* for two demonstration projects (£7,000);

Other
Home Improvement Trust*, pilot to set up a non profit company giving interest only
loans to elderly low-income owner-occupiers who need home refurbishment/
adaptation (£36,645);
Quest Trust*, to extend Estate Line to ethnic and other minority groups (£15,000).

**Grants marked with an asterisk show new projects supported in 1998/99. Other
grants are the annual allocations to schemes funded in the previous year/s.*

Exclusions: As funding 'of last resort', SGP grants are not available for work which is eligible for support under any other government grant programme, or which could proceed without SGP support or be carried out to an adequate standard without this funding.

Applications: These are sought during the summer with a deadline at the end of September. Approach the office for further information.

Contact: Charity McEvoy, Tel: 0171-890 3726; Fax: 0171-890 3719;
Web site: http://www.regeneration.detr.gov.uk/grants/vol/index/htm

Environmental Regeneration Branch (E H, 4/H9)

Groundwork

Grant-in-aid: £6.675 million (1997/98 and in 1998/99)

An annual grant is made to the Groundwork Foundation and its network of 41 autonomous trusts. This grant covers the core costs of the foundation, a contribution to the core costs of the trusts, and funding towards specific projects in England. (Welsh Groundwork Trust funding has been via the Strategic Development Scheme, see separate entry).

In July 1998 an increase was announced of more than £3 million over the three years (1999/02).

Contact: Peter Bates, Tel: 0171-890 3722; Fax: 0171-890 3709

Single Regeneration Budget

(see Regional section)

New Deal for Communities

(see Regional section)

Homelessness and Housing Management Policy Division (E H)

Single Homelessness (EH Zone 2/A2)

Grant total:	**£8.1 million (1998/99)**
	£7.9 million (1997/98)

Grants help voluntary organisations throughout England to meet the running costs of schemes providing practical help for single people needing accommodation.

In 1998/99 priority was given to innovative projects helping homeless young people or those in danger of becoming homeless and which had the support of their local authority. They included accommodation registers and resettlement schemes, emergency accommodation and rent/deposit guarantee schemes.

The National Homeless Advice Service run by Shelter/NACAB received the major allocation of just over £2 million.

A further 205 grants were made, 48 of which were new projects. These grants ranged between £5,200 and £200,000 and included:
   Bristol Cyrenians – The HUB Project (£200,000);
   Brighton Housing Trust (£150,000);
   Winter comfort – Cambridge (£47,000);
   NACRO Derbyshire (£39,000);
   Centrepoint – rent bond scheme/resettlement project (£30,000);
   The Children's Society – Newcastle (£22,000).

Applications: The deadline for 1998/99 applications was 5th December. Forms and guidance notes are available from the above address and enquiries are handled as follows:
London, Eastern region, Merseyside, North East, North West and South West –
Contact: Bryn Reynolds: Tel: 0171-890 3655; Fax: 0171-890 3649;
East Midlands, South East, West Midlands, and Yorkshire and Humberside
Contact: Gwen Roberts: Tel: 0171-890 3654; Fax: 0171-890 3649

Powers: Section 180 of the Housing Act 1996

Rough Sleepers Initiative (E H, Zone 2/A3)

> **Funding: £73 million for Phase 3 (1996/99) of which £3 million for new areas (1997/98-1998/99)**

The Rough Sleepers Initiative (RSI) started in 1990 to provide accommodation for people sleeping rough, together with outreach, resettlement and other support services. The bulk of RSI resources in the first seven years was directed to housing associations, funded through the Housing Corporation (see separate entry), to create permanent accommodation for "for people who have slept rough in central London".

RSI began in central London and subsequently expanded to Bristol and Brighton in 1996 and 1997. Both capital and revenue support have been available in these areas. By 1997 revenue funding was also given for outreach, resettlement workers and additional hostel staff in the following areas: Bath, Birmingham, Blackpool, Bournemouth, Bury, Cambridge, Canterbury, Chester, Exeter, Gloucester, Great Yarmouth, Guildford, Leicester, Manchester, Northampton, Norwich, Nottingham, Oxford, Plymouth, Portsmouth, Reading, Sheffield, Slough, Stoke on Trent and Southampton.

RSI is based on a collaborative approach with statutory and voluntary organisations working together as consortia. Projects are devised following a single night count and an assessment of current provision for rough sleepers. Voluntary agencies may *not* apply directly but should approach their local authority to conduct a count and develop a strategy.

Applications: Please note the proviso to liaise in the first place with the local authority. The Rough Sleepers Initiative is due to end in March 1999. Bidding rounds closed in December 1997.

Organisations should contact Ian Brady (deputy chief executive of Centrepoint on secondment to RSI), Tel: 0171-890 3675; Fax: 0171-890 3649

Powers: Section 180 of the Housing Act 1996

Homelessness Action Programme (E H, Zone 2/A2)

> **Grant total: £34 million (over 3 years, 1999-2002)**

The government has set itself a target of reducing by two-thirds the numbers of people sleeping rough by 2002. This programme, announced in September 1998, builds on and replaces the Section 180 Single Homelessness grant and the Rough Sleepers Initiative (both of which are outlined above and end in March 1999). It has been developed as a result of the *Report on Rough Sleeping* by the Social

Exclusion Unit (SEU) (July 1998). The programme will help voluntary organisations throughout England to combat rough sleeping.

It includes an enhanced programme of revenue funding in areas outside London to tackle aspects of single homelessness and rough sleeping. Funding is available on a pump-priming, tapered basis.

In London, a new body will be set up to prevent rough sleeping following the recommendations of the SEU report. This new body will have a flexible budget, integrating funding from different government departments.

What types of project may qualify for grant in 1999/2000? Grants are intended to assist with the revenue costs of NEW projects that will economically provide practical and effective assistance to rough sleepers and other single people in housing need. Typically the types of projects funded to date have included:
- accommodation registers;
- lodgings/volunteer host schemes;
- outreach workers;
- resettlement schemes;
- rent deposit/guarantee schemes.

Applications are welcomed for innovative projects, particularly those that tackle youth homelessness. National projects can also be funded. See examples in the notes on the previous schemes.

Most grants fall within the range of £20,000 to £50,000 but larger bids will be considered.

Applications: Voluntary organisations should make bids to the DETR. Local authorities will then be consulted before money is allocated to ensure that projects fit in with local homelessness strategies. The closing date for applications was the end of October for funding schemes starting in April 1999. For application forms and further details contact Gwen Roberts (Tel: 0171-890 3646).

Housing Management & Tenant Participation Grant (E H, 2/A4)

Section 16 Grant Programme

> Total Funding: £6.175 million (2000/02)
> £5.975 million (2000/01)
> £5.575 million (1999/00)
> £5.175 million (1998/99)

It has been the department's policy in recent years to use the powers under the act (see below) to help set up Tenant Management Organisations (TMOs) under the Right to Manage (RTM); to fund national and regional tenant training; to sponsor a national Tenant Participation Help Line, and generally to promote tenant participation.

Ministers have reviewed the Section 16 grants programme. Its scope has been broadened to made available a package of Tenant Empowerment Grants which will:

■ ensure that tenants have access to independent information and advice about tenant participation and the option for involvement in the management of their homes;

■ offer a structured framework for effective and appropriate training courses;

■ encourage tenant capacity building and networking;

■ support the development of TMOs through the RTM process and to fill in some of the gaps identified by the research at the University of Salford on the RTM process.

There will also be new opportunities to promote and deliver innovation and good practice in tenant participation by inviting bids to run a selection of good quality innovative projects (with built-in evaluation) capable of being replicated on a national scale.

The new programme of grants is not intended to replace local authorities' responsibilities towards meeting tenants' needs, and funding models of participation, other than TMOs. It will, however, provide pump-priming to stimulate tenants' awareness, understanding and skills development. It will also ensure that tenants are involved as fully and effectively as possible so that they can help take forward the new tenant participation agenda being developed through the Housing Investment Programme process, Best Value in Housing implementation and Tenant Participation Compacts.

Timing

The department aims to implement as many of the new grant elements as possible during 1997/98 and in full from April 1999. Further announcements were still to be made at the time of writing.

The grant programme continues to support:

TMOS under the Right to Manage – grant is available to tenants who want to set up a TMO on their estate. Where tenants want to serve a Right to Manage notice on their council, a 100% *feasibility* grant is paid to an 'approved agency' to carry out a six-month feasibility study. If tenants then decide to develop a TMO, *development grant* is paid to the tenants' group to buy in training and support from an "approved agency" over the two year development programme and to negotiate a management agreement with their council. The cost of developing a TMO is shared 75/25 between the department and the council.

National Tenant Training – training is provided on a national basis by the Priorities Estate Project (PEP) and the Tenant Participation Advisory Service

(TPAS) with Section 16 grant. The programmes aim to provide a range of appropriate and accessible courses designed specifically to enable tenants and residents to participate effectively in the management of their homes.

Further information about the programmes can be obtained by writing to the two agencies or telephoning the following contacts:
PEP, Sandra Young (Tel: 0171-281 0438);
TPAS, Fola Agbalaya (Tel: 0161-745 7893).

Tenant Participation Help Line – the TPAS Tenants' Help Line receives Section 16 grant to provide information to tenants on all aspects of tenant participation. Tenants can write to TPAS or call free on 0500-844111.

Approved Agencies – the list of 21 agencies approved by the department for the purposes of the Right to Manage Regulations.

Applications: Tenants should approach general enquiries first. Then they are referred to the approved agency which helps prepare the application to the department.

General enquiries: Tel: 0171-890 3488; Fax: 0171-890 3489.
Other Contacts: S16 Grant Programme Manager: Paul Spearman,
Tel: 0171-890 3486.

Allocations and Payments Managers: Clint D'Souza Tel: 0171-890 3493; Bryan Lea, Tel: 0171-890 3485; Andy Swyer Tel: 0171-890 3492.

Powers: Section 16 of the Housing and Planning Act 1986

Transport

Planning, Roads & Local Transport Directorate

Mobility Unit (G M H, Zone 1/11)

Grant-in-aid:	£140,000 (1998/99)
	£105,000 (1997/98)

The Unit supports two organisations which promote the mobility of disabled and elderly people. These grants in 1998/99 were:
  The Community Transport Association, for information/advice service on

voluntary and community transport and training for operators of such transport schemes (£70,000);
Mobility Choice, to promote personal mobility of disabled and elderly people, including Mobility Roadshows (£70,000).

The Unit does *not* invite bids for grants.

Contact: Ann Frye, Head of Mobility Unit, Tel: 0171-890 4460;
Fax: 0171-890 4460; E-mail: mu.dot@gtnet.gov.uk
Web site: www.mobility-unit.detr.gov.uk

Powers: Section 17 of the Ministry of Transport Act 1919

Road Safety Division (G M H, Zone 2/14)

Grant-in-aid: £310,000

Two grants are paid annually and reviewed every three years: Royal Society for the Prevention of Accidents (RoSPA), (£260,000); Medical Commission on Accident Prevention (£8,000).

Road Safety Small Grants

> **Budget: around £40,000 annually**

Criteria for grant-making are based on a "hierarchy of benefits which reflect and complement" the work of the department. These include proposals which improve:
- new (especially new young) driver safety;
- child safety, especially pedestrian;
- driver attitudes to speed;
- safety of other vulnerable users – pedestrians, cyclists, motorcyclists;
- 'hard-core' drink/driving psychology.

The small budget is used for short-term projects, or those which need finance to get an initiative started but which have a reasonable prospect of self-financing.

Grants in 1997/98 included:
Child Accident Prevention Trust's Child Safety Week.

Contact: Hilary M Davies, Tel: 0171-890 2025; Fax: 0171-890 2029

Powers: Section 40 Road Traffic Act 1988

Ⓔ *Housing Corporation*

149 Tottenham Court Road, London W1P 0BN

Tel: 0171-393 2000; Fax: 0171-393 2111
Web site: http://www.open.gov.uk/hcorp

Contact: Investment Division

Grant total:	**£972+ million (capital)**
	£165 million (revenue) (1998/99)
	£1,108 million (capital)
	£208 million (revenue) (1997/98)

The Housing Corporation is a non-departmental public body funded by the Department of Environment, Transport and the Regions. It regulates and funds registered social landlords (RSLs), the non-profit bodies run by voluntary committees, most of which are housing associations. The corporation maintains a register of over 2,200 RSLs which are the major providers of new subsidised housing in England. Its provides the following grant schemes and also commissions research as necessary.

Social Housing Grant (SHG)

(previously Housing Association Grant)

Grant total: £972+ million (1998/99)
£1,108 million (1997/98)

These capital grants fund new schemes to build, renovate and repair homes. They are only open to registered social landlords.

Supported Housing Management Grant (SHMG)

(previously Special Needs Management Allowance)

Grant total: £138 million (1998/99)
£130 million (1997/98)

These revenue grants support the higher management and service costs of schemes for residents with special needs.

Innovation and Good Practice (IGP) Grants

Grant total: **£7.4 million (1998/99)**
£9.9 million (1997/98)
£6.9 million to 575 projects (1996/97)

These revenue grants support innovation, good practice and promotion. They aim to test new approaches for the benefit of all RSLs. Proposals which can demonstrate that their findings could improve the service to tenants other than the ones they represent are particularly likely to receive support. Proposals should meet at least one of the current themes outlined in the corporation's information materials. New themes phased in from 1998 were:

■ Sustainability – covering communities; tenancies & management; buildings;
■ Effectiveness of RSLs – covering accountability, participation and development;
■ Housing strategy development – covering regeneration & partnerships; identifying and meeting needs especially of black and minority ethnic people; new methods and approaches;
■ Regional initiatives – covering local priorities and partnerships.

Information: The corporation has an excellent publications service providing many useful advice booklets. In the special series about Innovation and Good Practice Grants *Advice 2* includes detailed case studies of exemplary projects and a full list of grant-aided schemes.

Applications: National projects should approach the Investment Division at The Housing Corporation's Headquarters. Regional or local projects should apply to the relevant regional office. Forms and guidance notes are available from Headquarters, or regional offices.

Regional Offices:

London region: Waverley House, 7-12 Noel St, London W1V 4BA
Tel: 0171-292 4400; Fax: 0171-292 4401

South East region: Leon House, High St, Croydon, Surrey CR9 1UH
Tel: 0181-253 1400; Fax: 0181-253 1444

South West: Beaufort House, 51 New North Rd, Exeter, Devon EX4 4EP
Tel: 01392-428200; Fax: 01392-428201

East region: Attenborough House, 109/119 Charles St, Leicester LE1 1FQ
Tel: 0116-242 4800; Fax: 0116-242 4801

West Midlands region: Norwich Union House, Waterloo Road,
Wolverhampton WV1 4BP; Tel: 01902-795000; Fax: 01902-795001

North East region: St Paul's House, 24 Park Square South, Leeds LS1 2ND
Tel: 0113-233 7100; Fax: 0113-233 7101

North West region: Elizabeth House, 16 St Peter's Square, Manchester M2 3DF
Tel: 0161-242 2000; Fax: 0161-242 2001

Merseyside region: 6th Floor, Corn Exchange Building, Fenwick Street,
Liverpool L2 7RB; Tel: 0151-242 1200; Fax: 0151-242 1201

Powers: The Corporation was created under the Housing Act 1964. Its powers have changed as a result
of various housing acts, the latest being the Housing Act 1996

Home Improvement Agencies, Care & Repair England Ltd.

Castle House, Kirtley Drive, Nottingham NG7 1LD

Tel: 0115-979 9091; Fax: 0115-985 9457

Contact: Mike Ellison, Policy and Monitoring Officer

Funding from DETR: £5,200,000 (1998/99)
£4,400,000 (1997/98)

There are 162 Home Improvement Agencies (HIAs) providing independent advice
and help to elderly and disabled people and people on low incomes to undertake
building repairs, improvements and adaptations to their properties. They are usually
small schemes, staffed by three or four people, operating on a district-wide basis.
HIAs are managed by a variety of organisations, often housing associations, but
also local authorities and voluntary organisations. Grants (of up to 50% of revenue
costs of HIAs) are channelled through local authorities which are responsible for
assessing the need for HIA services in their area and for bidding on their behalf.
Bids from local authorities are submitted in the autumn.

Grants made in 1998/99 ranged between £17,000 and £80,200 with the majority
receiving between £20,000 and £35,000. DETR funding represents 32% of total
HIAs budgets for 1998/99, although this varies between individual HIAs from 18%
to 46%.

Applications: Prospective applicants for funding should approach their local housing
authority. Further information can also be obtained from the national coordinating
body for HIAs, see above address.

It should be noted though that present funding arrangements end in 2000. Changes will follow those proposed in a consultation paper produced in summer 1998.

Housing Action Trusts (HATs)

HATs were set up under the 1988 Housing Act to take over and regenerate former local authority inner city housing estates. There were a total of six trusts (three in London boroughs) each with a ten year programme to redevelop, refurbish and manage their housing and to improve the physical, social and environmental conditions in their areas. They set out to encourage community participation and each HAT is run with a board of representatives from people who live on the estates.

In pursuit of their aims HATs can give grants to individuals, organisations (including charities) and businesses.

Details are available direct from the HATs:
Liverpool 0151-227 1099;
Castle Vale (Birmingham) 0121-776 6784;
North Hull 0148-285 6160;
Tower Hamlets 0181-983 4698;
Waltham Forest 0181-539 5533;
Stonebridge (Brent) 0181-961 0278.

General information can also be obtained from the relevant government office for the region.

New Countryside Agency

Title not known at the time of editing.
(formed from merger of Countryside Commission & Rural Development Agency)

The merged agency, to be formed on 1st April 1999 from the Rural Development Commission and the Countryside Agency, aims to develop a more integrated approach to issues affecting rural communities and the countryside.

The new organisation will retain the statutory responsibilities of the two existing bodies:
- to advise the government on, and to conserve and enhance the natural beauty and amenity of the English countryside, and increase opportunities for the public to enjoy it;

- to review and advise the government on social and economic development of rural areas in England and promote such development as necessary.

It will take on the existing bodies' current programmes and commitments, *excluding those that it has already been announced are to be transferred to the Regional Development Agencies.* There seems to be some questioning about the scope and definition of the regeneration work which will be transferred.

Considerable locational changes will be involved. Both the CC and RDC have similar regional boundaries but their head and regional offices are in different towns.

The following information is provided, even if it rapidly becomes historical, to give future readers, unaware of the work of either of these agencies, a review of their functions and relevance to the voluntary sector prior to merger.

Until the merger takes place regional bodies will be working 'as usual' in their relationships with organisations seeking grants.

Countryside Commission

John Dower House, Crescent Place, Cheltenham, Gloucestershire GL50 3RA

Tel: 01242-521381; Fax: 01242-584270
Web site: http//www.countryside.gov.uk

Grant total:	£13.8 million (1997/98)
	£14.7 million (1996/97)

The Countryside Commission, funded by the Department of the Environment, Transport and the Regions, is the government's principal adviser on landscape, conservation and countryside recreation. It also raises funds from other sources – The National Lottery, the European Union and business sponsorship. The commission gives grants and financial support for a range of countryside conservation and recreation activities in England.

The commission allocates most of its grant (79%) to programmes with local authorities and public bodies. About 20% (£2.7 million) is paid to "private persons and non-public bodies". The remainder (some £1/4 million in 1997/98) is via special schemes.

In 1996 the commission produced *A Living Countryside* – its strategy for the next ten years. This set out seven main themes to be developed depending on "resources available and guidance from the Ministers". Grant-aid is directed at projects which support the priorities identified in the Strategy and Corporate Plan. In summary these were:

- the encouragement of local pride so that local communities and public organisations strengthen the special character of each part of the English countryside;
- the promotion of sustainable leisure activities including such features as 'Greenways' – links between town and countryside, 'Quiet Roads', 'Millennium Greens', rights of way, green tourism, including doubling the area of woodland in England and promoting products from land managed to benefit landscape, wildlife and recreation;
- the achievement of long-term benefits from farms and woodlands by finding a sound basis for the stewardship of land;
- sustainable development in the countryside, including experiments and advice on managing transport;
- better information about the countryside;
- protection and promotion of the areas of finest landscape – national parks, areas of outstanding natural beauty and heritage coasts;
- Improvement of the countryside around towns including 'Community Forests' and 'Green Corridors into the Cities'.

For many years the commission promoted many different types of grant in separate leaflets. It has recently run a more flexible arrangement which follows the strategy outlined above but also allows for the differing regional character and needs of the countryside. Regional offices may have their own particular priorities within these, depending on the pressures and issues affecting the countryside in their area. Interested applicants should be in contact with their relevant office. National, regional and local voluntary organisations are all eligible for support. Each application is assessed by a project officer in the relevant office. Grants of between 20% and 50% of the total cost may be offered. The level of grant is discretionary and only in exceptional circumstances has it exceeded 50%.

If the project has secured funding from other Exchequer sources (ie. from other government agencies or departments but not including local authorities) then the combined grant cannot exceed 50%. All other sources of funding or involvement in other schemes must be set out in the application.

Grants cannot be made retrospectively for work already undertaken.

Applications: Obtain a copy of *Grants and Payment Schemes Booklet CCP 422.* Approaches can be made at any time of the year. How quickly applications and grants are processed depends upon the size and complexity of the application. In all cases, preliminary enquiries should be made to the commission's regional offices at the addresses listed below.

Regional Offices
Northern: Warwick House, Grantham Road, Newcastle-Upon-Tyne NE2 1QF
Tel: 0191-232 8252; Fax: 01242-584270

North West: 7th Floor, Bridgewater House, Whitworth Street, Manchester M1 6LT
Tel: 0161-237 1061; Fax: 0161-237 1062
Yorkshire and Humberside: 2nd Floor, Victoria Wharf, Embankment 1V, Sovereign
Street, Leeds LS1 4BA; Tel: 0113-246 9222; Fax: 0113-246 0353
Midlands: 1st Floor, Vincent House, Tindal Bridge, 92-93 Edward Street,
Birmingham B1 2RA; Tel: 0121-233 9399; Fax: 0121-233 9286
Eastern: Ortana House, 110 Hills Road, Cambridge CB2 1LQ
Tel: 01223-354463; Fax: 01223-313850
South West: Bridge House, Sion Place, Clifton Down, Bristol BS8 4AS
Tel: 0117-973 9966; Fax: 0117-923 8086
South East: 4th Floor, 71 Kingsway, London WC2B 6ST
Tel: 0171-831 3510; Fax: 0171 -831 1439

Rural Development Commission

(addresses in 1998)

141 Castle Street, Salisbury, Wiltshire SP1 3TP

Tel: 01722-336 255; Fax: 01722-432773
E-mail: rdc.general@argonet.co.uk
Web site: http://www.argonet.co.uk/rdc

London HQ: Dacre House, 19 Dacre Street, London SW1H ODH

Tel: 0171-340 2900; Fax: 0171-340 2911

The RDC's rural regeneration work will transfer to the new Regional Development Agencies in 1999.

The Rural Development Commission was set up as the government agency 'concerned with the well-being of the people who live and work in rural England'. It has concentrated the largest share of its resources in Rural Development Areas (RDAs), the parts of rural England experiencing the greatest concentrations of economic and social problems. Here the commission aimed to diversify and strengthen their local economies, and also strengthen communities and help disadvantaged groups. The development of partnerships with public and private sectors has been central to its strategy.

The account which follows is given to indicate the funding programmes that the Regional Development Agency may inherit.

Rural Development Programmes

Funding total: Around £13 million annually

These programmes have provided advice and funding for a range projects, from village halls, to voluntary transport services, re-use of redundant buildings, green tourism and the regeneration of small towns and villages. The focus has been on the needs of a local community and its economy. Attractions important for residents as well as visitors, such as crafts, heritage and exhibition centres, museums, festivals and countryside education, have also been assisted to develop.

Rural Transport Development Fund

Grant total: £1.6 million (1997/98)
**   £1.7 million (1996/97)**

Nearly half of the 140-150 projects supported have been community projects.

Rural Challenge

Annual funding total: £5 million (1997/98)
**   £2.82 million (1996/97)**

This competition has provided prizes of £1 million each year for winning projects put forward by local partnerships within Rural Development Areas (RDAs). The prize has paid out over three years. RDAs have competed in alternate years except for the four largest which have competed annually. The commission has aimed to co-ordinate with the Single Regeneration Budget (SRB) Challenge Fund (see separate entry) by running to a similar timetable for bids and joint evaluation of SRB bids with a significant rural component.

The commission also provides funding to and works closely with ACRE, the co-ordinating body for rural community councils. Its combined funding to ACRE and RCCs has been about £3 million annually. ACRE also administers programmes for the commission (see separate entry).

RDC regional offices in 1998: For information about specific schemes and individual projects contact the relevant area office.

North West – Cumbria, Cheshire, Lancashire
Hawesworth Road, Penrith, Cumbria CA11 7EH
Tel: 01768-865752; Fax: 01768-890414

North East – Cleveland, Durham, Tyne & Wear, Northumberland
Morton Road, Yarm Road Industrial Estate, Darlington, Co Durham DL1 4PT
Tel: 01325-487123; Fax: 01325-488108

Yorkshire & Humber
Spitfire House, Aviator Court, Clifton Moor, York YO3 4UZ
Tel: 01904-693335; Fax: 01904-693288

West Midlands

Strickland House, The Lawns, Park Street, Wellington, Telford, Shropshire TF1 3BX;
Tel: 01952-247161; Fax: 01952-248700

East Midlands

18 Market Place, Bingham, Nottingham NG1 8AP
Tel: 01949-876200; Fax: 01949-876222

East Anglia

Lees Smith House, 12 Looms Lane, Bury St Edmunds, Suffolk IP33 1HE
Tel: 01284-701743; Fax: 01284-704640

South West

3 Chartfield House, Castle, Street, Taunton, Somerset TA1 4AS
Tel: 01823-276905; Fax: 01823-338673

27 Victoria Park Road, Exeter, Devon EX2 4NT
Tel: 01392-421245; Fax: 01392-421244

2nd floor, Highshore House, New Bridge Street, Truro, Cornwall TR1 2AA
Tel: 01872-273531; Fax: 01872-275646

South East

Sterling House, 7 Ashford Road, Maidstone, Kent ME14 5BJ
Tel: 01622-765222; Fax: 01622-662102

The Chantry House, 29-31 Pyle Street, Newport, Isle of Wight PO30 IJW
Tel: 01983-528019; Fax: 01983-825745

English Nature

Northminster House, Peterborough PE1 1UA

National office switchboard: 01733-455000
Enquiry Service: 01733-455100-102
Fax: 01733-455103
E-mail: enquiries@english-nature.org.uk
Web site: http://www.english-nature.org.uk

Contact: Margaret Robinson, Grants Officer

Grant-aid:	£1,616,000 (1998/99)
	£1,704,000 (1997/98)
	£1,839,000 (1996/97)

English Nature is the government funded body set up to promote the conservation of England's wildlife and natural features. "Biodiversity and sustainability are at the heart of its work." It advises government and other bodies, implements European and other international agreements, notifies outstanding areas as Sites of Special Scientific Interest (SSSIs) or, additionally, as National Nature Reserves (NNRs) and Marine Nature Reserve (MNRs). It works closely with public, private and charitable landowners and occupiers in various forms of co-operative and partnership arrangements for improved land management and wildlife enhancement. It also runs an extensive research programme and a popular public enquiry service.

Its grants programme consists of a number of targeted national schemes and support for local projects and volunteer action at local team level. Most of the funding is devoted to national work with local schemes absorbing about 18-20% of total grant aid. The programme reflects the organisation's nature conservation priorities:

- SSSIs;
- species recovery;
- Biodiversity Action Plan habitats and species;
- sustainability;
- Natural Areas;
- habitats and species directives;
- increasing public opportunities for wider public involvement.

The agency was not happy to give any more detailed information about its grants programmes or examples of recent beneficiaries for use in this guide lest it become outdated and misleading to applicants. "Schemes are sometimes changed or even cancelled and the accuracy of information given months in advance cannot be guaranteed... funding levels are also subject to our annual grant-in-aid."

All interested groups and individuals are advised to telephone the enquiry line (see above) for grants information or contact their local EN office (see list below) to find out the current situation. Local offices have interests specific to their own areas. It is important for potential applicants to build up a working relationship with them. All groups whether rural, urban and urban fringe may be considered, but priorities will, of course, vary according to the needs and natural features of the different areas.

Exclusions: Work in National Nature Reserves (with some exceptions), building works, projects outside England (except GB projects in co-operation with Scottish Natural Heritage and Countryside Council for Wales), compensation payments, expeditions and student projects (except those eligible for fieldwork projects by final year undergraduates, HND students and one-year postgraduates doing Masters degrees). Grants are not normally offered for ongoing office and administration costs, survey, research or data collection, books and periodicals.

Applications: Potential applicants are advised to contact the Enquiry Service (Tel: 01733-433101) or their appropriate Local Team as early in the project planning stage as possible. They can then receive specific advice on relevant schemes, eligibility, availability of funds and required procedures.

Voluntary organisations, local authorities, other non-profit-making organisations and individuals are eligible to apply for the discretionary grants provided they are able to find *at least 50% of the project costs from non-exchequer sources.* Grants are normally paid in arrears on satisfactory completion of objectives and there is usually a requirement to submit project reports with claims.

Local Area Teams
Bedfordshire, Cambridgeshire and Northamptonshire
Peterborough Tel: 01733-391100; Fax: 01733-394093

Cumbria
Kendal Tel: 01539-792800; Fax: 01539-792830

Devon
Okehampton Tel: 01837-55045; Fax: 01837-55046

Cornwall & Isles of Scilly
Truro Tel: 01872-262550; Fax: 01872-262551

Dorset
Wareham Tel: 01929-556688; Fax: 01929-554752

East Midlands – Lincolnshire, Leicestershire, Nottinghamshire
Grantham Tel: 01476-568431; Fax: 01476-570927

Essex, Hertfordshire and London
London Tel: 0171-831 6922; Fax: 0171-404 3369

Hampshire and the Isle of Wight
Lyndhurst Tel: 01703-283944; Fax: 01703-283834

Gloucestershire, Herefordshire and Worcestershire (listed as 'Three Counties')
Eastnor Tel: 01531-638500; Fax: 01531-638501

Humber to Pennines
Wakefield Tel: 01924-387010; Fax: 01924-201507

Kent
Wye Tel: 01233-81252; Fax: 01233-812520

Norfolk
Norwich Tel: 01603-620558; Fax: 01603-762552

North and East Yorkshire
York Tel: 01904-435500; Fax: 01904-435520
Leyburn Tel: 01969-623447; Fax: 01969-624190

North West
Wigan Tel: 01942-820342; Fax: 01942-820364

Northumbria
Newcastle-Upon-Tyne Tel: 0191-281 6316; Fax: 0191-281 6305

Peak District and Derbyshire
Bakewell Tel: 01629-815095; Fax: 01629-815091

Somerset and Avon
Taunton Tel: 01823-283211; Fax: 01823-272978

Suffolk
Bury St Edmunds Tel: 01284-762218; Fax: 01284-764318

Surrey and Sussex
Lewes Tel: 01273-476595; Fax: 01273-483063

Thames and Chilterns
Crookham Common/Newbury Tel: 01635-268881; Fax: 01635-268940

West Midlands
Shrewsbury Tel: 01743-709611; Fax: 01743-709303

Wiltshire
Devizes Tel: 01380-726344; Fax: 01380-721411

Powers: Environment Protection Act 1990

Rural Action for the Environment

see ACRE entry

The Forest Authority

231 Corstorphine Road, Edinburgh EH12 7AT

Tel: 0131-334 0303; Fax: 0131-316 3943
Web site: www.forestry.gov.uk

Contact: Gordon Inglis, Grants and Licences Division

Grants to private woodland owners:	£41 million (1998/99)
	£36 million (1997/98)
	£33 million (1996/97)

The Forestry Authority is part of the Forestry Commission, the government agency responsible for forestry in *Britain*. Its other components are Forestry Enterprise and Forestry Research. The Authority sets standards for the whole of the forestry industry, both private and public, ensures compliance with plant health and tree felling regulations and also administers grant schemes to help private landowners, known as the Woodland Grant Scheme.

Woodland Grant Scheme (WGS)

Woodland Grant Scheme (WGS) aims:

- to encourage people to create new woodlands and forests to increase the production of wood, to improve the landscape, to provide new habitats for wildlife and to offer opportunities for recreation and sport;
- to encourage good management of forests and woodlands, including their well-timed regeneration, particularly looking after the needs of ancient and semi-natural woodlands;
- to provide jobs and improve the economy of rural areas and other areas with few other sources of economic activity;
- to provide a use for land instead of agriculture.

All woodlands and forests can be considered for grants under the WGS, except those which are too small or too narrow. Normally the woodland must be a quarter of a hectare in area and at least 15 metres wide, but smaller woods may be eligible if the aims of the scheme are met.

These aims are pursued by a range of grants under three main categories: New Woodlands; Existing Woodlands and Challenge Funds.

New Woodlands

Planting Grants encourage the creation of new woodland. They are paid as part of a contract in which the applicant agrees to look after the woodlands and do the approved work to reasonable satisfaction. Supplements are also paid in priority areas. These are:

- Better Land Supplement for the planting on arable or improved grassland;
- Community Woodland Supplement where access is given to local people;
- Locational Supplement for new planting in specific areas over a limited period of time. Check for details with local office.

Short Rotation Coppice for poplars and willows.

Farm Woodland Premium Scheme (FWPS) encourages the creation of new woodlands for certain types of farm land to enhance the environment and as a productive alternative land use. The Forestry Authority is responsible for administering the scheme (though payments are made from the Agriculture Departments).

Existing Woodlands

Woodland Improvement Grants assist projects which provide public recreation in woodlands, to improve under managed woods, and enhance woodland biodiversity.

Natural Regeneration Grants may be made as an alternative to planting.

Restocking Grants towards the cost of replanting an existing wood.

Annual Management Grants towards the cost of work to safeguard or enhance the special environmental value of a wood, improve woods which are below current environmental standards, or create, maintain or enhance public access.

Livestock Exclusion Annual Premium is paid if agricultural stock are removed from and kept out of ancient woodlands in the uplands.

Forest Expansion Challenge Funds

These funds were launched in 1996/97 to encourage the planting of new woodlands in specific areas of the country. These projects run for three years. Each year, applicants are asked to 'bid' for the amount of money they require to carry out the planting. The bids are judged on a competitive basis. Contact local offices for details of locations.

Applications: Detailed guidance about these schemes, financial rates and application forms are given in the pack available from the above address or from the Woodlands Officer in local Forestry Authority Offices. Check your telephone directory or ring the following national offices for the contact you need in the conservancies in your country:

Scotland, Edinburgh office for contacts in its 6 conservancies:
Tel: 0131-334 0303; Fax: 0131-334-3943

England, Cambridge office for contacts in its 7 conservancies:
Tel: 01223-314546; Fax: 01223-460699;

Wales, Aberystwyth office for contacts in its 3 conservancies:
Tel: 01970-625866; Fax: 01970-626177

(For Northern Ireland see entry under Department of Agriculture, Northern Ireland – DANI)

The National Forest Company (NFC)

Enterprise Glade, Bath Lane, Moira, Swadlincote, Derbyshire CE12 6BD

Tel: 01283-551211; Fax: 01283-552844
E-mail: nationalforest@mcmail.com
Web site: www.nwleicsdc.gov.uk

Contact: Dr Hugh V Williams, Grants & Land Management Adviser

The National Forest, devised by the Countryside Commission and announced in 1990, links the ancient forests of Needwood and Charnwood and spans three counties in the English Midlands – Derbyshire, Leicestershire and Staffordshire. Its mostly rural landscape of mixed farmland is one of the least wooded areas of the country. It also suffers from economic decline and dereliction from mining and clay working. Its principal towns are Burton upon Trent (brewing), Coalville and Swadlincote (mining) and Ashby de la Zouche (historic).

The National Forest Company was set up in 1995 to create this new forest. It aims to promote nature conservation and cultural heritage; assist provision for sport, recreation and tourism; encourage agricultural and rural enterprise; stimulate economic regeneration; encourage community and business participation. Central to its work are its partnerships with local authorities, farmers, landowners, companies, local communities and people all over Britain. Whilst the company receives grant-aid from government this is pump priming finance and covers a proportion of the project's total costs. It has its own specialists to generate further funds, investment opportunities and together with other partners has made ambitious bids to the Heritage Lottery Board and the Millennium Commission.

A National Forest Tender Scheme

£1.8 million (1997/98)

The Tender Scheme was launched in 1995 jointly with the Forestry Authority, for rapid conversion of farm and derelict land to forest. An estimated two thirds of the planting needed during the Forest's first 10 years will be achieved through this scheme. In Round 3 (1997/98), 13 out of 27 bids were successful. Many of these were from local farmers planting new woods and giving access for walkers and horse riders. Others were urban such as a new woodland around playing fields, or planting on land restored after mineral workings between a brick factory and a row of houses.

Land Acquisition Fund

£100,000 (1997/98)

The company has funds to buy land itself or to assist others in acquiring it, as part of its work to develop a wide range of partners in its work. Grant aid is usually made for up to 50% of property's value, or 75% in exceptions.

Development Programme Fund

£150,000 (1997/98)

This fund allows for strategic acquisition of land and site management agreements. It also supports community and arts projects within the National Forest Areas with maximum grants of £2,000 and £3,000 respectively per project. Around 30 local projects are supported each year including parish-based wildlife surveys, heritage and art projects and specific features at forest sites. Both BTCV and Leicestershire and Rutland Trust for Nature Conservation have received support under this fund.

Major Forest Related Bids

The company will act as a catalyst giving advice and assistance for national and European Union funding. The National Forest has obtained Millennium funding of some £6.75 million for the National Forest Millennium Discovery Centre.

Countryside Commission

(see new Countryside Agency)

ENTRUST – Landfill Tax Credit Scheme

(see Appendix)

Ⓔ DEPARTMENT OF HEALTH

The departmental addresses occurring in this guide are:

Richmond House (R H)
79 Whitehall, London SW1A 2NS

Tel: 0171-210 3000; Fax: 0171-210 5523
Web site: www.open.gov.uk/doh/dhhome/htm

Wellington House (W H)
133-155 Waterloo Road, London SE1 8UG
Tel: 0171-972 2000

Quarry House (Q H)
Quarry Hill, Leeds LS2 7UE
Tel: 0113-254 5000

Health care, disability and the welfare of those people suffering from particular physical and mental problems have long been at the core of the work of the voluntary sector. The following outline is provided to help readers identify and target areas of potential interest.

In 1998 the department had two main sections with most relevance to the voluntary sector – the Social Care Group and the Health Promotion Division of the Public Health Policy Group. Both are based at Wellington House.

The Social Care Group covers social work and social service aspects of the services for which the department is responsible. It is comprised of the following branches:

- Branch SC1/2 – General social services policy and Personal and Social Services training (Section 64 grants);
- Branch SC3 – Children's services;
- Branch SC4 – Children's residential care, secure accommodation and juvenile justice;

- Branch SC5 – Community care, elderly social care;
- Branch SC6 – Disabilities, mental illness, deprivation issues.

The Health Promotion Division, a subdivision of the Public Health Policy Group, comprises:

- HP 1 Health of the Nation, health strategy and survey, Health Education Authority Ethnic Minority health;
- HP 2 Alcohol and drugs misuse, domestic violence;
- HP 3 Notifiable and other communicable diseases;
- HP 4 Birth control, family planning, fertility, genetics etc.

The National Health Service Executive (NHSE) is an integral part of the department, not a separate agency as the name suggests. The voluntary sector will have many varieties of working relationships with the regional offices of the NHE, the Health Authorities, the NHS Trusts and the proposed Primary Care Groups of GPs, but these relationships are outside the scope of this guide.

Contents

Related Agency
Health Education Authority

Social Care Group (W H)

Grants Administration Unit

Grants to national voluntary organisations Section 64

Grant total:	**£21,173,142 (1998/99)**
	£20,800,000 (1997/98)

Grants are made to national voluntary organisations whose activities consist of or include the provision of services similar to relevant services provided under statutes in the *health and personal social services* fields. Grants are restricted to England. Similar schemes operate in Scotland, Wales and Northern Ireland.

National Project Grants

Such grants must further the department's policy objectives by testing an innovative idea or by helping to develop a particular pattern of service. Arrangements for monitoring, evaluation and dissemination must be agreed before a grant is given. A grant is normally limited to a maximum of about half the total project costs. The source/s of funding for the balance of the costs must be clearly shown before a grant is approved. Such grants are given for a maximum of three years, plus another year for evaluation and dissemination. No extension to these periods is allowed.

Core Grants

These grants help with central administration costs of national organisations which demonstrate clearly defined objectives. Grants usually amount to only a small percentage of headquarters' administrative expenditure. Since the department does not wish for over-reliance on government funding, organisations are expected to demonstrate that other sources of funding have been also explored. Grants are usually for three years at a fixed cash level, tapered downwards over the grant period.

Local Project Grants

Local and health authorities also have powers to make grants to voluntary organisations. Local projects should seek funding from these sources though Section 64 project grants may be made exceptionally as follows:
- pump-priming to meet exceptionally high initial costs over a limited period (where local or health authorities are unable to meet these);

- where a project spans a number of local or health authorities which are unable or unwilling to provide the necessary finance;
- where an innovative local experiment has potential national significance and the local or health authority is unable or unwilling to meet the cost;
- where the department on it own initiative wishes to test certain proposals for client care.

As with national projects arrangements for monitoring, evaluation and dissemination must be agreed before a grant is given. Local project grants may be given for up to three years, plus one further year for evaluation.

Capital Grants

Grants for land, building or movable assets are only awarded in exceptional circumstances. This type of funding has a low priority within Section 64 funding. The applicant must demonstrate that it cannot achieve its objectives by other means and within its own resources. The purpose of the capital grant must rank very highly amongst the department's policy objectives.

Small movable assets (up to £5,000) such as office equipment may be considered as part of a core or project grant application and need not be separately requested.

In 1998/99 a total of 624 grants were given. Of these, 262 were 'new grants' in a rolling programme, ie. the first year of a round of core funding or of a specific project.

Individual grants ranged from £5,000 to over £350,000 with the largest being core grants. Many major core grants were given in conjunction with other grants eg. the Standing Conference on Drug Abuse (SCODA) received a total of £499,000, of which the core grant of £290,000 was accompanied by five other grants: First Key received £225,000, a core grant of £125,000 plus another £100,000 for its National Voice project, England; British Agencies for Adoption and Fostering (received £277,613 of which £200,000 was for core costs plus three other project grants); Action on Elder Abuse was awarded a total of £135,000, a modest core grant of £12,500 plus £63,000 for its response line and £60,000 for video and booklet production.

Major 'new' core grants of over £100,000 in 1998/99 included:
    Alcohol Concern (£370,800);
    Institute for the Study of Drug Dependence (£300,000);
    NACRO (£275,000);
    Family Service Units (£230,000);
    Carers' National Association (£120,000);
    Haemophilia Society, National Youth Advocacy Service (£100,000 each).

Continuing major core grants included:
  Family Service Units (£230,000);
  National AIDS Trust (£225,000);
  Mencap (£175,000);
  Mildmay Mission Hospital (£150,000);
  Childline (£163,000 + £10,000 project);
  Terrence Higgins Trust (£150,000);
  Family Planning Association (core – £100,000 + 3 other grants totalling £89,400);

Examples of smaller core grants were:
  Makaton Vocabulary Development Project (£30,000);
  Zito Trust (£15,000);
  Pain Concern UK (£13,000);
  Action Against Allergy (£7,000).

The wide ranging project grants included:
  CRUSE Bereavement Care (£150,000 in 4 grants);
  Centrepoint (£50,000);
  The Continence Foundation (£30,000);
  Theatre in Health Education (£30,000);
  Cystic Fibrosis Trust, advocacy project (£25,000);
  Vietnamese Mental Health Services (£21,000).

Exclusions: Funding is not given for research projects, or to voluntary organisations serving a particular profession or sphere of employment.

Applications: Guidance notes and application forms are available from late summer each year. The deadline for completed application forms is September/October for grants starting the following April. Notification of the outcome of the application can be expected around February/March.

Organisations should have or should be in the process of producing an equal opportunities policy.

Contacts: Allison Noterman, Policy Manager, SC2, Room 610,
Tel: 0171-972 4093; Becky Harrison, Tel: 0171-972 4109

Powers: Section 64, Health Services and Public Health Act 1968

Opportunities for Volunteering Scheme

> **Grant total: £9.1 million (1998/99 and in 1997/98)**

The General Fund of this programme which was first set up in 1982 is administered for the Department of Health by the Consortium on Opportunities for Volunteering (10 national voluntary networks). In addition *16 specialist charities* act as agents, each with their own cycle of grant applications. Scotland and Wales have their own separate arrangements (see separate entries).

This scheme aims to:

- develop opportunities for unemployed people to undertake voluntary work;
- expand voluntary work in the fields of health and personal social services.

Grants can only be given to voluntary organisations and groups. It is not a substitute for paid employment.

The voluntary work should help *people who need particular support* eg. elderly people, isolated young mothers, children in trouble, disabled people.

The definition of *voluntary work* for this scheme means:

- working as a volunteer in a voluntary organisation, or within a health authority or local authority social services department eg. arranging a programme of entertainment for residents of a hospital or old persons' home;
- contributing to a neighbourhood care group ie. one which reinforces the support provided by families, friends and neighbours to a range of people with particular needs;
- taking part in a community group, eg. helping supervise an adventure playground;
- participating in a self-help group eg. mother and toddler group.

The definition of *Unemployed*, for this scheme, means a person of working age who is not in full-time employment or education. It includes people who are sick or disabled, prematurely retired, or on short-term working as well as *unemployed people drawing Job Seekers' Allowance.*

Whilst a project must be designed to involve primarily unemployed volunteers, it is not a requirement that all volunteers must be unemployed.

Most work supported is outside the scope of services provided by health authorities and trusts, or local authority social services departments.

Exclusions: Grants are not given for activities more closely related to other government departments or public services eg. housing, environmental services, education, victim support services, information and advice about social security or housing benefits.

Contact: Allison Touboulic, Policy Manager, Tel: 0171-972 4104; Fax: 0171-972 4307

General Fund – Consortium on Opportunities for Volunteering

4th Floor, 35/37 William Road, London NW1 3ER
Tel: 0171-387 1673; Fax: 0171-387 1686

Contact: Jean Foster, Manager

The Consortium, now established as an independent charitable company, comprised in 1998:

Action for Communities in Rural England (ACRE);
British Association of Settlements and Social Action Centres (BASSAC);
Churches Together in England;
Community Matters;
National Alliance of Women's Organisations;
National Association of Councils of Voluntary Service;
National Association of Volunteer Bureaux;
National Coalition for Black Volunteering;
National Centre for Volunteering;
RADAR Royal Association for Disability and Rehabilitation.

Co-opted members include:
Asian People with Disabilities Alliance;
The Refugee Council.

Grants are made to voluntary organisations, collectives and self-help groups which develop projects involving volunteers in the delivery of *health and social care services to their local communities*. Priorities for 1998-2001 have been: women, disabled people, black and minority ethnic communities and people living in rural areas. Arts and environmental projects must demonstrate that the focus of their work is a health-related issue.

Start-up funds have been offered for a maximum of 36 months with an upper grant limit of £30,000 per year. These grants could be used for: salaries (all posts must be concerned with work which supports the involvement of volunteers); volunteers' out-of-pocket expenses; training; project and office equipment.

Funds have been fully committed for the three-year period 1998-2001.

The majority of grants have been between £20,000 and £30,000. Examples of projects supported during the 1995-98 funding programme include:
Refugee Volunteer Project, Africa Research and Information Bureau, Waterloo, London (£32,620);
Derby Homeless Advocacy Project (£30,926);
Children Affected by Alcohol Misusers, Birkenhead, Merseyside (£30,670);
Mental Health Volunteer Scheme SAVO, Ipswich (£28,858);
Cleveland AIDS Support, Middlesbrough (£27,876);

Drugline Lancashire, Preston (£21,685);
Salisbury and District Well Women Centre (£24, 190);
Hertsmere Domestic Violence Drop-in Centres, Herts (£5,516).

Exclusions: Applications from statutory bodies and individuals; schemes to set up volunteer bureaux or the core activities of a Citizens' Advice Bureau; organisations with an annual turnover of more that £100,000 at the time of applying – this limit does not apply to the member bodies of sponsoring organisations such as Councils for Voluntary Service, Rural Community Councils, Racial Equality Councils and Volunteer Bureaux; building work, except access arrangements for disabled people; projects for people over 55 – these projects should approach Age Concern England; work previously funded by the consortium or funded by one of the specialist agencies.

Applications: Grants are allocated for three years. Funds have been fully committed until 2001. Decisions for the 1998-2001 round were made in December 1997. Information about the fund after March 2001 should be available from the General Fund office early in 2000.

Specialist Agencies – Opportunities for Volunteering

Each of the 16 agencies listed below administers a funding programme specifically directed at the work of its own members, associates, linked projects, etc. Each has its own definition of the type of work it aims to support agreed with the Department of Health and its own administrative arrangements. Interested readers should contact the head office of each organisation to find out more details about its funding criteria and the timing of its funding cycles and application closing dates. In 1998 these were:

Age Concern, England
Grants Unit, Astral House, 1268 London Road, London SW16 4ER
Tel: 0181-679 8000

Barnardo's
Tanner's Lane, Barkingside, Ilford, Essex IG6 1QG
Tel: 0181-550 8822

British Association of Settlements and Social Action Centres (BASSAC)
Winchester House, 11 Cranmer Road, London SW9 6EJ; Tel: 0171-735 1075

Churches Together in England
Inter-Church House, 35-41 Lower Marsh, London SE1 7RL
Tel: 0171-523 2007

The Children's Society
Edward Rudolf House, Margery Street, London WC1X 0JL
Tel: 0171-837 4299

Community Service Volunteers (CVS)
237 Pentonville Road, London N1 9NJ; Tel: 0171-278 6601

Crisis
1st Floor, Challenger House, 42 Adler Street, London E1 1EE
Tel: 0171-377 0489

MENCAP
Clippers Quay, Salford Quays, Manchester M5 2XP; Tel: 0161-888 1200

MIND (National Association for Mental Health)
Granta House, 15-19 Broadway, Stratford E15 4BQ
Tel: 0181-519 2122; Fax: 0181-522 1725

NACRO (National Association for the Care and Resettlement of Offenders)
169 Clapham Road, London SW9 0PU; Tel: 0171- 582 6500

National Association of Leagues of Hospital Friend
2nd Floor, Fairfax House, Causton Road, Colchester, Essex CO1 1RJ
Tel: 01206-761 227

Pre-School Learning Alliance
69 Kings Cross Road, London WC1X 9LL; Tel: 0171-833 0991

RADAR
12 City Forum, 250 City Road, London EC1V 8AF; Tel: 0171-250 3222

Royal National Institute for the Blind (RNIB)
Voluntary Agencies Link Unit, 224 Great Portland Street, London W1N 6AA
Tel: 0171-388 1266

Scope (formerly The Spastics Society)
West Regional Office, 160 Pennywell Road, Easton, Bristol BS5 OTX
Tel: 0117-941 4421

United Kingdom Council on Deafness (UKCOD)
OFV Grants, P O Box 13, Abbots Langley, Herts WD5 ORQ
Tel: 01923-264 584 (voice and minicom); Fax 01923-261 635.

An application may be made to one agent only. In most cases funds are allocated on an annual basis.

Powers: Appropriation Act

Social Care Group 2 (WH)

Social Work Training, Education and Research

Grant total: **budgeted £912,000 (1998/99)**
£989,000 (1997/98)

These grants promote good practice and management, responsiveness to users, and the effectiveness of personal and social services staff. These also contribute to change in social policies and their implementation.

> National Institute for Social Work, London, to support its administrative infrastructure and a project on the Management of Practice Expertise (£517,000); Ruskin College, Oxford, to support a Diploma in Social Work course (£238,000); Selly Oak Colleges, Birmingham, to support a Diploma in Social Work course (£234,000).

This funding is not open to other applications. It is specific to the bodies funded and is fully committed to this purpose.

Contact: A R Parker, Room 620, Tel: 0171-972 4290

Social Care Group 3 (W H)

Children in need and their families

Grant total: **forecast £100,000 (1998/99)**
£300,000 (1997/98)

Funding is given to assist innovative schemes to help children *in need* and their families.

Grants in 1997/98 included:
> Council for Disabled Children at the National Children's Bureau, to mount seven workshops throughout England to disseminate current research and inspections relating to children with disabilities (£35,000);

National Children's Home (NCH), Action for Children South West for a collaborative project with Dartington testing ways of enabling children and their parents to make better use of educational opportunities (£30,000);

National Children's Bureau, to prepare an language assessment guide for children in need (£5,000);

NSPCC, North West Region, a project to promote effective family support, by monitoring of local authority budgets where these have been used successfully and quickly to refocus children's services.

Annual announcements are made calling for applications. Levels of funding vary annually and no calls for bids had been made for 1998/99 by early July 1998. Organisations within this area should also apply for Section 64 funding (available from the Department of Health and the Department for Education and Employment, see separate entries).

Contact: David Matthews, Room 101, Tel: 0171-972 4076

Women's Aid Federation (England)

Grant total: £49,000 (1998/99 and for 1997/98)

This funding supports the operation of a telephone helpline for the women victims of domestic violence.

Contact: Arran Poyser, Room 1116A, Tel: 0171-972 4261

Social Care Group 6 (W H)

Disability funding

Family Fund Trust (FFT)

Grant-in-aid UK wide:	**£24.18 million (1998/99 and 1997/98)**
England:	**£18,818,000 (1998/99)**
	£18,195,520 (1997/98)

The FFT provides grants to families with severely disabled children under the age of 16 who are being brought up in their own home. It funds items for which grants from other sources are not available (eg. washing machines, driving lessons and holidays). It operates UK-wide and receives funding from all four UK health departments.

The Family Fund was established in 1973 by the then SoS of Social Services in the wake of the Thalidomide tragedy and it was administered by the Joseph Rowntree Foundation in York on behalf of the government. The fund became an independent trust in 1996 with a cash-limited budget.

This grant is one of the DoH's Centrally Financed Services (CFS). The amount of the grant is determined annually and cash-limited dependent on need.

Contact: Sue Row, Room 242, Tel: 0171-972 4127

Disability equipment databases

Grant total: £106,000 (1998/99, and in 1997/98)

This funding for the development of disability equipment databases throughout the UK is a time-limited project:
Disability Living Foundation (£76,000);
Royal National Institute for the Blind (£30,000).

International disability action

Grant total: £72,978 (1998/99); £72,847 (1997/98)

These three grants, which are annually given, are made to support international disability action eg. international subscriptions, UK representation at conferences:
Disability Awareness in Action (£40,847);
Royal Association for Disability & Rehabilitation (£24,000);
British Council of Disabled People (£8,000).

Contact: David Wardle, Tel: 0171-972 4135

Shared Training Grant Programme

Grant total: £150,000 (1998/99 and 1997/98)

These grants are aimed to support services for people with learning disabilities. The priorities in 1998/99 covered the following areas but did not rule out consideration of bids received on other topics:
- involving and supporting parents and carers;
- meeting the needs of ethnic minorities;

- user involvement in planning and monitoring services;
- positive images;
- parents with learning disabilities;
- facilitating access to health care;
- identification and assessment of health needs;
- health promotion and education for people with learning disabilities generally and for those with particular syndromes;
- multi-agency audit.

Ten grants were given in 1998/99:
    British Institute of Learning Disabilities (£24,200, £11,920 and £3,920);
    University of Exeter (£29,000);
    Association of Practitioners in Learning Disability Services (£15,700);
    Tizard Centre (£15,000);
    Home Farm Trust Limited (£13,550);
    Strathcona Theatre Company (£11,780);
    Family Planning Association (£9,930).

There is no set limits to the grant given.

Applications: The scheme is run along similar lines to the Section 64 programme (see above). Publicity and access to this scheme is via the *Shared Training Newsletter* issued each summer which incorporates an application form.

Contact: Ms P Parris, Room 233, Tel: 0171-972 4501

Health Promotion Division (W H)

The health and access to health of ethnic minority groups

> **Grant total:**   **£638,000 (1998/99 and 1997/98)**

Funding is available for voluntary organisations, Health Authorities, NHS trusts, professional bodies and educational establishments to develop materials and projects to improve health and access to health services for all black and ethnic minority groups. Funding may be given for project work, the production of videos, guidance material, booklets, leaflets, and posters, or to organise conferences, seminars etc.

Grant may cover the full cost of the project or it may be a part contribution. Grants range in size but rarely exceed £40,000.

Voluntary organisations can apply for funding to:
- develop Health of the Nation and Patients' Charter projects to improve the understanding of these issues with ethnic communities and ensure their perspective of these issues is taken into account;
- develop communication and information dissemination with these groups;
- improve communications between service providers and users;
- carry out projects not covered in the Health of the Nation five key areas, but which are important to ethnic communities eg. diabetes and other health conditions such as sickle cell also other underlying issues affecting health;
- develop and improve access to Primary and Community Care Services.

Examples of grants to voluntary organisations in 1997/98 included:
Association of Guyanese Nurses and Allied Professions, good parenting skills amongst adolescent Caribbean and African women (£35,000 x 3);
Foundation for Women's Health and Research Development (FORWARD), female circumcision in the African community (£30,000 x 3);
Medical Institute of Tamils, coronary heart disease (£14,700);
Arab Health Project, for a directory of Arab organisations (£5,000);
Lifeline, towards a conference on drugs and the Asian community (£5,000).

Exclusions: Research projects.

Applications: Guidelines and criteria are available. Organisations must have or be in the process of producing an equal opportunity policy. Applications must have a built-in component for: pre-testing ideas; positive and measurable outcomes; national dissemination; evaluation and assessment.

In 1998 the programme planned to start to run an annual application 'round' with applications to be submitted by November for grants commencing the following financial year. Potential applicants should check the position.

Contact: Mrs Veena Bahl, Departmental Adviser on Ethnic Minority Health (HP1), Room 541, Tel: 0171-972 4671

Services for Drug and Alcohol Misusers

Voluntary Organisations Providing Services for Drug and Alcohol Misusers

> **Grant total: £2,500,000 (1998/99)**

During 1998/99 priority for funding was given to renewal applications which have successfully achieved the targets and milestones they agreed with the department at the outset of 1997/98. A balance of only £300,000 was available for new work in 1998/99. Instead of running a full bidding exercise for new projects involving local authorities, the department itself sought proposals for complex needs projects eg. those which involve mental health, as well as drug and alcohol, problems.

In early September 1998 the Health Minister announced that "My department will... be working very closely with the DETR's new Homelessness Action Programme... to give priority to rough sleepers projects in the bidding round for the Drugs and Alcohol Specific grant to 1999/2000". The details of future programmes were not finalised at the time of going to press.

Contact: Rob Jex, Team Leader, Alcohol (HP2)
Tel: 0171-972 4161; Fax: 0171-972 4218

Communicable Diseases Branch

HIV/AIDS Health Promotion

> **Grant total to voluntary sector: £2,815,000 (forecast 1998/99)**
> **£2,943,000 (1997/98)**
> **£2,490,000 (1996/97)**

National HIV/AIDS health promotion is undertaken by the statutory and voluntary sector. It supports the Secretary of State's objective "to reduce the incidence of avoidable illness, disease and injury of the population".

Planned expenditure for 1998/99 is approximately £4.640 million of which 60% (£2.815 million) will fund work by the voluntary sector through contracts with the department. This is in line with the UK Health Department's Report *HIV/AIDS Health Promotion: An Evolving Strategy* (Nov 1995) which stated that targeted work may be better undertaken by community-based and self-help groups.

Voluntary sector funding consists of:
i) targeted health promotion work for gay and bisexual men; a three year contract awarded in 1995 to the Terrence Higgins Trust (£1.1 million in 1998/99);
ii) work in support of World AIDS day; a three year contract awarded jointly to the National AIDS Trust and the Health Education Authority (£75,000 to each party in 1998/99);
iii) National AIDS Helpline and the National Drugs Helpline, a contract awarded by competitive tender in 1995 to Network Scotland. This contract ended in September 1998 and the department has been re-tendering (£1.640 million – 1998/99).

With the exception of the National AIDS/Drugs Helplines, all HIV/AIDS health promotion contracts from March 1999 will be subject to the outcome of an HIV/AIDS strategy review.

This funding has been handled in a proactive and strategic manner: it was not advertised. Voluntary organisations are expected to approach the Section 64 programme with their own funding proposals (see separate entry).

Contact: Kay Orton, Tel: 0171-972 4649

Primary Care Division

Dental & Optical Services (R H)

British Fluoridation Society
Forecast: £70,000 (1998/99)
          £66,000 (1997/98)

An annual grant for public education, public opinion surveys and research.

Contact: Jerry Read, Tel: 0171-210 5743; Fax: 0171-210 5774

NHS Executive

Child Health, Health Services Directorate (W H)

Training Clinicians and other Staff in Child Health Care

> **Total Budget: about £75,000 annually**
> **Grant total to voluntary organisations: £1,710 (1997/98)**

This budget is not restricted to applications from voluntary bodies, although applications from them are welcomed. Funds are mainly given on the basis of a detailed proposal which either directly delivers training for staff or develops new training methods. Whilst there is no set maximum size to grants awarded, individual grants are limited to £20,000 in any one year.

In 1997/98 two voluntary organisations were supported:
Laurence-Moon-Bardet Biedl Society, advice for GPs who encounter this rare condition (£1,100);
Association for Children with Life-threatening or Terminal Conditions and their Families, to publish guidance for professionals caring for these children (£610).

Contact: Keith Young, Room 509, Tel: 0171-972 4139

Patient's Charter Unit, Corporate Affairs – Quality Control (Q H)

Volunteering

> **Grant total: £14,000 (1997/98)**

In 1997/98 allocations were made in one-off payments from the Patient Partnership Budget following the recommendations of the NHS Executive report *Making a Difference: Strengthening Volunteering in the NHS*. Grants were given to:
National Centre for Volunteering, for survey (£4,550); towards a *Good Practice Guide* (£1,450);

National Centre for Volunteering, WRVS, League of Friends and Community Service Volunteers, to organise workshops on good practice in volunteering and spread the new guide's approach (£2,000 each).

The total funding for 1998/99 will include publication of the *Good Practice Guide* and further support to regional workshops.

Contact: Peter Burgin, Tel: 0113-254 6091; Fax: 0113-254 6114

Health Education Authority

Trevelyan House, 30 Great Peter Street, London SW1P 2HW

Tel: 0171-222 5300

Contact: Jane Greenoak, Deputy Chief Executive

The Health Education Authority, a public body funded by the Department of Health, promotes good health through education and awareness programmes.

It conveys its message through mass media advertising and educational materials and also through a wide network of alliances with voluntary bodies, local and central government, education, employers and the health and medical disciplines.

No special provision is made for grant-making. However, the potential exists for voluntary bodies working in relevant fields to receive programme funding for specific research, dissemination, education and training projects. For example in 1996/97 it formed a special working relationship with the National AIDS Trust to co-ordinate World AIDS Day. It also made arrangements with FOCUS, the umbrella group for the major mental health organisations, to support World Mental Health Day with a special local grants scheme.

Whilst the HEA works primarily in England it operates in close collaboration with corresponding bodies in Scotland (Health Education Board of Scotland) and Wales (Health Promotion Wales).

THE HOME OFFICE

The Civil Service Yearbook describes the Home Office as dealing with "those internal affairs in *England And Wales* which have not been assigned to other government departments". Whilst its work spans a variety of responsibilities its role is more coherent than those words would suggest since it is concerned with all aspects of law and order. Most of its functions relate to these in some way.

The Home Secretary is particularly concerned with the administration of justice, criminal law, the treatment of offenders including probation and the prison service, the police, immigration and nationality, community relations, race relations policy, certain public safety matters, fire and civil defence service services, and passport policy matters.

Amongst its wide ranging remit the Home Office deals also with firearms, dangerous drugs and poisons, laws in relation to shops, liquor licensing, gaming, theatre and cinema licensing.

It is also responsible for a special governmental unit concerned with the voluntary and community sector nationally. This unit advises government on this sector, conducts surveys of its health and vitality and also administers grant programmes to support it.

50 Queen Anne's Gate (Q A G)
London SW1H 9AT
Tel: 0171-273 4000
Fax: 0171-273 2190

Horseferry House (H H)
Dean Ryle Street,
London SW1P 2AW

Block A Whitgift Centre (W C)
Wellesley Road, Croydon,
London CR9 2BY

Contents

Voluntary and Community Unit
  Main Grants Programme
  Volunteering Section
  Voluntary Groups working with Families
Refugees – Reception/Resettlement
Racial Disadvantage Grants
Section 11 Grants (successor programme)
Immigration Asylum and Appeals
Probation Unit Grants
Approved Hostels (Probation/Bail)
  Victim Support and SAMM
  Homestart
  Crime Concern
  NACRO, Mental Health Unit
Innovative Projects in Crime Reduction
Drug Prevention Initiative
  RoSPA – Water Safety
  Prisoners Abroad
  NACRO Prisons Link Unit
  CSV – for Voluntary Work by Offenders Pre-Release Scheme

Related Agencies

Commission for Racial Equality
Alcohol Education & Research Council

Voluntary and Community Unit (HH)

The VCU is concerned with work and issues relevant to the voluntary and community sector as a whole in the UK. The main but not exclusive focus of its funding is England. It works closely with its counterparts in the Scottish, Welsh and Northern Ireland Offices and has a UK co-ordinating role.

The Minister of State in early 1998 described the VCU's work as ranging from the "better co-ordination of existing voluntary activity" and the "maintenance of established organisations" to being a "springboard to imaginative and diverse new work" which was innovative and "at the cutting edge of social exclusion".

Main Grants Programme

> **Grant total:** **£11.4 million (1998/99)**
> **£11.5 million (1997/98)**
> **£11.7 million (1996/97)**

The priorities for grants are:

Increasing the effectiveness of the UK voluntary sector
- supporting infrastructure organisations which develop the effectiveness of national, regional or local voluntary organisations;
- supporting the development of volunteering and voluntary organisations within black and minority ethnic communities;

Promoting voluntary activity generally
- developing and promoting volunteering by under-represented groups;
- increasing awareness of the benefits of volunteering;

Promoting community development and self-help
- developing and promoting work which engages with volunteers at a local community level;
- developing and promoting voluntary activity at a neighbourhood level among under-represented groups;
- developing and promoting work which helps agencies (statutory or non-statutory) to work together more effectively at neighbourhood level.

A leaflet, *Grants to Voluntary Organisations*, includes the VCU's Strategy Statement in full which, because of its length, is not reproduced here.

Support is available to national organisations. It is also given to projects sponsored by national, *regional or local* voluntary organisations which are a) 'innovative' (ie. new within the voluntary sector as a whole) and likely to provide lessons over a wider area, and b) likely to promote the VCU's strategy.

At least 45 organisations were funded in 1998/99 and grants ranged from £7,200 to £5.3 million. All but ten of the grants were to organisations which had previously received funding. The largest grant, absorbing 46% of funding, was made to the Women's Royal Voluntary Service. No other grants were over £1 million. Other major core grants over £250,000 were awarded to:
   Community Development Foundation (£901,000);
   National Council for Voluntary Organisations (£851,000);
   National Centre for Volunteering (£765,000);
   Community Service Volunteers (£653,000).

Other recipients included:
   SIA, the National Development Agency for the Black Voluntary Sector (£154,000);
   SCADU – Student Community Action Development Unit (£77,500);
   Telephones Helplines Association (£45,000);
   Churches Community Work Alliance (£44,500);
   The Media Trust (£32,000).

Organisations which received core grant for the first time in 1998/99 included:
   Neighbourhood Initiatives Foundation (£50,000);
   The Chinese in Britain Forum (£40,000);
   Consortium of Lesbian, Gay and Bisexual organisations (£30,000);
   National Federation of Youth Action Agencies (£7,200).

Exclusions: Work/organisations in which another government department or funder would have a greater interest (eg. crime prevention, assisting new refugees); work outside the UK; grants to individuals; match funding; religious activity; applications from regional and local voluntary organisations, with the exception of those which meet definition of 'innovative' projects (see above).

Applications: Queries about the application process and funding criteria may be made at any time of year.

New, or previously unsuccessful applicants, are invited to send an outline of their proposal before completing the application form. Three advisers, each with experience in the voluntary and community sector, are employed to help potential applicants prepare their applications.

Three types of grant are given: core (or strategic) funding, project and capital. Multiple applications are allowed – in 1997/98 one organisation received four grants: one core, two project and one capital. Funding is for work undertaken in England, but does not have to be exclusively confined to England.

Joint bids from more than one organisation are welcome.

Deadlines: Core and project grant applications must be sent by 30th September for grants paid from the following April. Applications for small capital grants from organisations already funded by VCU may be submitted later in the year.

The first issue of *VCU News* appeared in summer 1998.

Contact: Alison Patten, Tel: 0171-217 8565; Fax: 0171-217 8572
E-mail: grants.vcu@btinternet.com
Web site: www.homeoffice.gov.uk/vcu.htm (application forms can be downloaded from the Web site)

Ⓔ Volunteering Section

Total grant:	**£2,759,214 (1998/99)**
	£4,812,345 (1997/98)
	£3,707,984 (1996/97)

The following grant programmes, which have been run on a competition basis, have been part of the *Make a Difference Initiative*, which has aimed to broaden and strengthen the local volunteering infrastructure. Grants have been spread over 2-3 years, with later years receiving tapered funding.

Youth Volunteer Development Programme

Grant total: £1,078,355 (1998/99)
A major part (39%) of the total funding shown above was absorbed by a grant to the National Youth Agency (see separate entry) for the administration and onward grant making of this programme.

Local Volunteer Development Agency Grants (LVDA)

Grant total: £1,108,117 (1998/99)
The first round of these grants was held in 1995 and grants for the third round will continue to be paid until 1999/2000. Successful applicants were funded to establish a volunteer development agency in certain chosen areas. Individual voluntary organisations or a locally based consortia (including at least one voluntary organisation) were invited to apply for three-year funding with a maximum total grant of £120,000 (up to £60,000 in the first year, £40,000 in the second and £20,000

in the third), with a possible additional £5,000 as a continuation fund if alternative funding did not follow immediately.

Volunteer Bureaux (VB) Strengthening Grants

Grant total: £557,742 (1998/99)

These grants, for core services only, were to help volunteer bureaux extend their operations and/or increase their functions. Individual volunteer bureau, or group of volunteer bureaux, could apply for maximum funding over three years of £35,000 (up to £20,000 in first year, £10,000 in the second and £5,000 in the third).

Pre-start and ongoing development support has been available from:
National Association of Volunteer Bureaux, New Oxford House, 16 Waterloo Street, Birmingham B2 5UG (Tel: 0121-633 4555).

Community Service Volunteers received £15,000 to co-ordinate 'Make a Difference Day'.

At the time of writing this entry (autumn 1998) these programmes were completing their lifespan (see above). Consideration was being given to what form of funding to support local infrastructure may be made in the future, but plans were undeveloped and may not translate into grant programmes.

Contact: Janet Cross, Tel: 0171-217 8674; Fax: 0171-217 8572

Voluntary Groups working with Families

> **Grant total:**   £3 million (2000/01 and 2001/02)
>   £1 million (1999/00)

A total of £2 million has been allocated for grants for work by voluntary organisations concerned with family and parenting support work in 1999/00. £1 million of this will be allocated through an open competitive application process.

The criteria for making grants are expected to parallel those of the main grants programme of the VCU.

The VCU's Family Support Grants programme will be split into 3 strands:
- increasing the effectiveness of family and parent support services provided by voluntary organisations;
- innovative national or local projects aimed at developing new forms of support services to families and parents;

- work under an annually set theme. During 1999-2000, the theme is likely to be work with boys and fathers.

Applications: Criteria, guidance and application forms are expected to be available from December 1998 and announcements on successful applications will follow in April 1999.

Contact: Virginia Burton, Tel: 0171-217 8108 (for advice on applications); Matthew McGahran, Tel: 0171-217 8545; Fax: 0171-217 8800 (for grant leaflets and application forms).

This part of the VCU is providing the administration for the establishment of the National Family and Parenting Institute (see separate entry) which arose from discussions within the Ministerial Group on the Family (including Education, Health, Social Security, Lord Chancellor's and Home Office) and will receive start up interdepartmental funding of £2 million.
Contact: Katharine Bramwell, Team Leader, Tel: 0171-217 8475;
Marianne Lister, Tel: 0171-217 8453; Fax: 0171-217 8500.

Constitutional and Community Policy Directorate (QAG)

Race Equality Unit

 **Reception and Resettlement of Refugees**

Grant total:	£3,789,000 (1998/99)
	£4,303,200 (1997/98)

Grants are made to voluntary organisations to support the development of refugee self help community groups, and to promote networking between refugee groups and other local agencies to improve their access to statutory services.

In 1997/98 nearly half the total funding (£2,090,100) was given to 8 national and regional refugee councils with grants ranging from £32,640 to £1,274,000. They were:

Refugee Council (£1,274,000);
Refugee Action (£477,900);
Scottish Refugee Council (£32,640);
Welsh Refugee Council (£32,640);
Midlands Refugee Council (£32,640);
Northern Refugee Centre (£32,640);
North of England Refugee Services (£32,640).

Other grants were made to voluntary organisations involved with the reception of asylum seekers to enable them to advise on statutory services and to help with emergency accommodation and maintenance costs of destitute asylum seekers until they can access the statutory services. In 1997/98 these were made to:

Refugees Arrivals Project (£1,300,000);
Refugee Council Panel of Advisers for Unaccompanied Minors (£428,000);
Migrant Helpline (£85,100).

An additional grant was also given to Refugee Action Monserrat Project (£400,000).

Funding is given to groups with a national or regional remit. Emerging groups receiving this funding need first to be recognised by the National Development Working Group which draws together *existing* refugee organisations to implement a national framework for assisting refugees.

Contacts: Richard Brett (0171-273 3400); Ian Barton, Room 1276, Tel: 0171-273 3053; Fax: 0171-273 4198.

Section 11 Group

Reduction of Racial Disadvantage Grants

Grant total:	£175,000 (1998/99)

A small number of grants are given to projects that fit Government objectives aimed at reducing racial disadvantage, especially in employment and business. Grants have included:

Windsor Fellowship, to assist ethnic minority graduates to find employment;
Manchester City Football Club for anti-racism projects.

Applications: Information and application forms from Ceri Leech, Room 1286 at above address (Tel: 0171-273 4220).

Successor Programme to Section 11 Grant for Ethnic Minorities

Following a review of Section 11 provision, the major part of Section 11 funding will transfer to the Department for Education and Employment. These grants to overcome the barriers of language or culture have been made to local authorities, grant maintained schools and further education colleges to employ staff to support ethnic minorities. The majority are for teachers of English as a second language. Other educational support areas include social services, housing and employment, training and enterprise.

A new grant programme to tackle racial disadvantage and to promote racial equality *in fields other than education* will start in 1999 and be made up of those resources formerly spent under Section 11 on non-education projects and from resources from government spending plans announced in July 1998.

The new grant aims to be:
- flexible;
- be concerned with a wider range of types of disadvantage than Section 11, and include tackling racism, racial harassment and racial discrimination;
- be open to voluntary organisations and others as well as to local authorities.

For further information contact:
Bob Wright (Room 1279, Tel: 0171-273 2145);
Michael Dewey (Room 1385, Tel: 0171-273 4222).

Powers: Section 11 of the Local Government Act 1966

New Grant Scheme for Ethnic Minority Voluntary Groups

A new funding programme is likely to start from 1999 but at the point of editing no further information was available. For further information, interested organisations should contact:
Bob Wright (Room 1279, Tel: 0171-273 2145);
Michael Dewey (Room 1385, Tel: 0171-273 4222).

ⓊⓀ Asylum and Appeals Policy Directorate (WC)

Immigration Asylum and Appeals

> **Grant total:**   **£5.9 million (1998/99)**
> **£6.7 million (1997/98 and 1996/97)**

Discretionary grants can be made to voluntary organisations providing free advice and assistance to people with rights of appeal. Eligible organisations must be able to provide a comprehensive service.

Two independent organisations receive core-funding. In the two years preceding 1998/99 they also received short-term funding, under the Spend to Save Initiative, to help speed up the asylum decision-making process following the 1996 changes to benefit regulations.

Grants awarded in 1998/99 were:
Refugee Legal Centre, to help asylum seekers with rights of appeal (£3.2 million);
Immigration Advisory Service, to help people with immigration and/or asylum rights of appeal (£2.7 million).

Contact: Geoff Brindle, Tel: 0181-760 3486; Fax: 0181-760 3128

Powers: Section 23, I immigration Act 1971 (also under the Asylum and Immigrations Appeals Act 1993)

Criminal Policy Directorate (QAG)

Probation Unit

Probation Unit Grants

Grant total:	**£3.23 million (1998/99)**
	£3.28 million (1997/98)

Grants are made to organisations or individuals concerned with the rehabilitation of offenders or support for those on bail. Support is made available for projects or organisations that are national or serve a national purpose. Grants are also given as 'seed money' for innovative projects which support Home Office priorities. Funding is available for 100% of costs with no set minimum or maximum grant level.

A total of 15 projects were funded in 1998/99 with grants ranging between £25,000 and £900,000. They included:
  NACRO core grant (£500,000);
  Wolvercote Sex Offenders Clinic (£320,000);
  SOVA, core grants (£180,000);
  Prisoners Abroad, for outreach work with repatriated offenders (£60,000);
  RPS Rainer, for court desk help (£25,000).

Applications: Applicants need to have contacted the unit by November for grants in the following year. There is no standard form, but applications should be well-structured and include clear summaries of the purposes/s for which the grant is sought, evidence of need, precise objectives, breakdowns of proposed expenditure, time-scales and information about how the applicant would "demonstrate progress during the work and the achievement of objectives".

NB: Individual probation boards are expected to spend 7% of their budgets on partnerships with voluntary and private sector organisations. Contact should be made directly with the *local* probation services.

Contacts: Steve Pitts, General partnership grants (Tel: 0171-273 3278);
Marcus Smart, Education, training and employment of offenders (Tel: 0171-273 2874). Fax: 0171-273 3944.

Powers: Section 20 (1) (d) Probation Service Act 1993

Voluntary Managed Approved Hostels

> **Grant total:**   **£3,501,470 (1998/99)**

In July 1998 there were 101 approved hostels (8 bail and 93 probation/bail). The majority are managed by probation services and 13 by voluntary organisations. Approved hostels are intended as a base from which residents take full advantage of community facilities for work, education, training, treatment and recreation. Their primary purpose is to provide enhanced supervision.

Funding comes from three different sources: 80% of the net running costs from Home Office revenue grant; the remaining 20% from the relevant local authority plus a contribution from the residents towards their accommodation costs.

The grants to the 13 voluntary managed hostels ranged between £249,340 and £324,670 in 1998/99 and totalled £,3,501,470.

Contact: Mark Warren, Tel: 0171-273 3995; Fax: 0171-273 3944

Powers: Sections 20(2) (b & c) Probation Service Act 1993

Procedures and Victims Unit

Grant-in-aid in 1998/99 was given to two organisations and represented about 80% of their total income.

Victim Support

Grant-aid: £12.682 million (1998/99 and in 1997/98)

An annual grant is made to Victim Support which provides practical help and emotional support to victims of crime and support for victims/witnesses in the Crown Court. About 10% goes towards the costs of the national office while the major part supports the work of local victim support groups and witness services.

SAMM (Support After Murder and Manslaughter)

Grant-aid total: £43,000 (1998/99)

First grant to this young self-help organisation for the families and friends of homicide victims.

Contact: Richard Thew, Tel: 0171-273 3368; Fax: 0171-273 2967

Powers: Part 1 of the Estimate and Confirming Appropriation Act

ⓔ Juvenile Offenders Unit

Homestart

A one-off grant of £69,000 spread over three years (1996/97-1998/99) for two early intervention projects to help parents: the Castleford, Pontefract and District Project in Yorkshire and the Wycombe project in Buckinghamshire.

Contact: Hilary Jackson, Head of Unit, Tel: 0171-273 3161; Fax: 0171-273 4345

ⓔ ⓦ Crime Prevention Agency

Crime Concern

Grant-in-aid: £750,000 annually (1996/97-1998/99)

Crime Concern, an independent crime prevention charitable company set up in 1988 and based in Swindon, receives core-funding on a three-year basis from the agency. It is required to submit to the Home Office for a further three years funding for the period 1999/2002.

Contact: Jackie Westlake, Tel: 0171-273 2147; Fax: 0171-273 4037

Powers: Part 1, vote 3 of the Supply Estimates and confirming Appropriation Act

ⓔ Mental Health Unit

NACRO (National Association for the Care and Resettlement of Offenders)

Grant: £184,800 (1998/99); £145,656 (1997/98); £142,800 (1996/97)

The Mental Health Unit of NACRO has been funded since 1990, initially for a three year pilot project, then for a rolling programme of work to promote effective local inter-agency arrangements for dealing with mentally disordered offenders. Funding of a further three year programme of work has been agreed from 1998/99 which includes project development work with local groups; providing training and advisory services; and work with the Area Criminal Justice Liaison Committees.

In 1996/97 the Revolving Doors Agency, London, also received a non-statutory grant.

Contact: Helen McKinnon, Tel: 0171-273 3233; Fax: 0171-273 2937

Research and Statistics Directorate (QAG)

Programme Development Unit

Innovative Projects in Crime Reduction/ Prevention

> **Funding total:**　£680,000 per annum including evaluation costs for three year funding cycle 1996/97-1999/00

The Unit was set up in 1991 to test out innovative practical responses to problems of crime and criminality, the results of which could then inform policy development and practice. It encourages and funds the development of local projects which are independently evaluated and from which findings are widely disseminated.

Grants are usually for up to three years subject to annual review. They cover project costs but not core funding or major capital expenditure.

The current programme, concentrating on crime reduction issues relating to young people, supports six projects chosen after a two-stage application process from nearly 1,000 original applicants. The following examples are those with a voluntary sector lead organisation. The figures include evaluation costs.

> Chance, Islington, London, a mentoring programme for primary age children (£90,000);
>
> Dalston Youth Project, Crime Concern, a mentoring and supplementary education programme for 11 to 15 year olds (£105,000);
>
> Suffolk ACRE, social integration and crime prevention in rural areas (£75,000).

For further information about the Unit's programme contact:
Christine Lehman, Head of Unit (0171-273 3542);
Dr Lorna Smith (0171-273 3541).

Ministerial priorities for the new cycle were not known (or if programme would be continued) at time of editing this guide.

Ⓔ Central Drugs Prevention Unit (H H)

Drug Prevention Initiative

> **Grant total:** £1.9 million (1998/99)

The Drugs Prevention Initiative was launched in 1990 to test and pilot a community based approach to drugs prevention. As an *initiative* it is set to run until March 1999. It focuses on: young people; communities; parents; and the criminal justice system. There are 12 local Drugs Prevention Teams which work with a range of local partners, both statutory and voluntary, providing support both via grants and through advice.

Successor arrangements are planned for the initiative beyond March 1999 to support the government's anti drugs strategy and promote community based drugs prevention across England. On 1 April 1999 the Drugs Prevention Initiative will be replaced by the Drugs Advisory Service which will have nine regional teams covering the whole of England. Contact the unit for further advice.

Contact: Jim Nicholson, Head of Unit, Tel: 0171-217 8055; Fax: 0171-217 8230
Web site: http://www.homeoffice.gov.uk/dpi/dpiinf.htm

Ⓤ Fire Safety Unit (HH)

Water Safety

RoSPA (Royal Society for the Prevention of Accidents)

Grant-in-aid: £17,000 (1998/99); £16,000 (1997/98); £37,000 (1996/97)

Annual grant-in-aid is paid to RoSPA for its water safety education and publicity work throughout the UK. This covers coastal and inland waters as well as the home environment.

Contact: Mike Larking, Tel: 0171-217 8364; Fax: 0171-217 8722

H M Prison Service

Prison Service Headquarters, Cleland House (CH)
Page Street, London, SW1P 4LN
Tel: 0171-217 3000; Fax: 0171-217 6635

Abell House, (A H)
John Islip Street, London SW1P 4LH
Tel/Fax: see above

The Prison Service, which became an Executive Agency of the Home Office in 1993, is responsible for prison services in England and Wales.

Prisoner Administration Group (C H)

Prisoners Abroad

Grant-in-aid: £85,000 (1998/99 and in 1997/98)

An annual ongoing grant contributes towards the core costs of Prisoners Abroad. This charity works with British citizens detained overseas, their families in this country, and prisoners returning here, who have served custodial sentences abroad and have then been deported after their release from prison. There is no competitive funding system as this is the sole organisation working in this field.

Contact: John Edwards, Tel: 0171-217 6398; Fax: 0171-217 6280

Regimes Policy Unit (A H)

NACRO Prisons Link Unit

Grant-in-aid: £226,000 (1998/99 and in 1997/98)

NACRO Prisons Link Unit provides information and training on setting up and running housing and employment advice services for prisoners. All establishments are expected to have a pool of officers trained by the Prisons Link Unit. It has been fully funded since 1988 by the Prison Service.

Contact: Elizabeth Bernard, Tel: 0171-217 5086; Fax: 0171-217 5332

Community Service Volunteers

Grant-in-aid: £150,000 (1998/99); £200,000 (1997/98 and 1996/97)

This long-standing grant from the Young Offender Unit helps CSV to place offenders on a volunteer scheme for a period of time prior to their release.

Contact: Ron Le Maréchal, Tel: 0171-217 5123; Fax: 0171- 217 5227

Youth Justice Board for England & Wales

50 Queen Anne's Gate, London SW1H 9AT

Tel: 0171-273 3822; Fax: 0171-273 2258

Contact: Warwick Maynard

The Youth Justice Board for England & Wales was set up as a NDPB on 30th September 1998. It monitors and advises on: the operation of the youth justice system and the provision of youth justice services; how the principal aim of the youth justice system might most effectively be pursued; and the content of any national standards in respect of youth justice services or the accommodation in which children and young persons are kept in custody.

Development Fund

The chairman of the board announced a development fund for the next three financial years (starting April 1999). The purpose of the fund is to encourage the development of innovation and good practice in fulfilling the statutory aim of the youth justice system, ie. to prevent offending by young people.

The fund will invite competitive bids from those delivering youth justice services in England and Wales. No further information was available at the time of editing.

Alcohol Education and Research Council

Room 520 Clive House,
Petty France, London SW1H 9HD

Tel: 0171-271 8379/8337

Contact: Leonard Hay

> **Grant total: £350,000-£400,000 (anticipated for 1997/98)**

The council founded in 1981, administers the Alcohol Education and Research Fund, set up as a charitable foundation (number 284748) with assets from the former licensing compensation authorities. The fund finances projects within the UK concerned with "education and research and for novel forms of help to those with drinking problems, including offenders. The fund may be used to aid other charitable organisations having similar purposes". The council also runs a studentship scheme.

Its 15 council members are appointed by the Home Secretary from a variety of professional and business backgrounds.

In 1996/97 the most recent report sent by the council and filed at the Charity Commission, showed that the fund had assets of over £9.3 million with a gross income of over £533,000 from which grants of £345,600 were paid. The kinds of work it seeks to support include the following:

- researching socio-economic, culture and media influences on drinking;
- promoting public health and responsible drinking;
- understanding early drinking patterns among high-risk groups and providing advice and prevention projects;
- public education and effective co-operation between statutory and voluntary bodies.

Grants made in 1996/97 totalled £301,160, ranged from £335 to £68,440 and included:

Newcastle City NHS Trust (£68,440);
British Deaf Association (£23,410);
Alcohol Concern (£3,000);
Newham Alcohol Advisory Service (£2,000).

Applications: The council meets quarterly to consider applications and reports from grant holders. Applications are first assessed by independent assessors. All projects are expected to include proposals for monitoring progress, final evaluation and dissemination.

Commission for Racial Equality

Elliot House, 10/12 Allington Street, London SW1E 5EH
Tel: 0171-932 5412; Fax: 0171-630 7605

Funding to Racial Equality Councils

> **Funding total: £3,697,500 (1997/98)**

The commission, which receives grant-in-aid from the Home Office, provides financial support to 91 racial equality councils (RECs) around the country, all of which are set up as registered charities. The funding covers the employment costs of racial equality officers. This funding is matched by contributions from local authorities for project and administrative costs.

Reduced grant-in-aid to the Commission from Home Office in 1998/99 has led to the loss of the Project Grants Scheme which ran at about £375,000 in 1997/98.

Powers: Section 44 of the Race Relations Act

INTERNATIONAL SECTION

This section covers those departments where support to the voluntary sector is given to organisations working internationally.

Contents

Foreign Office

Department for International Development
- Non-Governmental Organisations Unit
- Development Awareness Fund
- Conflict & Humanitarian Affairs Department
- Know How Fund (including Environmental Know How Fund)

Related Agencies/Organisations
Charity Know How
British Council
- *Arts Division*
- *Visiting Arts*
- *Youth Exchange Centre*
Commonwealth Youth Exchange Council

ⓤ FOREIGN AND COMMONWEALTH OFFICE

> **Whitehall, London SW1A 2AH**
> **Tel: 0171-270 3000**

General grants to Voluntary Organisations

> **Grant-in-aid:**   £6,039,382 (1996/97)

In 1996/97, the most recent year for which the department could provide information, a total of 22 grants were made to organisations in the voluntary sector. Grants are awarded to organisations which help further foreign policy aims and objectives. Many are annual and long-standing. (In the three years since 1993/94 the department's total funding to the voluntary sector has dropped by £1.48 million.)

The larger grants were made to:
    Westminster Foundation for Democracy (£2,500,000);
    Commonwealth Institute (£1,580,169);
    ICRC – International Committee of the Red Cross (£550,000);
    Great Britain/China Centre (£345,847);
    British Russia Centre (£255,904);
    British Association for Central and Eastern Europe (£204,294);
    Anglo/German Foundation (£185,000);
    Atlantic Council of the UK (£131,000);
    Franco/British Council (£84,000);
    Canning House (£41,000);
    Encounter (£27,668);

Royal Commonwealth Society (£25,000);
UN Association (£24,000).

Smaller grants ranging between £3,000 and £18,000 included the UK/Canada
Colloquia, International Commission of Jurists, Hague Academy of International
Law, Spanish Tertulias, the Pontignano Seminar and the UK/Japan 2000 Group.

Contact: Steven Townson, Head of Section, Financial Policy Department
Tel: 0171-238 4019; Fax: 0171-238 4004

(UK) DEPARTMENT FOR INTERNATIONAL DEVELOPMENT

Abercrombie House (A H)
Eaglesham Road, East Kilbride,
Glasgow G75 8EA

Tel: 01355-844000; Fax: 01355-843457
E-mail: @dfid.gtnet.gov.uk

20 Victoria Street (20 V St)
London SW1H 0NF

Tel: 0171-210 0083

94 Victoria Street (94 V St)
London SW1E 5JL

Tel: 0171-917 7000/0494
Fax: 0171-917 0016

The department was set up by the incoming Labour government in May 1997. In November 1997 it published the White Paper on International Development, outlining its strategy for eliminating world poverty. One of the main sections of the White Paper deals with partnerships, spelling out the need for partnership with the developing countries themselves but also with other donors and NGOs.

In the Comprehensive Spending Review of July 1998, it was announced that the department's budget would rise from £2,326 million in 1998/99 to £3,218 million in 2001/02, a year-on-year increase in real terms of 8.8 per cent.

The department funds non-governmental organisations to carry out work in developing countries. Details of how NGOs can work with the department follow.

Non-Governmental Organisations Unit (A H)

Head: Robin Russell

> **Total grant-aid of programmes**   £63,919,124 (budgeted 1998/99)
> **listed below:**   £63,535,000 (1997/98)
>   £70,289,000 (1996/97)

Joint Funding Scheme

> **Total grant-aid:** £36,156,000 (1998/99 and 1997/98)
>   £40,214,000 (1996/97)

Contacts: First point: 01355-84 3445; Second point 01355-84 3585

The Non-Governmental Organisations (NGO) Unit co-funds projects in developing countries. Funding can only be made to UK charities which must carry out the formal funding agreements for reporting and accounting.

Any project which aims at improving conditions for the poorest groups of people in developing countries is eligible for support, provided that it is *developmental* in character rather than for the relief of immediate needs.

Grants, usually on a 50:50 basis, can be made for up to five years with a maximum contribution of £500,000. (The remainder must come from non British government sources eg. the Lottery or Comic Relief.) Only family planning and population projects can apply for grants of more than 50% of the total budget.

Whilst core funding is not given, the extra management and administrative costs of the project incurred under this scheme in the UK can be included in its budget (up to 10%).

JFS Block grants: £16,973,370 (1998/99)
                        £16,973,000 (1997/98)
                        £20,483,000 (1996/97)

Five major organisations receive notification of their guaranteed annual funding (block grants) under this scheme prior to each financial year. The block grant

allocation accounts for about 46% of JFS funding. The allocations for 1997/98 were:
Oxfam (£5,304,000);
Save the Children Fund (£4,583,000);
Christian Aid (£3,003,590);
Worldwide Fund for Nature (£2,164,000);
Catholic Fund for Overseas Development (£1,9219,688).

Other JFS grants: £19,183,000 (1997/98)
£19,730,000 (1996/97)

In 1997/98 grants were made to over 430 projects undertaken by some 130 organisations. Multiple grants in 1996/97 were given to Concern (16), Care International (15), ACTIONAID (15), Plan International (14), ITDG (13), Population Concern (12), Homeless International (12) and MSI (12). Whilst the majority of organisations were given funding for several projects, some were allocated grants for single projects. Grants ranged from £193,000 to Concern for a project responding to the social consequences of AIDS in Uganda, to £2,047 for the New Hope Rural Community Trust's women's savings and credit scheme in India.

Other grants included:
CODA International Training for a community radio station in South Africa (£132,891);
Tear fund for a TB control programme in Nepal (£131,624);
Plan International for 14 projects in South America, Africa, India, S E Asia including a permaculture project in Thailand (£29,600), integrated recycling in Colombia (£98,000);
Interfund for a peace education in schools programme in South Africa (£74,000);
Homeless International for a low cost housing and network project for poor farmers in India (£33,065);
ITDG for a cycle-based transport project in Sri Lanka (£32,395);
One World Action for a community health care project in Nicaragua(£31,577);
Aga Khan Foundation, for mobile crèches in India (£17,275);
Y Care International, for centre for organic gardening at Salto Grande, Argentina/ Uruguay (£13,541);
Rainforest Foundation, to protect Dong Nah Tom Forest in Thailand (£9,238);
World University Service for an educational publishing project for children in the Occupied Territories (£2,750).

Volunteers

> **Total grant-aid: £25,533,124 (1998/99)**
> **£ 23,769,000 (1997/98)**
> **£26,091,000 (1996/97)**

Contacts: Sharon Cairnduff, Tel: 01355-84 3248; Fiona Dogherty,
Tel: 01355-84 3548

Five grants were given to volunteering agencies in 1997/98. The major part of which
(82%) was given to VSO:
  VSO (£19,381,000);
  CIIR (ICD) (£1,975,750);
  Skillshare Africa (£1,466,000);
  UNAIS (£986,250);
  FORUM (£10,000).

Appropriate Technology Development Fund (ATPF)

> **Total grant: £1,500,000 (1997/98)**
> **£1,750,000 (1996/97)**

Grants were given to organisations such as Intermediate Technology Development
Group. ITDG funding has now been transferred to DFID Engineering Department.

Other NGO grants

> **Total grant-aid: £2,230,000 (1998/99)**
> **£2,110,000 (1997/98)**
> **£2,235,000 (1996/97)**

Six organisations receive annual support. Funds are also allocated for studies and
reviews. Grants in 1997/98 included:
  British Ex-Patriot Service Overseas (£772,000);
  Overseas Development Institute (£653,000);
  Overseas Training Programme (OTP) (£325,000);

WGDS (£180,000);
BOND, British Overseas NGOs for Development (£45,000);
Christians Abroad (£30,000).

Exclusions: JFS funding is not available for relief or welfare projects, ie. those that are clearly unsustainable, nor in general for the following:

- projects involving major construction works;
- single items of equipment or vehicles, other than as part of a larger project;
- conventional curative medical projects not combined with health education, preventative medicine or community-based programmes;
- environmental conservation projects in which the main objective is to conserve flora and fauna for their own sake, rather than for the benefit of poor communities;
- scholarships, even if part of a wider project;
- projects where proselytisation is a theme.

Applications are not accepted for Eastern Europe or the former Soviet Union (for these see entry for the Know How Fund).

Applications: Detailed guidelines on the Joint Funding Scheme are available from the NGO Section. New proposals can be submitted at any time until the end of the 30 November immediately preceding the financial year (beginning of April to end of following March) in which the project is scheduled to begin. Early submission of applications is helpful.

Contact: Switchboard: 01355-844000

Geographical Desks (94 V St & overseas)

NGOs can also apply to geographical desks direct for one hundred per cent funding.

Development Awareness Fund (AH)

Grant total:	**£1.5 million (1998/99)**
	£750,000 (1997/98)

Funding is available for organisations involved in "increasing public understanding of our mutual dependence and the need for international development by giving people the facts about the forces that are shaping the world and their lives".

A total of 16 organisations received grant in 1997/98. Major support (46% of total funding) continued to be allocated to World Aware (£250,000 and £94,241): a long-standing grant relationship. For others, contributions of up to £100,000 a year towards the total projects costs can be considered. These grants ranged between £1,335 and £74,319 and included:

Education Partners Overseas (£74,319);
The Panos Institute (£50,000);
Scottish Education and Action on Development (£32,000);
Tourism concern (£15,000).

The doubling of the resources of the fund and the new application system is likely to change this pattern of grant aid.

Applications: In 1998/99 the department started to invite applications to its expanded programme. These have to be submitted by November for a grant beginning the following financial year.

Contact: Frances Burns, Deputy Head of Information
Tel: 01355-843509; E-mail: f-burns2dfid.gtnet.gov.uk

In addition the following programme is available for local organisations.

Mini-Grant Programme
Grant total: £140,000 (1998/99)
Small grants are delegated to be administered by the Development Education Association in England and equivalent bodies in the other three countries. Applications under £10,000 in England and £5,000 in Northern Ireland, Scotland and Wales.

England
Grant sub-total: £85,000 for Mini Grants + £30,000 for Global and Development Awareness Fund for Black & Ethnic Minority Organisations (1998/99)

Development Education Association, 29-31 Cowper Street, London EC2A 4AP
Tel: 0171-490 8108; Fax: 0171-490 8123; E-mail: devedassoc@gn.apc.org

Scotland
IDEAS, 34-36 Rose Street, North Lane, Edinburgh EH2 2NP
Tel: 0171-490 8108

Wales
Cyfanfyd, Welsh Centre for International Affairs, Temple of Peace, Cathays Park, Cardiff CF1 3AP; Tel: 01222-757067

Northern Ireland
Coalition of Aid & Development Agencies (CADA), 52-54 Dublin Road, Belfast BT2 7HN

Conflict & Humanitarian Affairs Department (94 V St)

General Enquiries: Tel: 0171-917 0507; Fax: 0171-917 0502

Agencies seek support from the emergency funds of the department for:
- rapid onset disaster relief;
- DFID's geographical departments and overseas offices are responsible for gradual onset disaster relief and other complex political emergencies; technological, or natural disasters;
- national and technological disaster preparedness, prevention and mitigation;
- humanitarian assistance to Afghanistan and North Korea;
- conflict preparedness, prevention and reduction, and mitigation;
- policy and institutional development, including monitoring and evaluation, training and research.

Geographical range

The department can provide assistance in response to natural and technological disasters anywhere outside the UK.

This department was divided into the following three sections from April 1998.

Section One

Refugees and migration; disaster preparedness and mitigation; multilateral – UNHRC, IOM, UNDP; Afghanistan; emergency response/back up to regional departments (Europe, Africa, Middle East); EU and ECHO relations.
Section Head: Roger Clark
Tel: 0171-917 0792
E-mail: r-clarke@dfid.gnet.gov.uk

Section Two

Demining; humanitarian response capacity building; multilateral – Red Cross, WFP, UNICEF; emergency response/backup to regional departments (Asia, Pacific, Americas); North Korea.
Section Head: Peter Troy
Tel: 0171-917 0073
E-mail: p-troy@dfid.gnet.gov.uk

Section Three

Conflict policy and projects including human rights in conflict situations; humanitarian policy; technical & advisory; multilateral – OCHA, UN secretariat, OHCHR, UNESCO, WHO.

Section Head: Sara Todd

Tel: 0171-917 0599

E-mail: s-todd@dfid.gtnet.gov.uk

The largest tranches of funding are given in two areas: emergency response, and refugee and migration.

Emergency Response

> **Grant total:**   **£6,031,153 (1997/98)**
> **+ £15 million to the International Committee for the Red Cross (ICRC) for conflict reduction and humanitarian action**

These grants help preserve life and relieve suffering following natural and man-made disasters. The unit provides funds against need and does not set minimum or maximum levels. For rapid onset disasters a response can be made by DFID within a few hours.

A total of 78 grants were made in 1997/98 to 24 organisations. Individual grants ranged from £1,400 to £400,000. Examples were:

Oxfam for flood relief, Kenya (£400,000);

IFRC for earthquake relief, China (£200,000);

Action Against Hunger, for civil strife relief, Chechnya (£100,000);

Merlin, for civil strife relief, Congo (£94,790);

Lightforce International for civil strife relief, Albania (£56,023);

World Vision, for landslide relief, Peru (£20,657);

Project Hop UK, airlift of medical supplies to assist flood victims in South Poland (£10,000).

Refugees & Migration

> **Grant total:**   **£1,570,000 (1997/98)**

In 1997/98 a total of 16 grants were made to 15 organisations working in 10 countries. Grants ranged between £10,000 and £264,000 and were provided to assist NGOs working in refugee situation in mainly Africa and Asia.

NB The DFID NGO Refugee Fund ceased to exist from April 1998 after the establishment of a trust fund set up jointly with UNHCR (United Nations High Commission for Refugees). The purpose of the trust fund is to provide a continued source of funding for NGOs working with refugees overseas. Applications to this fund should be made direct to UNHCR.

Disaster Preparedness Mitigation

Grant total: £2,000,000 (1997/98)

In 1997/98 a total of 31 grants were made to 23 organisations. They ranged from under £5,000 to over £300,000. Ten of the grants were directed at work within specific countries whilst the majority were of wider significance. Examples of grants:

Pan American Health Organisation, to assist Latin American and Caribbean countries adopt disaster preparedness measures (£328,000);

Oxfam, for disaster relief programme in Bangladesh (£35,434);

British Red Cross, for a training programme (£41,669);

Coventry University, for student placements with the World Health Organisation (£31,437);

Overseas Development Institute, for relief and rehabilitation network (£23,168);

British Geological Survey, for volcanic hazard mapping in Chile (£5,141).

Conflict Policy and Projects
including human rights and humanitarian policy

Grant total: £1,294,000 (1997/98)

Grants were committed to 18 projects in 1997/98. They ranged from £13,000 to £200,000. Grants included:

University of Essex, human rights conference (£85,000);

Accord, support and development of the Conflict and Development of Peace (CODEP) Network (£80,000);

Oxfam, communities for peace project in Colombia (£54,230);

Saferworld, investigation coherence of EU approach to conflict prevention (£50,000);

Grants in the previous year had included:

BRCS for Jammu/Kashmir civil unrest (£150,000);

International Centre for Human Reporting (ICHR) strengthening lifeline media in regions of conflict (£80,000);

Conciliation Resources for Liberian Women's Initiative Voter Outreach Programme (£59,108).

Applications: The booklet, *Guidelines on Humanitarian Assistance*, covers **all** the areas of funding referred to above. It covers the format for making proposals, reporting, budgeting and appraisal systems, etc.

Geographical departments with responsibility for a country or region usually deal with "predictable emergencies" – long-running complex political emergencies or frequently recurrent natural disasters. Disaster preparedness and conflict reduction projects are also funded by geographical departments as well as from central budget.

If in any doubt as to where to send an application, contact this department for advice.

The Know How Fund (20 V St)

Grant total:	£80 million (1998/99 provisional)
	£81 million (1997/98)
	£89 million (1996/97)

The Know How Fund is Britain's programme of bilateral technical assistance to the countries of Central and Eastern Europe and Central Asia. It aims to support the process of transition to pluralist democracy and a market economy in a way which promotes and recognises the interests of all their people.

Although the KHF funds projects that involve governments in the region at national and local level, it is not a formal government-to-government programme. It supports a broad range of partnerships with regional and local authorities, private sector organisations, business and NGOs. Its programmes are tailored to specific country needs, but are based on one or more areas of activity identified in the government's 1997 White Paper on International Development.

These broadly are:
- The enabling framework: the creation of market institutions and systems, etc;
- An inclusive approach to economic management: employment increase, employee and consumer rights, protection of the most vulnerable in society, etc;
- Empowerment and participation: strengthening civil and economic rights and helping people to exercise them, etc;

- Environment: links between poor environment, health and livelihoods, etc;
- The global dimension: international political and economic links at all levels.

The programmes are administered by two departments:
- Central and South Eastern Europe Department (CSEED);
- Eastern Europe and Central Asia Department (EECAD).

These departments are staffed by officers from the Diplomatic Service, the Department for International Development and the Department of Trade & Industry who are backed up by a team of professional advisors. An Advisory Board chaired by the SoS for International Development meets three to four times a year to assist the two departments in their strategies for different countries and sectors.

British NGOs have been supported to assist in the development of a healthy third sector. The annual report for 1996/97 provides the following examples:

The Big Issue helped a sister magazine, *The Depths*, in St Petersburg (Russia);

Voluntary Service Overseas (VSO) East European Partnership sent volunteers on one to two-year assignments in healthcare, small business development and social work (Russia);

Wales Council for Voluntary Action assisted Centar Supolnose, an NGO umbrella development organisation, with its work to foster the sector (Belarus);

Save the Children Fund organised training placements for NGO staff working with young people and their families (Bulgaria);

Save the Children Fund supported NGOs (Slovenia);

Charities Aid Foundation ran seminars for NGOs about improving women's access to political and economic decision-making (Bulgaria);

Charities Evaluation Services ran a programme to develop sustainable NGOs (Federal Republic of Yugoslavia);

Law Society organised training workshops for English speaking law students (Tzbekistan);

British Executive Service Overseas sent nearly 100 volunteers, mostly from the business community, on short attachments of up to three months eg. training for staff at a Russian hospice in methods of palliative care and administration.

KHF also co-funds **Charity Know How (CKH)** (see separate entry), a joint initiative with a number of charitable trusts which is administered by the Charities Aid Foundation. CKH supports the development of the voluntary sector in the region.

Exclusions: The KHF is **not**: a disaster relief organisation; an organiser of, or sponsor for non-KHF conferences; a supplier of goods or of capital equipment; a bank; an export support fund; an export credit agency. Full details about their policies programmes from the relevant department /country of the KHF.

Applications: Contact the relevant country unit for specific details.

General enquiries: Tel: 01710-210 0083

In 1998 all telephone numbers started with 0171-210, followed by the four digits for the relevant area:

Central and South Eastern Europe Department, Fax: 0171-210 0010
Albania – 0012;
Baltic States – 0078;
Bosnia Herzegovina – 0077;
Bulgaria – 0020;
Croatia – 0077;
Czech Republic – 0022;
Hungary – 0007;
FYR of Macedonia – 0012;
Poland – 0015
Romania – 0016;
Slovak Republic- 0022;
Slovenia – 0003;
FR of Yugoslavia – 0077;

Eastern Europe and Central Asia, Fax: 0171-210 0098
Russia – 0028/0041;
Ukraine, Belarus, Moldova – 0029;
Armenia, Azerbaijan, Georgia – 0065;
Kazakhstan, Kyrgyzstan, Tajikistan, Turkmenistan, Uzbekistan – 0065.

Environmental Know How Fund

Grant-aid:	£2 million annually

The KHF also jointly manages the Environmental Know How Fund (EKHF) with the Department of the Environment, Transport and the Regions. The EKHF supports the transfer of UK skills and expertise to the countries of Central and Eastern Europe and Central Asia, to help those countries improve their environmental performance. It supports policy reform, better environmental management, institutional capacity building and the preparation of priority investments with the international financial institutions. EKHF projects are designed to support the strategy on environmental aid to the countries of Central and Eastern Europe and Central Asia (the Environmental Action Programme) endorsed by European Environment Ministers.

The EKHF is the environmental tranche of the Know How Fund and operates in addition to the environmental projects supported by the main Know How Fund.

Assisted projects with relevance to this guide have included:

University of Cambridge, for regional land-use planning summer schools held annually (£50,000 pa);

Field Studies Council, to develop a management strategy with the National Environmental Education Centre, Warsaw (£176,000 over 3 years between 1993/96);

Lancashire Wildlife Trust for work with the Upper Tisza Foundation in Hungary (£7,100 between 1992/95);

TVE/WWF-UK, for environmental education and public awareness in Hungary (£29,750 in 1994/95);

Conservation Foundation, environmental law summer school in Georgia, Russia (£3,150 in 1996);

Living Earth, environmental education/NGO strengthening (£25,000 1996);

National Trust for environment exchange with Russia (£17,700 in 1996).

Exclusions: Disaster relief.

For further information contact:

Will Morlidge, Executive Officer, European Environment Division, Department of Environment, Transport and the Regions, Ashdown House, 123 Victoria Street, London SW1E 6DE; Tel: 0171-890 6222; Fax: 0171-890 6249

Charity Know How

114-118 Southampton Row, London WC1B 5AA

Tel: 0171-400 2315; Fax: 0171-404 1331
E-mail: ckh@caf.charitynet.org
Web site: www.charitynet.org/charityknowhow/

Contact: Nev Jefferies, Director

> **Funding from the Department for International Development:**
> **£335,823 (1997/98) 50% of total budget**

Charity Know How is an initiative funded by a group of grant-making trusts and the Department of International Development. It was set up in 1991 to assist the revitalisation of the voluntary sector in Central and Eastern Europe (CEE) and the Newly Independent States (NIS). It aims to enhance the transfer of skills and know how and to form productive and supportive links between NGOs in the region and the UK.

It makes two kinds of grant:
- Regular grants for projects which meet CKH criteria
- Exploratory grants to enable potential partner organisations to meet and decide if a proposed partnership is appropriate.

Funding is made available for work in 27 countries: Albania, Armenia*, Azerbaijan*, Belarus, Bosnia-Hersegovina, Bulgaria*, Croatia, Czech Republic, Estonia, FR of Yugoslavia, Georgia*, Hungary, Kazakhstan, Kyrgyzstan, Latvia, Lithuania Macedonia, Moldova, Poland, Romania*, Russia, Slovakia*, Slovenia, Tajikistan, Turkmenistan, Ukraine*, Uzbekistan.

* Proactive programmes were being developed in 1998 in the countries marked with and asterisk, and in the Arkangelsk region of Russia. They were expected to last between 18 months and 2 years. The proactive programme arose from a major strategic review.

Funding is given for skill-sharing partnership projects between UK charities and NGOs in these countries, or between NGOs in different countries of the region. All applications must be joint projects.

In 1997 more than 80 grants were made which ranged between £200 and £12,000. Examples included:

Animus Association, Bulgaria, and Women's Aid Federation of England, National Helpline, for 2 visits to England to examine setting up a similar project (£11,385);

Nottingham Play Centre for Children with Disabilities and their Families, and the Lesenka Centre, Chelyabinsk in Russia, for a study visit to the Nottingham centre by 6 people (£8,816);
Clydebank Unemployed and Community Resource Centre and Stowarzyszenie Inicjatyw Lokalnych, Poland for Scottish trainers to lead workshops (£800);
Powerful Information and ALTAIR, Moldova, an exploratory visit to Moldova to make new contacts for the provision of environmental information (£200).

Exclusions: These include: individuals, core and capital costs, youth artistic and cultural exchanges; retrospective grants. Full details with the guidelines.

Applications: Full guidelines are available with the application form. Application deadlines are in February, April, July and October. Be sure to check the exact date.

The British Council

Arts Division

11 Portland Place, London W1N 4EJ
Tel: 0171-930 8466; Fax: 0171-389 3199

The Arts Division of the British Council promotes cultural, educational and technical co-operation between Britain and other countries. Its work is designed to develop worldwide partnerships and improve international understanding. It promotes British ideas, talent and experience primarily through the provision of education and training services, books and periodicals, English language teaching and the management of arts events. The council is represented in 224 towns and cities in 109 countries. It provides an impressive network of contacts with government departments, universities, embassies, professional bodies, arts organisations and businesses in Britain and overseas.

Only a small percentage of its total expenditure is devoted to arts (around 5%) and only a small part of this sum was given in direct subsidies. Each year the council assists about 2,000 British drama, dance, music, literature and arts events, tours or exhibitions to take place in a variety of countries. It does not usually make 100% grants but contributes to certain expenses involved in the presentation of arts events abroad.

The council's Arts Division consists of five departments: Visual Arts; Drama and Dance; Music; Literature; Film, Television and Video. Each department is supported by an advisory committee of specialists in the relevant fields. Expenditure figures for each department vary widely from year to year, depending on whether major exhibitions, tours etc. are being mounted by a department in any one year. It also has an Exhibitions and Audio Visual Unit which produces exhibitions and displays and gives advice on design promotion.

The British Council also administers the Visiting Arts Office of Great Britain and Northern Ireland (see separate entry) on behalf of the Foreign and Commonwealth Office and the Arts Councils.

Visiting Arts Office of Great Britain and Northern Ireland

(based in same address as the Arts Division)

Tel: 0171-389 3019; Fax: 0171-389 3016
E-mail: office@visiting arts.demon.co.uk
Web site: http://www.britcoun.org/visitingarts/

Visiting Arts is a joint venture of the national Arts Councils (England, Scotland, Wales and Northern Ireland), the Crafts Council, the Foreign & Commonwealth Office and the British Council. It provides consultancy, advisory services, information, training, and publications. It funds specific research in current Visiting Arts priority areas and the following project development grants.

Country Project Awards

Grant total:	**about £420,000 annually**

These awards, mostly between £2,000 and £5,000, cover a wide range of art forms with particular emphasis on contemporary work. They are available to promoters and venues to help them present quality foreign companies or artists not previously presented in the UK.

Applications: There are no deadlines but applications must be made at least 3 months prior to the start of the project. An early approach to VA needs to be made as most successful applications are either initiated, encouraged or developed with their help. Applicants should write giving an outline of the project proposal.

Contacts: Performing Arts: Nelson Fernandes, Tel: 0171-389 3107;
Visual Arts: Camilla Edwards, Tel: 0171-389 3018

🆄🅺 Youth Exchange Centre

10 Spring Gardens, London SW1A 2BN
Tel: 0171-389 4030; Fax: 0171-389 4033

> **Grant total: £2,069,000 (1997/98 and 1996/97)**

The Youth Exchange Centre is a department of the British Council which receives funding from the Foreign and Commonwealth Office, the Department of Education and Employment and the European Commission. Grants are given towards exchanges between groups of young British people aged between 15 and 25, and young people in other countries. They are designed to encourage the exchange of ideas as well as to increase mobility. Most European countries are included as well as China, Israel, Japan, USA, West Bank and Gaza. They must be for a minimum of seven days and be theme based. The average grant is about £100 a person.

Exclusions: Tours to several countries, or cities in one country; competitions; purely touristic visits; exchanges that are part of an educational curriculum; youth wings of political parties; individual young people proposing to live, work or study in another country.

Applications: Contact the Regional Committee, listed below:

East Midlands
Rosemary Beard, Deputy Principal Youth Officer, Youth Service, Education Department, PO Box 149, County Hall, Guildhall Road, Northampton NN1 1AU
Tel: 01604-237442; Fax: 01604-237532

Eastern Region
Karen Williams, Youth Services in the Eastern Region, Regional Office, School Lane, Sprowstone, Norwich NR7 8TR
Tel/Fax: 01603-488824

London
Nicci Carter, Youth Officer, Education Department, London Borough of Richmond, Regal House, London Road, Twickenham TW1 3QB
Tel: 0181-891 7502; Fax: 0181-891 7714

North
Tony Halliwell, Regional Development Officer, RYCDU, Pendower Hall Education Development Centre, West Road, Newcastle-Upon-Tyne NE15 6PP
Tel: 0191-274 3620; Fax: 0191-274 0727

North-West
Janet Preece, North-West RYSU, Derbyshire Hill Youth Centre, Derbyshire Hill Road, Parr, St Helens WA9 3LN
Tel: 01744-453800; Fax: 01744-453505

South

Tina Saunders, County Youth & Community Officer, County Hall, Chichester, West Sussex PO19 1RF
Tel/Fax: 01243-777771

South-West

Dillon Hughes, South-West Association for Further Education & Training, Bishops Hull House, Bishops Hull, Taunton, Somerset TA1 5RA
Tel: 01823-335491; Fax: 01823-323388

West Midlands

Chris Knapper, Youth & Community Service, Education Department, Tipping Street, Stafford ST16 2DH
Tel: 01785-278762; Fax: 01785-2785-278764

Yorkshire/Humberside

Peter Davie, Youth Exchange Committee, c/o Batley Community Resource Centre, 90 Commercial Street, Batley WF17 5DS
Tel: 01924-326330; Fax: 01924-326340

Scotland

Jim Bartholomew, SCEC, Rosebery House, 9 Haymarket Terrace, Edinburgh EH12 5EZ
Tel: 0131-313 2488; Fax: 0131-313 6800

Wales

Jean Reader, Wales Youth Exchange Committee, Wales Youth Agency, Leslie Court, Lon-y-Llyn, Caerphilly, Mid-Glamorgan CF8 1BQ
Tel: 01222-880088; Fax: 01222-880824

Northern Ireland

Chuck Richardson, Youth Council for Northern Ireland, Lamont House, Purdys Lane, Belfast BT8 4TA
Tel: 01232-643882; Fax: 01232- 643874

Commonwealth Youth Exchange Council

7 Lion Yard, Tremadoc Road, Clapham, London SW4 7NQ

Tel: 0171-498 6151; Fax: 0171-720 5403

Contact: Máire Ní Threasaigh, Exchanges Officer

Grant total:	**£242,000 (1998/99)**
	£237,604 (1997/98)

The Commonwealth Youth Exchange Council (CYEC) is a charity financed largely by the government through the Youth Exchange Centre (see separate entry) and the Education and Employment Department via its National Voluntary Youth Organisations Scheme (see separate entry). It promotes two-way educational exchange visits between groups of young people in the UK and their contemporaries in all other Commonwealth countries by providing advice, information, training and grant aid.

CYEC's funding priorities are: young people who would not normally have the opportunity to take part in an international project; exchanges with Commonwealth countries in Africa, Asia and the Caribbean; local British groups rather than national ones. Groups should normally number between 5 and 13 participants, excluding leaders. At least two-thirds of the group must be within the age-range 16-25. UK groups must host as well as visit. One-way visits are not eligible for funding. Return visits should take place within two years. Visits must last at least 21 days for exchanges outside Europe, and at least 14 days for Cyprus, Malta and Gibraltar. Grants are given on a per head basis and represent up to 35% of international travel or hosting costs. A total of 74 projects were funded in 1998/99 equally split between incoming and outgoing trips.

Applications: Detailed guidelines and application forms are available on request (SAE required). Potential applicants should make contact with CYEC as early as possible to discuss their proposals. Applications must be submitted during the autumn and at least nine months prior to a visit.

LORD CHANCELLOR'S DEPARTMENT

 Legal Aid Board

85 Gray's Inn Road, London WC1X 8AA

Tel: 0171-813 1000; Fax: 0171-813 8638

The Legal Aid Board is a non-departmental public body set up in 1988 which is responsible for ensuring the provision of legal advice and assistance to persons of small or moderate means.

Contracts to Agencies in the Not-for-Profit Sector

Pilot Scheme

Total funding:	**£8,314,319 (1998/99)***
	£3,178,820 (1997/98)
	£2,704,532 (1996/97)

* The actual amount committed up to May 1998. This is subject to variation and is likely to be greater as more contracts are let and others due to expire are extended. The maximum funding available in 1998/99 is £14 million.

The Legal Aid Board contracts with some non-for-profit agencies (including Citizens' Advice Bureaux, members of the Federation of Independent Advice Centres, and Law Centres) to provide legal services in an expanding pilot scheme. Contracts are to provide specified numbers of casework hours in categories of law to specific quality standards.

The Board has been asked to prepare plans to move to contracting of all civil advice and assistance in 1999. Whilst the majority of these contracts will be with solicitors in private practice the not-for-profit sector will play a part in the new scheme. In early 1998 the Board was in the process of establishing Regional Legal Services Committees (RLSCs) to advise on needs and priorities for contracts.

Contracts with not-for-profit agencies for legal advice are in the following categories of social welfare law: Debt, Employment, Housing, Immigration and Welfare Benefits. Most contracts are for work in one or two of the categories, although some agencies, in particular law centres, do cover all areas. In 1997/98 a total of 84 contracts were let and the amount spent on these was £3.179 million. By May 1998 this number had increased to 159 and a total of £8.314 million had been committed from a potential funding of £14 million. This amount is likely to increase as more contracts are agreed.

Examples of organisations awarded contracts in 1998/99:
Acton Law Shop Law for All, covering all categories of advice (£138,094);
Tyneside Housing Aid Centre (£100,739);
Cambridge Independent Advice Centre, for housing, debt and employment advice (£99,881);
Birkenhead CAB for debt advice (£53,931).

Applications: Only organisations which are part of an existing advice network, and which have a relatively stable funding base, can take part. There are 13 area offices of the Legal Aid Board, each with a responsibility for funding in their region: London, Brighton; Reading; Bristol; Cardiff; Birmingham; Manchester; Newcastle; Leeds; Nottingham; Cambridge; Chester; Liverpool.

Funding of Law Centres

Grant total:	**£969,465 (annually 1996/97-1998/99)**

Nine law centres (all but three in London) and the Law Centres Federation have received grants. These grants are separate from any payment that can be claimed on a case by case basis for legal aid work. They ranged between £37,000 and £169,000 in 1997/98, and included:
Law Centres Federation (£68,901);
Tower Hamlets Law Centre (£168,929);
Cardiff Law Centre (£105,739);
Harehill & Chapeltown (£115,999);
Saltley & Nechells Law Centre (£89,888).

The Board has been asked to prepare plans to move to the provision of all civil advice and assistance under contracts with quality assured suppliers. Law centres will be eligible to apply for such contracts.

Contact: Allison McGarrity, Policy Adviser, Policy and Legal Department
Tel: 0171-813 8671; Fax: 0171-831 8638

Powers: Part II of the Legal Aid Act 1988

Mediation Services

The London Area Office co-ordinates the arrangements for the provision and development of mediation services in England which are contracted to non-for-profit organisations and solicitors.

Mediation services for reaching agreement over divorce and separation (covering difficult issues – children, financial and property) were available to people eligible for legal aid in certain areas as at summer 1998: Newcastle-Upon-Tyne; Middlesbrough; Durham; Manchester; Birmingham; Coventry; Northampton; Cambridge; Peterborough; Bristol, Cardiff; Bromley and London (certain areas).

No information has been provided about the organisations funded/contracted to provide support advice.

Contact: Sarah White, Project Manager, London Area Office, 29-37 Red Lion Street, London WC1R 4PP; Tel: 0171-813 5300x4992; Fax: 0171-813 5330

REGIONAL, REGENERATION AND RURAL SECTION

(see also Environment)

Contents

Regional Development Agencies (RDAs)

The government has said that its approach to the English regions is based firmly on the principle that power should not be centralised in Whitehall and that it sees the regional economies as the building blocks of the UK economy.

Nine new Regional Development Agencies are being created to integrate the work of national, regional and local partners in economic development in its widest sense. They will have five core areas of responsibility:
- economic development and regeneration;
- competitiveness, business support and investment;
- skills;
- employment;
- sustainable development.

RDAs will take up their powers in April 1999 after a transitional period of a few months. Their powers will include responsibility for the following:
- Single Regeneration Budget;
- taking as leading role on European Structural Funds;
- the regional operations of English Partnerships;
- the rural development programmes of the Rural Development Commission (which otherwise is merging with the Countryside Commission into a new countryside body).

RDA boundaries
They will have the same boundaries as the current Government Offices for the Regions, with the exception that a single RDA will serve the whole North-West, including Merseyside.

Composition of boards, appointment of chairs and board members
The composition of the nine new NDPBs, or quangos, resembles that for Training and Enterprise Councils (TECs). The boards of the RDAs will be business-led, with other board members reflecting regional interests, such as the voluntary sector, rural areas, and tourism, and will include four local authority members. The chairmen were announced by the Prime Minister in July 1998.

Staffing

The RDA staff will be drawn largely from English Partnerships, the Rural Development Commission, and the Government Offices for the Regions, all of which are also contributing functions to the new RDAs. The Government Offices will continue their other current activities such as those relating to land use planning and housing.

Regional Chambers and their functions

The government has also said it is "committed to move to directly elected regional government in England where there is demand for it". As a 'first step' the development of nine voluntary Regional Chambers is being encouraged. These will bring together elected representatives from local authorities and other regional partners (started in some areas as at July 1998). Each RDA will be required *to have regard to* the regional viewpoint of the Chamber in preparation of its economic development strategy, *consult* the Chamber on its corporate plan, and be *open to scrutiny* by the Chamber. Their powers are indirect and imprecise. The role of these Regional Chambers seems solely advisory and precautionary.

The Greater London Authority (GLA) and the London Development Agency

The situation in Greater London is more complicated and extended. A whole new strategic body of government and democratic system is being developed. A Greater London Authority will be formed led by an elected Mayor and Assembly.

The GLA will co-ordinate and fund many basic services – the London Development Agency, Transport for London, the Metropolitan Police Authority, London Fire and the Emergency Planning Services. GLA will absorb the London Planning Advisory Committee, the London Ecology Unit and the London Research Centre.

The London Development Agency will be run by a chair and board appointed by the mayor and have a total of 12 members with 4 elected members as with other RDAs. It will be responsible for the economic and regeneration strategy for London as with other RDAs but with no specific mention of responsibility for environmental sustainability as with other RDAs (other arrangements with the mayor and the Assembly in London).

The LDA is scheduled to start in April 2000.

Web site: http://www.London-decides.detr.gov.uk

Regional networks of voluntary and community organisations are forming to start to address these new challenges (see separate listing).

Single Regeneration Budget

Since 1994 the Single Regeneration Budget (SRB) has been the major source of urban funding in England, contributing millions of pounds annually to a rolling programme. It then combined under one banner the 20 or so separate programmes which had previously been operated from different government departments. The main financial contributor has been the Department of Environment, Transport & the Regions, with contributions also from the Departments of Education and Employment, Trade and Industry and the Home Office.

The aim of SRB is to provide a flexible fund for local regeneration in a way which meets local needs and priorities. Earlier urban programmes which had formed part of the wider SRB included:

- Urban Development Corporations;
- City Challenge (the forerunner to the SRB Challenge Fund and based on the same principles of partnership and competition and now paid via a Challenge Fund), 31 City Challenge winners each received £7.5 million a year over a 5 year period for the social, economic and environmental regeneration of their areas.

Both these programmes had wound up by the end of March 1998.

Most of the regeneration budget is administered by the *Government Offices for the Regions* which co-ordinate the main programmes and policies at local level and ensure that businesses, local government and voluntary agencies have just one port of call.

This responsibility will transfer to the *Regional Development Agencies* from April 1999.

From 1995/96 a proportion of regeneration resources (until 1998 known as the **SRB Challenge Fund**) has been devoted to partnerships which encourage local communities to come up with comprehensive programmes to improve the quality of life in their area. These partnerships are expected to involve a diverse range of organisations in their management and harness the talent, resources and experience of local business people, the voluntary sector and the local community. Bids are expected to achieve some or all for the following objectives and to aim to:

- enhance the employment prospects, education and skills of local people, particularly the young and those at a disadvantage, and promote equality of opportunity;
- encourage sustainable economic growth and wealth creation by improving the competitiveness of the local economy, including support for new and existing businesses;

- protect and improve the environment and infrastructure and promote good design;
- improve housing and housing conditions for local people through physical improvements, better maintenance, improved management and greater choice and diversity;
- promote initiatives of benefit to ethnic minorities;
- tackle crime and improve community safety;
- enhance the quality of life, health and capacity of contribute to regeneration of local people, including the promotion of cultural and sports opportunities.

Funding is made available in response to bids submitted to the relevant regional offices. Bids are expected to generate the greatest possible investment from the private sector and support from European Structural Funds as well as involving local communities and drawing on "the talents and resources of the voluntary sector". A strong emphasis is placed on local partnerships between relevant bodies: local authorities, TECs, other public bodies, the private sector, the voluntary sector and the local community. Funding is available for bids lasting from one to seven years, resources permitting.

Resources can contribute to a comprehensive strategy concentrated on a relatively small area eg. a rundown town centre, one or more housing estates or a large, multi-faceted development site. But small *free-standing* schemes, which do not link into a wider local regeneration strategy, are unlikely to be successful.

Advisory groups assist in each of the 10 regions (see list below) with voluntary sector representatives on each. For instance, the London Council for Voluntary Service serves on the London group.

Single Regeneration Budget – Round 4

> **Grant total for Round 4: £14.6 million (1998/99)**

Ministers announced at the end of March 1998, the names of the 121 successful Partnerships under Round 4 of the SRB which stand to get a total of over £300 million over a period of years. Nearly all these successful schemes have multiple objectives, which include social exclusion, employment and training, education, community safety, prevention of drug misuse, health care and child care. Over half the schemes include support for ethnic minorities as an explicit objective. This reflects local needs and priorities and the need to look across traditional boundaries in finding solutions.

The Round 4 schemes aim to attract private sector support of over £400 million and other public sector contributions, including European funding, of over £500 million over their lifetime of up to seven years. Further figures given by the department indicate that this investment should benefit over 600,000 school children, provide training for 86,000 people, provide jobs for over 50,000 target area residents and benefit over three million people by means of community safety initiatives.

New Deal for Regeneration

Single Regeneration Budget (1999-2000)

Round 5 onwards

The government announced in mid July 1998 the conclusions of the Comprehensive Spending Review which included a re-shaped SRB. This is one of two strands of a **New Deal for Regeneration**, the other being the **New Deal for Communities**.

The reshaped SRB will receive over £2.3 billion over the three years, 1999-2002. Of this figure £800 million is new money, with the rest of the funding to cover existing commitments under SRB Rounds 1-4.

The major part of the new money (80%) will be targeted on the areas of greatest need, while the balance of the resources (20%) will tackle pockets of need elsewhere including rural areas and former coal field areas.

Resources will be concentrated so that most will go on over 50 major new schemes (about £20 million each) in the most deprived areas. These schemes will be running by the end of the three year period (2002).

The reshaped SRB gives an emphasis to local partnerships and value for money including:
- a new emphasis on partnership capacity building so that the local community is equipped to participate fully in the regeneration of its area;
- partnerships will have to demonstrate that local communities are directly involved in and supportive of schemes;
- the release of funding will depend on adequate management systems including project appraisal.

New Deal for Communities (NDC)

Total funding over three years:	**£800 million (1999/00-2001/02)**
Pathfinder funding:	**£15 million, of which £12 million to England (1998/99)**

This new programme, the second strand of the New Deal for Regeneration, will tackle the multiple-deprivation in the very poorest areas, taking forward the government's commitment to tackle social exclusion in the 'Worst Estates'. Resources of £800 million have been set aside to support the programme over the three years, 1999-2002.

The announcements about the NDC stated that the programme will:

- "bring housing and regeneration spending together to achieve improvements which last. It is vital that housing and other capital spending is integrated with regeneration spending. A comprehensive approach is essential to achieve the sustainable regeneration of the most deprived areas.
- "extend economic opportunities for local people. The NDC will help people back into work through locally devised solutions tailored to circumstances in each area. It will link with **Welfare to Work New Deals** and, where appropriate, **Employment Zones**, to maximise the beneficial impact of those programmes on local people.
- "improve neighbourhood management and the delivery of local services. The NDC is an excellent opportunity to test our new and more effective models of neighbourhood management of the kind being examined by the Social Exclusion Unit as part of their broader work on worst estates".

The NDC will operate only in neighbourhoods with the highest concentrations of deprivation.

In September 1998 the government invited the following 17 Pathfinder authorities to prepare bids – Liverpool, Manchester, the London Boroughs of Newham, Hackney, Tower Hamlets and Southwark, Newcastle-Upon-Tyne, Middlesborough, Nottingham, Leicester, Birmingham, Sandwell, Hull, Bradford, Brighton and Hove, Norwich and Bristol. The experiences of these Pathfinders will inform future rounds. A list of *areas eligible for support* under the full programme will be announced later in 1998.

Bids under both strands of the New Deal for Regeneration will have to show how these fit with other new area-based initiatives and strategies. Regeneration partnerships will have to make clear the linkages between housing, regeneration and other initiatives and demonstrate that their local strategies complement the regional strategies that the Regional Development Agencies will develop.

General information about regeneration programmes:

Regeneration Policy Unit, DETR Regeneration Division 2, Zone 4/A6, Eland House, Bressenden Place, London SW1E 5DU; Tel: 0171-890 3801/2.

The SRB Challenge Fund: A Handbook of Good Practice in Management Systems is available from the Government Office of your region (see below). *Involving Communities in Urban and Rural Regeneration*, published by HMSO for DETR, £10.00; ISBN 185 1120 483.

These publications cover general policy rather than the practical details of negotiations, work relationships and activities. Voluntary groups are advised to approach their own local co-ordinatory body, the council for voluntary service, for further information and assistance.

The Urban Forum was set up as the voluntary sector voice on regeneration policy and has over 300 local and national community and voluntary organisations as members, with associate members from other sectors. Its activities include an information service for members, representing the sector on urban policy issues and lobbying for increased community involvement in regeneration.
Co-ordinator: John Routledge, 4 Dean's Court, St Paul's Courtyard, London EC4V 5AA; Tel: 0171-248 3111; Fax: 0171-248 3222.

Applications: *Always first approach the Government Office for your region/ Regional Development Agency to obtain full information and guidance about the details of the programme currently operating.* Ask to be put on the mailing list for information about the new programme. When a new programme starts, make sure to arrange a meeting to discuss the information and how to proceed further in forming a partnership.

Ask for contacts with other voluntary organisations in your region which are part of a successful bid/programme of activities. This should help strengthen your resolve if the processes seem difficult and laborious and you need greater understanding of official practices.

Also ask about any co-ordinatory services provided in their area to assist voluntary organisations, for example *Pan London Community Regeneration Forum* provides training, advice and support to organisations in the Greater London area (see more details under 'Supportive Organisations' section).

The contacts below work with SRB. For full GOR addresses see the special list.

Government Office for the Eastern Region
Tel: 01234-796154; Fax: 01234-276252
Contact: Rom Hirst

Government Office for the East Midlands
Tel: 0115-971 2444; Fax: 0115-971 2558
Contact: Pam Hough

Government Office for London
7th Floor, Riverwalk House, 157-161 Millbank, London SW1P 4RT
Tel: 0171-217 3062; Fax: 0171-217 3461
Contact: Malcolm Sims

Government Office for the North West
(including former Government Office for Merseyside)
Tel: 0161-952 4351; Fax: 0161-952 4365
Contact: Helen France

Government Office for the North East
Tel: 0191-202-3649; Fax: 0191-202 3768
Contact: Derek Burns

Government Office for the South East
Tel: 01483-882322; Fax: 01483-882309
Contact: Jane Couchman

Government Office for the South West
Tel: 0117-900 1854; Fax: 0117-900 1917
Contact: Robin Morris

Government Office for the West Midlands
Tel: 0121-212 51194; Fax: 0121-212 5301
Contact: Ruth Dudley

Government Office for the Yorkshire and Humberside
Tel: 0113-283 6402; Fax: 0113-283 6653
Contact: Alison Biddulph

English Partnerships

16-18 Old Queen Street, London SW1H 9HP
Tel: 0171-976 7070; Fax: 0171-976 7740

3 The Parks, Lodge Lane, Newton le Willows, Merseyside WA12 OJQ
Tel: 01942-296900; Fax: 01942-296927

The new Regional Development Agencies take over the regional regeneration functions of English Partnerships in April 1999 (with the exception of the London Regional Development Agency scheduled to start in April 2000).

The following historical information, put together before the RDAs were operational, is provided to give some background to help new readers to appreciate the EP's functions and what the RDAs regional responsibilities might include.

The Community Investment Fund is the function specially directed at the voluntary sector.

English Partnerships was set up in 1993 to regenerate derelict, vacant and under-used land and buildings throughout England. It has been funded through the Department of the Environment, Transport and the Regions and has a network of regional offices (see below) each headed by a Regional Director. It works in partnership with the public, private and voluntary sectors and focuses on the following areas:
- long-term area regeneration;
- individual land reclamation projects;
- job-creating investment opportunities;
- community development.

English Partnerships Investment Fund
It promotes a broad range of projects from large-scale regionally planned schemes through to local initiatives. It has wide powers to:
- assist developers and others to carry out regeneration and to offer necessary financial assistance closely linked to the needs of individuals projects;
- promote and enter into joint ventures;
- carry out development on its own account.

All English Partnership projects must achieve one or more of the following outputs:
- jobs created;
- jobs safeguarded;
- development of floor space for industry, commerce, housing or leisure;

- land (and infrastructure) made available for employment space or housing;
- land brought back into use or made safe for green/recreational purposes.

Areas of Operation

The following list is not exhaustive. The agency can respond to urgent needs. Each regional office identifies its own priorities.

- European Objective 1 and 2 areas;
- coalfield closure areas;
- City Challenge and other inner city areas;
- other assisted areas;
- rural areas of severe economic need, chiefly European Objective 5b.

Operation of the Investment Fund

A broad range of support is available: help and advice; joint ventures; rental guarantees; loan guarantees; gap funding and other forms of partnership investment; direct development.

English Partnerships Community Development Work

The agency has a commitment to work with local communities to achieve its objectives and has done so by:

- appointing Community Development Managers in each region to build links with local communities and involve them in setting investment priorities;
- enabling local authorities to participate in the decision-making process in many of its major projects;
- establishing a Community Investment Fund that distributes funds to capital projects devised by community groups.

Community Investment Fund – about £3 million annually

The fund is designed to help local communities participate more effectively in local regeneration. It recognises that community groups find difficulty in accessing small amounts of capital funding to realise their goals with land or property regeneration projects.

The fund is for projects which are:

- put forward by voluntary groups based in and involving local communities;
- non-profit-making;
- involve capital works to provide or improve land and buildings;
- need a contribution from EP that will usually be below £100,000;
- contribute to EP's regeneration aims;
- produce social and economic benefits at community level;
- tie in with and contribute towards other local regeneration strategies;
- practicable and financially sustainable.

No revenue funding is available. All projects must adhere to the criteria set out in *The Community Investment Guide*. Appraisal, selection and monitoring of projects takes place at regional level. Projects should not be able to go ahead without EP support, and separate, clear benefits should be attributable to it. Applications are restricted to local, grass-roots, community/voluntary, non-profit distributing organisations. They need not necessarily be registered charities.

The Land Reclamation Programme may support small environmental improvement schemes. Funding is available for land improvement schemes which become public open space. Guidelines prepared for local authorities may be obtained. Groundwork Trusts have helped instigate as well as support several schemes assisted from this programme.

Applications: Obtain the full guides from your regional EP office (see list below) and then contact the Community Development Managers for further advice and to discuss your proposal.

London
Devon House, 58-60 St Katharine's Way, London E1 9LB
Tel: 0171-680 2000; Fax: 0171-680 2040

Eastern
Berwick House, 22 Thorpe Road, Norwich NR1 1RY
Tel: 01603-617006; Fax: 01603-664375

South East
Bridge House, 3rd Floor, 1 Walnut Tree Close, Guildford GU1 4GA
Tel: 01483-882347; Fax: 01483-882348

South West
North Quay House, Sutton Harbour, Plymouth PL4 0RA
Tel: 01752-234821; Fax: 01752-234840

Midlands
Osiers Office Park, Braunstone, Leicester LE3 2DX
Tel: 0116-282 8400; Fax: 0116-282-8440

Yorkshire & Humberside
Hall Cross House, 1 South Parade, Doncaster, South Yorkshire DN1 2DY
Tel: 01302-366865; Fax: 01302-366880

North West
Lancaster House, Mercury Court, Tithebarn Street, Liverpool L2 2QP
Tel: 0151-236 3663; Fax: 0151-236 3731

North East
St George's House, Kingsway, Team Valley, Gateshead, Tyne & Wear NE11 0NA
Tel: 0191-487 8941; Fax: 0191-487 5690

Corporate offices are based in London, Merseyside and Gateshead (see address above).

Rural Development Commission

(see New Countryside Agency)

Government Offices for the Regions

Many of the responsibilities of these offices were to be transferred to the new **Regional Development Agencies** (see separate entry) from April 1999. These offices retain responsibility for land use planning and housing.

Central Unit, Department of Environment, Transport and the Regions
1st Floor, Eland House, Bressenden Place, London SW1E 5DU
Tel: 0171-890 5157; Fax: 0171-890 5091

Government Office for the Eastern Region
Heron House, 49-53 Goldington Road, Bedford MK40 3LL
Tel: 01234-796332; Fax: 01234-276252

Victory House, Vision Park, Histon, Cambridge CB4 4ZR
Tel: 01223-346700

Building A DTI, Westbrook Centre, Milton Road, Cambridge CB4 1Y
Tel: 01223-346700

Government Office for the East Midlands
The Belgrave Centre, Stanley Place, Talbot Street, Nottingham NG1 5GG
Tel: 0115-971 9971; Fax: 0115-971 2404

Government Office for London
Riverwalk House, 157-161 Millbank, London SW1P 4RR
Tel: 0171-217 3456; Fax: 0171-217 3450

Government Office for the North West (including the former office for Merseyside)
Sunley Tower, Piccadilly Plaza, Manchester M1 4BE
Tel: 0161-952 4000; Fax: 0161-952 4099

Government Office for the North East
Wellbar House, Gallowgate, Newcastle-Upon-Tyne NE1 4TD
Tel: 0191-202-3300; Fax: 0191-202 3744

Government Office for the South East
Bridge House, 1 Walnut Tree Close, Guildford, Surrey GU1 4GA
Tel: 01483-882255; Fax: 01483-882259

Government Office for the South West
Bristol: The Pithay, Bristol, BS1 2PB
Tel: 0117-900 1700; Fax: 0117-900 1900

Plymouth: Mast House, Shepherds Wharf, 24 Sutton Road, Plymouth PL4 OHJ
Tel: 01752-635000; Fax: 01752-227647

Government Office for the West Midlands
77 Paradise Circus, Queensway, Birmingham B1 2DT
Tel: 0121-212 5050; Fax: 0121-212 1010

Government Office for the Yorkshire and Humberside
City House, New Station Road, Leeds LS1 4US
Tel: 0113-280-0600; Fax: 0113-233 8301

Regional Voluntary Networks

Networks are developing to address and mirror the new Regional Development
Agencies and Regional Chambers. These emerging fora are listed below. At the
time of compiling this guide some under represented and overlapping areas were
apparent. Changes will inevitably occur to this list and it should not be further
reproduced without checking its current status.

East Midlands
East Midlands Voluntary Sector Firum
C/o Derby CVS, 4 Charnwood Street, Derby DE1 2GT
Tel: 01332-346266; Fax: 01332-205069; E-mail: cvs@cvsderby.co.uk
Contact: Kevin Curley

Nottingham CVS
33 Mansfield Road, Nottingham NG1 3FB
Tel: 0115-947 6714; Fax: 0115-924 2863; E-mail: ncvs@ncvs.demon.co.uk
Contact: David Hughes

Eastern Region
COVER (Community & Voluntary Forum: Eastern Region)
C/o 28 Westerfield Road, Ipswich, Suffolk IP4 2UJ
Tel: 01473-222276; Fax: 01473-210303

London Region
London Regeneration Network
C/o London Voluntary Sector Resource Centre, 356 Holloway Road,
London N7 6PA
Tel: 0171-7008124; Fax: 0171-7008108

Merseyside
Merseyside Urban Forum
C/o European Institute for Urban Affairs, 51 Rodney Street, Liverpool L1 9AT
Tel: 0151-231 3430; Fax: 0151-708 0650; E-mail: h.russell@livjm.ac.uk
Contact: Hilary Russell

North East
C/o Newcastle-Upon-Tyne CVS, Mea House, Ellison Place,
Newcastle-Upon-Tyne NE1 8XS
Tel: 0191-232 7445; Fax: 0191-230 5640
Contact: Carolle Howells

North West
Voluntary Sector North West
C/0 Greater Manchester Centre for Voluntary Organisations
St Thomas Centre, Ardwick Green North, Manchester M12 6FZ
Tel: 0161-273 7451; Fax: 0161-273 8296; E-mail: gmcvo@mcr1.poptel.org.uk
Contact: Judy Robinson or Phil Langslow

South East
South East Voluntary & Community Network
C/o Community Action Hampshire, Beaconfield Road, Winchester SO22 6AT
Tel: 01962-854971; Fax: 01962-841160; E-mail: helen.horton@action.hants.org.uk
Contact: Helen Horton

South West
South West Forum
C/o VOSCUR, Greats Centre, Smeaton Road, Bristol BS1 6XN
Tel: 0117-909 9949; Fax: 0117-929 7283
Contact: Jean Erskine

Community Regeneration in the Southwest Partnership
C/o Progress, Unit 40 Easton Business Centre, Felix Road, Easton,
Bristol BS5 OHE
Tel: 0117-941 5849; Fax: 0117-941 5844; E-mail: crisp@kparade.demon.co.uk
Contact: Lin Whitfield

West Midlands
Voluntary & Community Sector Network Steering Group
C/o Wolverhampton VSC, 2/3 Bell Street, Wolverhampton WV1 3PR
Tel: 01902-773761; Fax: 01902-310270
Contact: Chris Bonnard

Yorks/Humberside
Yorks & The Humber Regional Forum for Voluntary & Community Organisations
C/o Charities Information Bureau, 11 Upper York Street, Wakefield WF1 3LQ
Tel: 01924-382120; Fax: 01924-387406; E-mail: funding@the-cib.demon.co.uk
Contact: Chris Hollins

Regional Cultural Bodies (proposed)

In July 1998 proposals were announced from the Department of Culture, Media and Sport, to shift more funding decisions on the arts, heritage and sports to regional level.

Regional cultural bodies were also proposed to co-ordinate the work of the regional arts boards, area museums councils, tourist boards, the regional offices of English Heritage and the English Sports Council.

Lottery funding decisions would also be delegated to the boards of the new regional bodies and would work alongside the new Regional Development Agencies.

Consultation on these proposals continued till October 1998.

Regional Arts Boards

The Regional Arts Boards (RABs) are partners with the Arts Council of England (ACE), British Film Institute, Crafts Council, and local authorities in the system for sustaining, promoting and developing the arts in England. RABs are concerned with all the arts and plan jointly with their major strategic and funding partners. They work as arts development agencies (in the broadest sense) identifying needs and formulating strategies for arts provision in conjunction with their key partners, other government departments, non-arts agencies and the private sector.

Financial support: The RABs provide financial support for professional theatre companies, dance and mime companies, music ensembles, literature, arts centres, galleries, community projects, arts education and training and a wide range of local arts bodies which promote arts events. The greater part of RAB funding is allocated to the professional sector, largely because of the greater expenses of professional arts companies and because amateur activities are more generally seen as the responsibility of local rather than regional authorities. Nevertheless some assistance is provided to support amateur work. Changes in Lottery distribution roles and greater decentralisation is also expanding the possibilities for supporting participation.

Priorities: Each RAB establishes its own priorities from year to year, in line with a strategy agreed with the Arts Council. Generally, RABs are concerned with developing ventures in areas where provision is poor.

Services provided: RABs employ specialist officers to deal with particular art forms or combinations of these. Other officers provide financial, marketing, PR, publications and administration services. RABs offer a range of marketing services to regional and touring arts organisations and many co-ordinate with the Association of Business Sponsorship of the Arts (ABSA) on advice sessions about how to raise sponsorship. Via these staff and reference facilities, the RABs provide funding, information, publicity, planning and guidance to arts organisations and individual artists in their regions.

Contact the RABs to obtain further information on policies and grant guidelines. Their annual reports list grant recipients during that year providing helpful background information for new applicants.

The Lottery: The RABs act as agents for the ACE in the assessment of applications for awards. RABs are also able to help potential applicants with advice and discussion of their Lottery bids before applications are formally made.

The new (1988) Lottery Act is giving rise to substantial changes. Owing to existing committed schemes, Lottery capital funding will be more difficult to access than hitherto. RABs will be handling the decisions on all capital bids up to £100,000. Other Lottery allocations to support development work are likely to be dealt with at regional level.

Local authorities: RABs can be very useful to help locate the relevant arts officer for funding from local authorities and the local arts councils/associations which are usually funded by local authorities and often help support amateur activities.

Film and video: Not all RABs fund film, video and broadcasting. At the time of writing there were separate organisations in London (the London Film and Video Agency) and in the South West (the South West Film and Video Agency). It is possible that more such organisations may be formed during the next few years.

The following brief information on individual RABs indicates the scale of their annual funding from the Arts Council of England. The lion's share of their grant-aid is absorbed by their 'revenue clients'. These organisations are funded over a number of years or on an annual basis. A small proportion of RAB funds, usually between only 10 and 20%, is devoted to funding schemes for projects. These are usually advertised according to art form. These are usually heavily over-subscribed.

The Future

It is highly likely that from April 1999 the Arts Council of England will be devolving a high proportion of responsibility and money to RABs on the basis of three-year strategies. RABs would then be able to direct money strategically in line with policy rather than through small, art-form dedicated schemes.

The co-ordinating body for the boards is:
English Regional Arts Boards, 5 City Road, Winchester, Hampshire SO23 8SD
Tel: 01962-851063; Fax: 01962-842033
Chief Executive: Christopher Gordon

Eastern Arts Board

Cherry Hinton Hall, Cherry Hinton Road, Cambridge CB1 4DW
Tel: 01223-215355; Fax: 01223-248075

Area covered: Bedfordshire, Cambridgeshire, Essex, Hertfordshire, Lincolnshire, Norfolk, Suffolk, and unitary authorities of Luton, Peterborough, Southend on Sea, Thurrock.

Grant-in-aid from Arts Council of England: £5,223,780 (1998/99)

Information Officer: Jane Moss.

East Midlands Arts Board

Mountfields House, Epinal Way, Loughborough LE11 OQE
Tel: 01509-218292; Fax: 01509-262214

Area covered: Northamptonshire, Leicestershire, Derbyshire (excluding the High Peak district), Nottinghamshire, unitary authorities of Derby, Leicester, Nottingham, Rutland.

Grant-in aid from Arts Council of England: £4,732,820 (1998/99)

Customer Information: Deborah Duggan.

London Arts Board

Elme House, 133 Long Acre, Covent Garden, London WC2E 9AF
Tel: 0171-240 1313; Helpline: 0171-670 2410; Fax: 0171-670 2400

Area covered: The 32 London boroughs and the Corporation of the City of London.

Grant-in-aid from Arts Council of England: £14,154,170 (1998/99)

Head of Press and Information: Purba Choudhury.

Northern Arts Board

9-10 Osborne Terrace, Newcastle-Upon-Tyne NE2 1NZ
Tel: 0191-281 6334; Fax: 0191-281 3276

Area covered: Cumbria, Durham, Northumberland; unitary authorities of Darlington, Hartlepool, Middlesbrough, Redcar and Cleveland, Stockton; metropolitan districts of Newcastle-Upon-Tyne, Gateshead, North Tyneside, Sunderland, South Tyneside.

Grant-in-aid from Arts Council of England: £6,165,587 (1998/99)

Press and PR: Jo Beddows.

North West Arts Board

Manchester House, 22 Bridge Street, Manchester M3 3AB
Tel: 0161-834 6644; Fax: 0161-834 6969

Area covered: Cheshire, Lancashire, Merseyside, Greater Manchester and the High Peak of Derbyshire; unitary authorities of Blackburn with Darwen, Blackpool, Halton, Warrington.

Grant-in-aid from Arts Council of England: £8,070,729 (1998/99)

Information Officer: Ian Gasse.

Southern Arts Board

13 St Clement Street, Winchester, Hampshire SO23 9DQ
Tel: 01962-855099; Fax: 01962-861186

Area covered: Buckinghamshire, Hampshire, Oxfordshire, Wiltshire south east Dorset: unitary authorities of Bournemouth, Bracknell Forest, Isle of Wight, Milton Keynes, Poole, Portsmouth, Reading, Sough, Southampton, Swindon, West Berkshire, Windsor and Maidenhead, Wokingham.

Grant-in-aid from the Arts Council of England: £3,924,648 (1998/99)

Information & Marketing Officer: Paul Clough.

South East Arts Board

Union House, Eridge Road, Tunbridge Wells, Kent TN4 8HF
Tel: 01892-507200; Fax: 01892-549383

Area covered: Kent, Surrey, East and West Sussex; unitary authorities of Brighton and Hove, Medway.

Grant-in-aid from Arts Council of England: £3,079,240 (1998/99)

Research & Information Officer: Jill Hogan.

South West Arts Board

Bradninch Place, Gandy Street, Exeter EX4 3LS
Tel: 01392-218188; Fax: 01392-413554

Area covered: Cornwall, Devon, Dorset (except districts of Bournemouth, Christchurch & Poole), Somerset, Gloucestershire; unitary authorities of Bath and North East Somerset, Bristol, North Somerset, Plymouth, South Gloucestershire, Torbay.

Grant-in-aid from Arts Council of England: £4,810,707 (1998/99)

Information Advisers: Clare Frank & Kirsty Prabucki.

West Midlands Arts Board

82 Granville Street, Birmingham B1 2LH
Tel: 0121-631 3121; Fax: 0121-643 7239

Area covered: Worcestershire, Shropshire, Staffordshire, Warwickshire; metropolitan districts of Birmingham, Coventry, Dudley, Sandwell, Solihull, Walsall and Wolverhampton; unitary authorities of Hereford, Stoke-on-Trent, Telford and Wrekin.

Grant-in-aid from Arts Council of England: £6,047,582 (1998/99)

Senior Information Officer: Ann Smith.

Yorkshire & Humberside Arts Board

21 Bond Street, Dewsbury, West Yorkshire WF13 1AX
Tel: 01924-455555; Fax: 01924-466522

Area covered: North Yorkshire; unitary authorities of East Riding, Kingston Upon Hull, North East Lincolnshire, North Lincolnshire, York; metropolitan districts of Barnsley, Bradford, Calderdale, Doncaster, Kirklees, Leeds, Rotherham, Sheffield, Wakefield.

Grant-in-aid from Arts Council of England: £7,117,244 (1998/99)

Information Officer: Ian Aspinall.

Area Museum Councils

> **Grant total: about £4 million (for councils in England)**

The Area Museum Councils (AMCs) are the regional development agencies charged with the support of charitable trust, university and local authority museums. They are independent charitable companies run by their members; these include virtually all the 1,650 registered museums in the UK. They offer their members a range of advisory services and training, as well as (in some cases) technical services like design and conservation.

They work very closely with other regional agencies (eg. Regional Arts Boards) and government departments, and can provide a strategic overview and information on the museum scene in their regions. AMCs advise the Heritage Lottery Fund and the Regional Government Offices on grant applications from museums. They are particularly well placed to advise on proposals to set up new museums or redevelop existing ones. They can also recommend consultants for more detailed studies.

The AMCs receive grant from the government channelled through the Museums & Galleries Commission. They offer grants to their members in support of improvements. For further information consult the relevant office.

Committee of Area Museum Councils (the co-ordinatory body for all 10 councils including those for Scotland, Wales and Northern Ireland)
Tel & Fax: 01730 893750

West Midlands Area Museums Service
Hanbury Road, Stoke Prior, Bromsgrove B60 4AD
Tel: 01527-872258; Fax: 01527-576960

North East Museums Service
House of Recovery, Bath Lane, Newcastle-Upon-Tyne NE4 5SQ
Tel: 0191-222 1661; Fax: 0191-261 4725

East Midlands Museums Service
Courtyard Buildings, Wollaton Park, Nottingham NG8 2AE
Tel: 01602-854534; Fax: 01602-280038

North West Museums Service
Griffin Lodge, Cavendish Place, Blackburn BB2 2PH
Tel: 01254-670211; Fax: 01254-2681995

Area Museums Council for the South West
Hestercombe House, Cheddon Fitzpaine, Taunton TA2 8LQ
Tel: 01823-259696; Fax: 01823-413114

Yorkshire & Humberside Museums Council
Farnley Hall, Hall Lane, Leeds LS12 5HA
Tel: 0133-263 8909; Fax: 0113-279 1479

South Eastern Museums Service
Ferroners House, Barbican, London EC2Y 8AA
Tel: 0171-600 0219; Fax: 0171-600 2581

See separate entries for the museums councils in Scotland, Wales and Northern
Ireland.

Ⓔ Training and Enterprise
Ⓦ Councils

TEC National Council, Westminster Tower,
3 Albert Embankment, London SE1 7SX
Tel: 0171-735 0010; Fax: 0171-735 0090

Combined TEC contracts with government: around £1.4 billion annually.

There were 78 TECs, covering *England and Wales* (as of August 1998), of which
14 had merged with Chambers of Commerce and were known as Chambers of
Commerce Training and Enterprise (CCTEs). Contact details can be found in the
local telephone directory. In Scotland, similar work is the responsibility of the
network of local enterprise companies.

Training and Enterprise Councils (TECs) have had responsibility for the delivery
of youth and adult training mainly through a number of government programmes.
Each TEC has its own priorities and methods of operating and links can be made
by voluntary organisations in a number of ways. The main programmes through
which they have worked are: Training for Work; Youth Training; Investors in
People, the staff development programme; New business start-up schemes providing
business skills training and support; Business Training Schemes – specialist and
high quality training. TECs are also playing a key role in New Deal Partnerships.

The role of TECs was expanded in line with a consultation paper issued in July 1998.
The stated aim was to "build on the strengths of TECs and enable TECs to contribute
to six challenges:
- Create and sustain an internationally competitive economy;
- Raise standards of education and training to internationally competitive levels;
- Promote lifelong learning;

- Help people move from welfare into sustainable employment;
- Tackle deprivation;
- Support regeneration of local communities".

TECs work with a broad range of partners including voluntary and community organisations. It is envisioned that they will have a 'collaborative' relationship with Regional Development Agencies (RDAs), with TECs responsible for delivery programmes on the ground whilst RDAs set up regional strategies. Future funding arrangements were expected to reflect TEC's widening role.

Being part of the TEC network at a local level is vital to find out how decisions are made and priorities are determined.

See separate entry for Local Enterprise Councils (LECs) in Scotland.

ⓔ ACRE – Action with Communities in Rural England

Rural Action National Team, Somerford Court, Somerford Road, Cirencester, Gloucestershire GL7 1TW

Tel: 01285-653477; Fax: 01285-654537
E-mail: acre@acre.org.uk
Web site: http://www.acreciro.demon.co.uk

Contact: Sue Pope, Information Officer.

Rural Development Commission grant-in-aid:

To county-based Rural Community Councils: £2.98 million (1998/99 and in 1997/98).
To ACRE: £60,000 (1998/99 and in 1997/98).

ACRE is the national association of Rural Community Councils which have the shared purpose to improve the quality of life of local communities, particularly of disadvantaged people in rural England.

Rural Action for the Environment

Grant total: around £1 million a year (£800,000 to community groups via county/local networks; £200,000 to networking organisations for their services)

Rural Action is a partnership of organisations working for a better environment throughout England. It is managed by ACRE from its national office, but grants and advice are administered locally, usually by the rural community council. Information is also available from most country wildlife trusts, BTCV, many community and environmental organisations and local authorities. It is funded by grant-in-aid of some £1.1 million (1998/99) from the Countryside Commission, English Nature and the Rural Development Commission.

Rural Action aims to make life easier for people in rural communities to undertake almost any project which benefits their local environment or increases the understanding and care of it. Any group of people within a village, small town or parish can apply for a grant. They may be an existing group (WI, youth group, village hall committee, town or parish council etc.), local people coming together for a specific project, or just a group of friends.

Projects must concern some aspect of the environment and be in a rural area of England. Local people must be actively leading and carrying out the project and the expected benefits should be sustainable. For site-based projects there must be full public access. The types of projects receiving support include: local surveys (eg. wildlife, trees, traffic), practical tasks (eg. creating or managing woodlands, footpaths, rebuilding drystone walls), feasibility studies, setting up recycling and community composting schemes, tackling litter, graffiti or noise problems, management plans for wildlife areas, landscape improvements around community buildings, energy audits and creating parish maps.

Rural Action can identify people who can give expert advice and help a group develop the skills and knowledge needed for the project.

Project grants can cover the cost of specialist help and training and can also help with publicity, feasibility studies, consulting other local people, obtaining maps and other materials for surveys, hiring equipment and venues for meetings etc. Grants cannot be used to buy equipment or tools, but may fund some materials as part of a package including advice etc.

If the project is tackled in stages (eg. feasibility study, public meeting, skills training), grant applications can be made for each stage, before applying for further funding.

Project grants can be for up to £2,000, although most are smaller. A group must provide 50% of the total value of the project, which can include the time spent carrying it out (valued at £46 per day) and 'in kind' donations of materials and services, as well as cash raised from other sources.

Applications: Contact any of the organisations in the Rural Action network in your county – the local Wildlife Trust, BTCV or RCC – to develop the project. Then meet a Rural Action advisor to discuss how Rural Action can help. A Registration of Interest card will be completed before a Rural Action Project Grant application form is obtained.

When completed the application form is sent to the Project Grant Administrator in the county.

Project grants are usually paid in advance, so work can start once the application is approved. A feedback report is needed within six months. Repeat applications are welcome.

Village Halls Loan Fund

Fund total:	£500,000

ACRE administers a loan programme for the Rural Development Commission towards capital improvements, such as extension or rebuilding costs. The building must be open to use by all members of the community.

Loans do not usually exceed £20,000. At least 20% of the total cost, or £1 per head of the population, whichever is the less, must come from local funds. Interest is laid down by the Treasury under the 'broadly commercial' rate. Loans are repaid over a period of five or eight years.

Exclusions: Loans cannot be offered to parish councils or towards work on buildings owned or run by individual organisations eg. church halls, WI halls.

Applications: Guidance notes and applications forms are available. Applications can be processed within three weeks.

Countrywork

In 1997/98 the Rural Development Commission contributed £125,000 as a third of the costs of a partnership with the Post Office and BT to fund a grants scheme for local community-based projects. This scheme aimed to generate employment, training and income-earning opportunities. Applications were processed by the county-based rural community councils. In 1998/99 ACRE was endeavouring to develop a successor partnership.

DEPARTMENT OF
SOCIAL SECURITY

Adelphi, 1-11 John Adam Street,
London WC2N 6HT

Tel: 0171-962 8000

The department has a series of addresses with a leading office close to Parliament
in Richmond House, 79 Whitehall London SW1A 2NS. The address above is the
one where funding relevant to this guide has been identified.

Resettlement Section

Grant total: £18.7 million – 29% capital and 71% revenue (1998/99)
                £21.3 million – 41% capital and 59% revenue (1997/98)

Discretionary payments, both capital and revenue, are made mainly to voluntary
organisations providing supported accommodation to single homeless people.
Projects must involve an active resettlement programme. The provision covers
England, *Scotland* and *Wales*.

Capital grants (up to 100% of costs), have been reducing in number and have been
predominantly committed to the refurbishment/replacement of former DSS
Resettlement Units. This programme was near completion in 1998/99. Revenue
funding is given for up to the amount needed to make a project 'break even'.
Revenue grants vary from £1,000 to £500,000.

The department has written that in 1998/99 over 100 organisations were supported
to provide resettlement beds in about 260 projects. It has also stated that its rules
on confidentiality do not allow it to give information about grant awards *even though
these are to organisations and not individuals* [Ed.]. Its own background note refers
to the autumn 1997 announcement of a £1.5 million capital grant to the St Mungo
Association.

Contact: Arlene Olver, Monitoring Officer, Tel: 0171-712 2487; Fax: 0171-712 2480

Applications for funding are initiated by the DSS.

Powers: Section 30 of the Jobseekers Act 1995

Disability and Carer Benefits

Increasing the Independence of Disabled People

Grant-in-aid: £123.3 million (1997/98)

Annual grants are *only* made to the following organisations for their work *UK wide* to increase the independence of disabled people. Grants in 1997/98 were:
Independent Living Funds enable people to live independently in the community who would otherwise be unable to do so (£115,500,000);
Motability (£3,050,000 for Mobility Equipment Fund which funds the cost of vehicle adaptations, plus £4,640,000 for administration);
BLESMA (Ex Serviceman's Limbless Association), an annual allocation for administrative costs and grants to purchase specialist adaptations (£10,000).

Contacts: Geraldine Darcy re Independent Living Funds; Steve Walsh re Motability Tel: 0171-712 2252; Fax: 0171-962 8494

Powers: Disability Grants Act 1993
Powers: Section 64 of the Health Services and Public Health Act 1968

ⓊⓀ DEPARTMENT OF TRADE & INDUSTRY

---

1 Victoria Street, London SW1H 0ET
Tel: 0171-215 5000; Fax: 0171-222 2629
Web site: http://www.dti.gov.uk/

Consumer Affairs & Competition Policy Directorate

The Consumer Affairs and Competition Policy Directorate sponsors bodies which represent the *UK consumers' interests* and promote consumer safety and is responsible for ensuring that they operated according to the terms and conditions of their funding.

Branch 1

Grant-in-aid: £170,000 (1998/99 and 1997/98)

This regular grant to the Royal Society for the Prevention of Accidents (RoSPA) Home & Leisure Safety Division funds Home Safety Officers in England and Wales.

Contact: Jan Krefta (Tel: 0171-215 6723; Fax: 0171-215 0357)

Branch 2

Grant-in-aid: £22,182,600 (1998/99)
£20,948,000 (1997/98)

Branch 2 is responsible for funding official consumer bodies and also for ensuring that these bodies represent consumers effectively. It regularly funds nine organisations: the national consumer councils, the national industry consumer councils for gas, telecommunications and the Post Office and the two national CABx. Funding for 1998/99 shows the major part of this funding (72%) allocated to:

National Association of Citizens' Advice Bureaux (£14,416,000);

Citizens' Advice Scotland (£1,455,000).

Contact: Jaqui Entwistle, Tel: 0171-215 0318/19; Fax: 0171-222 6260

Powers: Section 20 of the 1980 Competition Act

THE SCOTTISH OFFICE

**St Andrew's House,
Edinburgh EH1 3DG**

**Tel: 0131-556 8400
Web site: www.scotland.gov.uk**

The Scottish Office is made up of five departments listed below with their main responsibilities:

Agriculture, Environment and Fisheries
- agriculture
- environment
- natural heritage

Development
- housing
- transport
- regeneration
- built heritage

Education & Industry
- arts
- youth and community services
- public education

Health
- public health policy
- National Health Service in Scotland

Home
- social services
- law and order including prisons

Funding of the voluntary sector

A breakdown of total funding in 1998/99 to voluntary organisations from the Scottish Office is given in the pie-chart. It shows over three quarters of the funding to Scottish Homes, with allocations to the Scottish Arts Council and 'All other grants' (programmes only open to the voluntary sector) absorbing the remainder in similar proportions.

The following graph breaks down the section 'All other grants' in the pie-chart. It shows the different contributing departments within the Scottish Office and the relative proportions of funding they made available via programmes aimed exclusively at voluntary organisations in 1998/99.

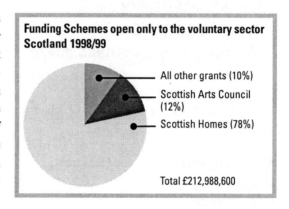

Funding Schemes open only to the voluntary sector
Scotland 1998/99

All other grants (10%)
Scottish Arts Council (12%)
Scottish Homes (78%)

Total £212,988,600

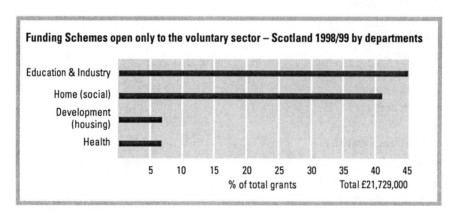

Funding Schemes open only to the voluntary sector – Scotland 1998/99 by departments

Education & Industry
Home (social)
Development (housing)
Health

5   10   15   20   25   30   35   40   45
% of total grants   Total £21,729,000

Notes on graph

The Education and Industry Department funding covers cultural organisations, special needs and community education.

The Home Department funding covers social welfare as well as voluntary action.

The Development Department funding covers housing and homelessness.

The Health Department funding covers general health.

Detailed Breakdown of 'All other grants'
Grant Schemes for Voluntary Organisations

	£'000	
Development Department		
Housing and Homelessness Grants	1,403	
		1,403
Department of Education & Industry		
Special Schools Grants	7,760	
Community Education Grants	1,217	
Cultural Organisations Grants	812	
		9,789
Home Department		
Social Welfare – Section 10 Grants	5,400	
Victim Support Schemes Grant	1,505	
Unemployed Voluntary Action Fund	868	
Social Welfare – Training Grants	706	
Ethnic Minority Grant	275	
		8,754
Health Department		
Health Grants	1,219	
Health Education Board for Scotland	264	
		1,483
Agriculture Department		
Forward Scotland	300	
		300
TOTAL		**21,729**

Devolution

The Scottish Parliament will be elected in May 1999 and then sit in transitional mode for six months with full powers coming into force from early 2000. Devolution will give Scotland new powers among which is the ability to vary income tax. Other powers to be devolved to the Scottish Parliament are set out in the White Paper *Scotland's Parliament*. Westminster reserves the following functions: constitution, foreign policy, employment legislation, fiscal policy, social security and defence.

Contents

AGRICULTURE, ENVIRONMENT AND FISHERIES DEPARTMENT

**Pentland House,
47 Robb's Loan,
Edinburgh EH14 1TY
Tel: 0131-556 8400**

The responsibilities of the department include the agriculture and fishing industry as well as environment and the natural heritage. It sponsors Scottish Natural Heritage and the Scottish Environment Protection Agency.

Scottish Rural Partnership Fund

The Scottish Rural Partnerships Fund supports a system of national and local partnerships throughout rural Scotland announced in the Scottish White Paper on Rural Policy, *People, Prosperity and Partnership*. It aims to 'move decision-making closer to the local level and encourage communities to self-start'. Three broad categories of partnerships can be identified: strategic, area or topic-oriented.

Local Capital Grants Scheme for Community Facilities

Grant total:	£1.427 million (1998/99)
	£1.054 million (1997/98)

Grants are made to help local voluntary and youth organisations provide new facilities, or improve existing premises, for educational, social or recreational activities. Facilities should be open to all sections of the community, with priority given to:

- areas with the greatest social needs;

- rural areas;
- projects catering for all ages of the community;
- in the case of youth projects, those which cater for the 15-25 age group but mainly for the 15-19 age group.

The maximum grant aid is £100,000 and will not exceed 50% of eligible costs. The local authority contribution is normally 25% with the applicant meeting 25% of costs. The average grant is £24,000.

A total of 38 grants were made in 1997/98 including:
    Uig Community Centre, Western Isles (£100,000);
    Northmuir Village Hall, Angus (£52,100);
    Gulberwick Hall, Shetland Islands (£2,300).

Applications: Local authorities annually print a list of projects they are prepared to support during the following year in order of priority.

Powers: Education (Scotland) Act 1980 (a), Further Education (Approved Associations) (Scotland) Grants Regulations 1989

Rural Strategic Support Fund

Grant total:	**£1.601 million (1998/99)**
	£1.6 million (1997/98)

Three types of support are available:

■ Local Rural Partnerships

Funding is available for organisations forming a Local Rural Partnership or providing assistance to a partnership. A special guidance note on the formation of these partnerships is available. It cites the Moray Firth Partnership as an example of a topic-based partnership including local authorities, local enterprise companies, port authorities, wildlife, nature protection and environmental organisations, the Forestry Commission and RAF Kinloss. The partnership is developing an integrated management strategy of the natural, economic, recreation and cultural resources of the area.

Powers: Housing grants, Construction and Regeneration Act 1996, Sections 126-128

■ Councils for Voluntary Service (CVSs)

Support is available only for rural and semi-rural CVSs. New applicants should ensure there is no overlap with existing councils. The Scottish Office maintains contact with those currently receiving a grant.

Powers: Social Work (Scotland) Act 1968, Section 104

■ Scottish National Environmental Organisations

Organisations undertaking environmental improvement projects throughout Scotland may apply for core funding.

Powers: Environmental Protection Act 1990, Section 153

Contact: Gavin Gardener, Room 259, Tel: 0131-2240469; Fax: 0131-244 3110; E-mail: gavin.gardiner@so061.scotoff.gov.uk

Rural Challenge Fund (RCF)

> **Total grant-aid:** £1,220,000 (1998/99)
> £1,220,000 (1997/98)

This competitive fund is open primarily to applications from rural communities and voluntary organisations in Scotland, though commercial concerns may bid for innovative transport-related projects (formerly run as a separate funding scheme).

Rural communities and voluntary organisations will be expected to have applied to the 'normal sources of funding' for their projects *before* submitting a bid to RCF to close any funding gap. 'In essence the RFC is a source of funding of last resort.'

In 1998/99 a total of 25 grants were made for projects ranging from one to three years, including the following:

The Royal Scottish Forestry Society, acquisition of Cashel Forest (£50,000);

The Land Sea and Islands Centre at Arisaig old Smiddy (£45,000);

Forres Area Action Group, A Riverside Challenge Project (£33,400);

Duff House, Banff, events and grounds programme (£36,800 over two years);

Helter Skelter, for teenagers in Largs (£50,000 over three years).

Applications: The deadline for bids in 1998 was 28th November. Guidance about sources of funding is available from:

Rural Forum, Highland House, 46 St Catherine's Road, Perth PH1 5RY
Tel: 01738-634565, or a local Council of Voluntary Service.

Contact: Raymond Evans, Room 259, Tel: 0131-244 6945; Fax: 0131-244 3110; E-mail: raymond.evans@so061.scotoff.gov.uk

Powers: Housing Grants, Construction and Regeneration Act 1996, Sections 126-128; Environmental Protection Act 1990; Section 153 transport Act 1985, Section 108

Forward Scotland

c/o Scottish Power, St Vincent Crescent, Glasgow G3 8LT

Tel: 0141-567 4334; Fax: 0141-567 4339

> **Grant total:**   **£300,000 (budgeted 1998/99)**
> **£300,000 (1997/98)**

Forward Scotland (FS), formerly UK 2000 Scotland, is a charitable company funded annually by the Agriculture, Environment and Fisheries Department of the Scottish Office (with about £1/2 million). It is committed to putting the concept of sustainable development into practice throughout Scotland and works with communities, voluntary organisations and others.

It works in partnership with the public, private and voluntary sectors. FS has changed the emphasis of its programmes from those which concentrate solely on the environment towards programmes which also address social and economic concerns. 'The range of actions undertaken... will follow closely the areas set out in LA 21 and the UK Strategy for Sustainable Development.'

Partnership Fund

> **Grant total:**   **£260,000 (budgeted 1998/99)**
> **£260,000 (1997/98)**

With this fund FS plays a financial, advisory and partnership role in larger scale sustainable development projects and initiatives. It works proactively and monitors the achievements.

Recent partnerships include:
Sustainable Communities, for partnership community programmes with Stirling, Edinburgh, Glasgow and Renfrewshire Councils (£56,000);
Scottish Wildlife Trust, towards 37 teams working on environmental issues, biodiversity training and community based initiatives at 18 different locations (£35,000);
East of Scotland Waste Minimisation Project, a programme bringing together East of Scotland Water, British Oxygen Company Foundation, Scottish Power, Scottish Environmental Protection Agency, and the Environmental Technology Best Practice Programme (£15,000);
Scottish Conservation Projects Trust, for 5 programmes of work: Glasgow Community Projects providing training and employments on environmental

projects in areas of need; Dundee Waste and Environment Trust which was established to disburse landfill tax credits; Highland Environmental Network; Conservation Local Area Networks (CLAN) who assist small voluntary groups taking environmental action; Action Recycle, doorstep recycling service in central Scotland (£35,000).

Contact: Andrew Lyon, Development Manager

Small Projects Grant Fund

Grant total:	**£23,000 (1998/99)**
	£40,000 (1997/98)

This fund gives support, advice and grants to community-led projects. Most grants are around £500 with £1,000 being given in exceptional cases. An organisation must be able to comply with FS's sustainability check-list and have the necessary permissions and community support. Recent grants have included:

Scottish Pensioner Power Welfare Services (£1,000);

Dighty Environmental Group and North Arran Community Growers (£500 each).

Applications: An introductory leaflet and contact form, *Small Grants Big Ideas*, is available.

Contacts: Alison Quinn and David Airlie

Scottish Natural Heritage

12 Hope Terrace, Edinburgh EH9 2AS

Tel: 0131-447 4784

Contact: National Grants Officer, at Battleby, Redgorton, Perth PH1 3EW (Tel & Fax – see below under Eastern Area)

Grant total:	**£7 million (1997/98)**
	about 30% to the voluntary sector

Scottish Natural Heritage (SNH) is the government agency working with others to conserve and enhance Scotland's wildlife, habitats and landscapes. It is responsible to and funded by the Secretary of State for Scotland (and replaced the Countryside Commission for Scotland and the Nature Conservancy Council for Scotland in the early 1990s). It advises on policies and promotes projects which improve the natural heritage and support its sustainable use. Grants are available for a wide range of projects which:

- improve the conservation of species, habitats and landscapes;
- promote public enjoyment of the natural heritage;
- increase awareness and understanding of the natural heritage.

SNH particularly fosters the development of working partnerships with all kinds of interested parties – voluntary bodies, other public sector agencies (including local authorities), individuals and businesses.

Community and voluntary action

Grants for environmental projects; establishing and promoting local community-based organisations; information and assessment of local sites of natural heritage value; volunteer involvement, travel costs and training; and project/development officers for voluntary groups.

SNH funds a number of national voluntary and community organisations which are able to offer further information and advice to groups: Scottish Conservation Projects, Scottish Wildlife Trust, Rural Forum, Highland Forum and Scottish Wildlife and Countryside Link.

Environmental education and interpretation

Grants for site interpretation; demonstration and display areas; interpretative strategies/plans; visitor reception facilities; publications, exhibitions and campaigns; seminars, training and fieldwork courses; schools.

SNH supports the Scottish Environmental Education Council and Regional Environmental Education Forums (based at the Department of Environmental Science, Stirling University) which can give further advice.

Land managers, farmers and crofters

Grants are given for landscape features, nature conservation, geological features, species, access and recreation. Management agreements may be arranged for ongoing programmes. Projects eligible for funding under other governmental schemes (agricultural, forestry or agri-environment) are not usually considered.

SNH supports the Farming & Wildlife Advisory Group, based near Newbridge, Midlothian, and encourages applicants to seek its advice.

Applicants for all schemes must demonstrate that they have sought resources of support in kind and/or moral support from other people. They also need to consider carefully whether any of the other agencies giving overlapping areas of grant-aid are more appropriate to their project ie. the Forestry Commission, SOAEFD, Scottish Tourist Board, Scottish Sports Council, Historic Scotland, Local Enterprise Company or local authority.

Grants rarely exceed 50% of the total eligible expenditure. Higher rates may be offered for a limited number of priority projects. Grants range in size from under £100 to £1 million.

Exclusions: Work undertaken prior to submission of, and during consideration of an application; expeditions, research projects, conferences; publications; work required for planning consent or other statutory obligation.

Applications: Guidelines and application forms are available. Applicants are encouraged to discuss their proposals with the area officer nearest their project (see below) before submitting an application there. Projects relating to Scotland as a whole, or covering more than one region, should be sent to the National Grants Officer at the Battleby office. There are no deadlines but applicants are strongly advised to apply as far in advance of the start date as possible. Successful applicants are expected to monitor their projects and present a report.

Main Regional Offices:

North Areas
Northern Isles
Lerwick Tel: 01595-693345; Fax: 01595-692565
East Highland
Dingwall Tel: 01349-865333; Fax: 01349-865609
North Highland
Golspie Tel: 01408-633602; Fax: 01408-633071
West Highland
Fort William Tel: 01397-704716; Fax: 01397-700303
Western Isles
Stornoway Tel: 01851-705258; Fax: 01851-704900

East Areas
Grampian
Aberdeen Tel: 01224-312266; Fax: 01224-311366
Tayside
Battleby Tel: 01738-444177; Fax: 01738-442060
Forth & Borders
Dalkeith Tel: 0131-654-2466; Fax: 0131-6542477

West Areas
Argyll & Stirling
Stirling Tel: 01786-450362; Fax: 01786-451974
Strathclyde & Ayrshire
Clydebank Tel: 0141-951 4488; Fax: 0141-951 8948
Dumfries & Galloway
Dumfries Tel: 01387-247010; Fax: 01387-259247

DEVELOPMENT DEPARTMENT

Victoria Quay
Edinburgh EH6 6QQ
Tel: 0131-556 8400

The department's responsibilities include housing, roads and transport, urban regeneration, historic buildings and ancient monuments. It also funds the executive agency, Historic Scotland.

Area Regeneration Division

The Urban Programme – Priority Partnership Areas and Regeneration Programmes

Total funding: £34 million (1998/99)
                   £18 million (1997/98)

The overall purpose of the Urban Programme is to contribute to the improvement of the social, economic and environmental conditions of those who reside in the areas of worst deprivation. Currently, Urban Programme resources are targeted on 12 Priority Partnership Areas (PPAs) and 11 Regeneration Programme Areas (RP). In these areas, local regeneration partnerships have been set up to pursue comprehensive regeneration strategies. Each of these regeneration partnerships comprises the Council, Scottish Homes, the Local Enterprise Company, other relevant agencies and representatives from the private sector, the community and the voluntary sector. Partnerships in PPA and RP areas receive a block allocation of Urban Programme funds, with detailed decisions on how to use these funds being taken locally by the partnerships.

Currently, over 60% of projects supported by these partnerships are run by the voluntary sector. For example, the Project for Child and Family Wellbeing in Greater Easterhouse in Glasgow received over £100,000 from the Greater Easterhouse PPA in 1997/98 to provide childcare facility for under threes as well as providing some family support.

The Government has announced its intention to review the Urban Programme and set up new Social Inclusion Partnerships. The characteristics of these new Social Inclusion Partnerships will be that: they focus on the most needy members of society; they co-ordinate and fill gaps between existing programmes to promote inclusion; and they seek to prevent people becoming socially excluded. They will retain the key features of the existing PPAs, and are expected to start work in April 1999. Further details of the new arrangements can be obtained by contacting the Scottish Office.

Priority Partnerships Areas
Ardler, Dundee Tel: 01382-433617; Fax: 01382-433871
Craigmillar, Edinburgh Tel: 0131-4693821; Fax: 0131-4693574
North Edinburgh Tel: 0131-4693821; Fax: 0131-4693574
Glasgow East End Tel: 0141-5546252; Fax: 0141-5540323
Glasgow North Tel: 0141-2870329; Fax: 0141-2870431
Greater Easterhouse Tel: 0141-7719338; Fax: 0141-7713856
Great Northern, Aberdeen Tel: 01224-523035; Fax: 01224-522832
Inverclyde, Greenock Tel: 01475-731700; Fax: 01475-731800
Motherwell North Tel: 01698-302449; Fax: 01698-302489
North Ayr Tel: 01292-616180; Fax: 01292-616161
Paisley Tel: 0141-840 3228; Fax: 0141-8895140
West Dunbartonshire Tel: 01389-737401; Fax: 01389-737512

Regeneration Programmes
Angus Tel: 01307-473004; Fax: 01307-461874
Dundee Tel: 01382-433617; Fax: 01382-433871
East Renfrewshire Tel: 0141-5773144; Fax: 0141-6200884
Edinburgh Tel: 0131-4693821; Fax: 0131-4693574
Falkirk Tel: 01324-506004; Fax: 01324-506061
Fife Tel: 01592-416162; Fax: 01592-416020
Glasgow Tel: 0141-2870308; Fax: 0141-2875997
North Ayrshire Tel: 01294-324113; Fax: 01294-324114
North Lanarkshire Tel: 01698-302449; Fax: 01698-302489
South Lanarkshire Tel: 01698-454202; Fax: 01698-454376
Stirling Tel: 01786-442677; Fax: 01786-442538

Contact: Ann McVie, Tel: 0131-244 0808

Powers: Local Government Grants (Social Need) Act 1969, Section 1

Housing Division

Housing and Homelessness Grants

Grant total:	**£1,402,600 (1998/99)**
	£1,488,000 (1997/98)

Grants, for core funding or specific projects, are awarded to voluntary organisations tackling homelessness and other housing work on a short term basis. They were allocated between the following areas in 1998/99:

- Homelessness (£577,000), 41%;
- Community care (£238,000), 17%;
- Services to tenants (£208,600), 15%;
- General, including energy efficiency (£194,000), 14%;
- Education, training, research (£185,000),13%.

A total of 23 grants were made which ranged from £8,000 to £250,000 and included:
Shelter Scotland, Scottish Homeless Advisory Service (£250,000 a year for three years);
Housing Studentships (£130,000);
Energy Action Scotland (£53,000);
Tenants' Participation Advisory Service, TEPAS (£50,000);
Scottish Refugee Council (£40,000);
Disabled Persons Housing Service (£34,000);
Community Self Build Scotland (£22,500).

Applications: Application forms were available from the above address in early September for return by the end of October in 1998.

Contact: Fiona Ferguson, Tel: 0131-244 5525

Powers: Housing (Scotland) Act 1987, Sections 39 and 197. Local Government and Housing Act 1989, Section 168

Empty Homes Initiative

Grant total:	**£7 million (1998/99)**
	£2 million (1997/98)

The Empty Homes Initiative aims to bring vacant properties back into use through seed corn funding to innovative projects. Local authorities, in partnership with statutory, voluntary and private sector bodies, may apply for funding after assessing the extent of empty homes in their area. Funding is available for both capital and revenue expenditure and covers projects from empty homes registers to property refurbishment, from research to Empty Homes Officers. A total of 103 grants were made in 1998/99 to 27 local authorities. The payment of resources is administered by Scottish Homes to local authorities who distribute it to participating partners. Grants ranged between £5,000 and £400,000.

Exclusions: Grants are not available to replace funding for existing schemes.

Applications: Voluntary bodies may *not* approach the Scottish Office directly for funding but should work in partnership with the appropriate local authority. Local authorities should submit bids to the above address, following a survey of the extent of empty homes in the area. Guidelines are available from the Scottish Office contact above.

Powers: Section 2 of the Housing (Scotland) Act 1988

Rough Sleepers Initiative

Government funding:	**£7 million (1999/00)**
	£5 million (1998/99)
	£4 million (1997/98)

The Rough Sleepers Initiative is a pilot scheme funded from 1997 to 2000, to be evaluated in 1999. Local authorities work with partners from the statutory, voluntary and private sectors to identify the extent of rough sleeping in their area and devise innovative solutions. Schemes should identify current gaps in provision including rough sleepers with special needs and particularly the under 25s.

Funding is available for both capital and revenue expenditure for schemes that provide accommodation and support, information, advice, outreach and advocacy services for rough sleepers. The majority of funds (88% in 1999/00) is targeted at Glasgow and Edinburgh, with 24 grants made to these cities in 1999/00 ranging from £19,550 to £640,170 and including:

Turning Point, Glasgow, (£640,170);

Old Town Housing Association, Edinburgh (£252,000);

Homeless Outreach Project, Edinburgh (£141,000);

Shelter, Glasgow (£32,875).

The payment of resources is administered by Scottish Homes to local authorities which distribute it to participating partners.

Exclusions: Grants are not available to replace funding for existing schemes.

Applications: Voluntary bodies should *not* approach the Scottish Office directly for funding but should work in partnership with the appropriate local authority. Local authorities should submit bids to the Scottish Office, following a survey of the extent of rough sleeping in the area. Guidelines are available from the Scottish Office. Bids are assessed by an Advisory Group (chaired by the Scottish Office and involving representatives of local authorities, Scottish Homes, Shelter Scotland, the Scottish Council for Single Homeless and the Glasgow Simon Community) which provides advice to the Secretary of State on the merits of the bids.

Contacts: Lindsay Manson, Head of Unit; Catherine Hodgson,
Tel: 0131-244 5515

Powers: Section 2 of the Housing (Scotland) Act 1988

The future of the both the Empty Homes and the Rough Sleepers Initiatives was undecided in autumn 1998.

Care & Repair Forum Scotland

Grant-in-aid: £64,400 (1998/99)
                   £65,900 (1997/98)

Care and Repair Forum Scotland is the national co-ordinating body for Care and Repair officers in Scotland. It addresses the unsuitable living conditions of older people or people with a disability through advice and information, training, support, promoting policies which improve poor housing conditions.

Transport Division

Transport for Disabled People

Grant total:	£66,500 (1998/99)

Grants were made to the following three projects in 1998/99:
    Community Transport Association, for the Scottish Rural Transport Initiative (£39,000 p.a. for three years);
    Community Transport Association, for the Scottish Advice and Information Service (£15,000 p.a.);
    Disability Scotland, for biennial mobility roadshow (£12,500 p.a.).

Contact: John Stirling, Tel: 0131-244 0869

Historic Scotland

Longmore House, Salisbury Place, Edinburgh EH9 1SH

Tel: 0131-668 8600 See also below

Grant total: £13,600,000 (1998/99)
£14,115,000 (1997/98)
£13,440,000 (1996/97)
(30% grants, remainder contracts)

Historic Scotland aims to protect, present and promote Scotland's built heritage which includes ancient monuments and archaeological sites, historic building, parks and gardens, and designed landscapes. It was made an executive agency by the Secretary of State for Scotland in 1991.

Historic Buildings
Grant total: £11,700,000 (1998/99)

Grants are made available for the repair of buildings of outstanding architectural and historic importance and buildings in outstanding conservation areas. Buildings in the most urgent need of repair are given priority. Only buildings in categories A and B and buildings of prominence within outstanding conservation areas are considered eligible for grants. Modest buildings within Town Schemes established within outstanding conservation areas (partnerships with local authorities) may also receive assistance with repairs. The demand for grant regularly exceeds the provision and there can be a delay before monies are made available. The need for grant has to be demonstrated. Private owners normally receive up to 33% of eligible costs; trusts up to 40%; and churches-in-use up to 60%. There are no maximum or minimum grants sizes or inadmissible sources of matching funding. Partnership funding can include contributions from the European Regional Development Fund (ERDF), the Heritage Lottery Fund, as well as schemes jointly funded by other government agencies, such as LECs, Scottish Homes or local authorities.

Recent examples of grants/partnerships include:
26-31 Charlotte Square, Edinburgh (£1,600,000);
Argyll Motor Works, West Dumbarton – private sector (£400,000);
Former Glasgow Herald Building, Glasgow (£350,000).

Applications: Two booklets provide guidance: *Guide to Grant Applicants* and *Notes for Professional Advisers*. Awards are only made to the owner of the property. Conditions include a measure of public access, as appropriate, and a requirement to notify of disposal within 10 years of the award. Claims are accepted quarterly, in arrears, as work proceeds.

Regional Offices:
North – Inverness Tel: 01667-462777
Central – Stirling Tel: 01786-450000
South – Edinburgh, see above.

Contact: Edward Tait, Grants Manager, Tel: 0131-668 8600; Fax: 0131-668 8788
Grant Enquiry Section: 0131-668 8797

Ancient Monument Grants
Grant total: £200,000 (1998/99)

Applications are dealt with on a priority system according to the historical, archaeological and architectural importance of the monument and the feasibility of the proposed works. Whilst monuments do not necessarily have to be scheduled, in practice grants are only awarded to scheduled monuments or those of schedulable quality. Inhabited buildings and buildings in ecclesiastical use (including buildings undergoing restoration for such uses) are not eligible.

The need for a grant has to be demonstrated. There is no set maximum or minimum size of grant. Private owners and trusts normally get no more than 75% of eligible costs, local authorities, 50%. Partnership funding is the same as for historic buildings (see above).

Recent grants/partnerships have included:
   Uchdachan Bridge, Association for the Protection of Rural Scotland (£78,000);
   Dunure Castle, Strathclyde Buildings Preservation Trust (£18,000);
   Ancrum Old Bridge, private owner (£18,000);
   Amisfield Tower, private owner (£10,000);
   St Cuthbert's chapel, Moffat, private owner (£5,000).

Applications: A booklet, *Grants for Ancient Monuments (1997)*, provides guidance. The conditions attached to grant may include an undertaking to allow a measure of public access, as appropriate, and to ensure future maintenance.

Contact: A J Tasker, Tel: 0131-668 8775; Fax: 0131-668 8765

Rescue Archaeology
Grant total: £1,700,000 (1998/99)

Grants are given for investigation of archaeological sites and landscapes under threat; applied research into site conservation; contributions to costs of strategic conservation effects by others. Also see *State-Funded Rescue Archaeology in*

Scotland: Past Present and Future.

Recent grants have included:
Fordhouse Burial Ground, National Trust for Scotland, for cost of excavating burial round suffering from severe damage from erosion and rabbits (£12,043).

Applications: Approach the contact above for more information. Applications need to be made the September before the financial year of expenditure.

Contact: Gordon Barclay, Principal Inspector of Ancient Monuments
Tel: 0131-668 8758; Fax: 0131-668 8765

Scottish Homes

Thistle House, 91 Haymarket Terrace,
Edinburgh EH12 5HE

Tel: 0131-313 0044

Contact: Ian Williamson, 0131-479 5333

Government grant-in-aid:	**£267 million (1998/99)**
	£268 million (1997/98)

Scottish Homes aims to help provide good quality housing and enhance the social and economic quality of life in Scotland through community development. Its funding focuses on partnerships; using public sector resource as leverage for private and other public funding; improving housing quality, decreasing social exclusion through housing for a range of needs; and empowering communities through resident involvement. It provides the following grants relevant to the voluntary sector:

Housing Association Grant (HAG)

Grant total:	**£165.7 million (1998/99)**
	£173.8 million (1997/98)

HAGs are capital grants that support registered housing associations and co-operatives to provide good quality housing for rent and ownership. It represents 80% of Scottish Homes' Development Funding programme. Four key areas are supported by HAG funding: urban regeneration; rural policy; supporting care in the community;

and alleviating homelessness. A total of 175 Housing Associations received grants in 1997/98 ranging between £5 million and £10 million. Projects covered included new build schemes, community ownership projects, adapting of houses for people with disabilities and sheltered housing.

HAG funding only covers 100% of costs for highly specialised supported accommodation projects. For other projects a substantial proportion of costs are usually met, with the remainder coming from private sources.

A number of other grants are available to Housing Associations:

Seedcorn Grants support the formation of housing associations or cooperatives, primarily where they seek to acquire Scottish Homes' stock. Only small associations with under 250 houses are eligible.

Housing Association Revenue Support Grant covers additional management and maintenance costs incurred by a small organisation because of its size.

Housing Association Revenue Deficit Grant is an emergency grant to cover unforeseeable deficit.

Other grants are available to non-registered housing associations and co-operatives:

Central External Grants support the wider housing field especially through development and training.

HomePoint Grants. The Housing Information and Advice Unit (HomePoint) allocates grants for advisory services. The majority of funds go to support ongoing innovative projects.

Special Needs Allowance Package (SNAP) is a revenue grant that supports the cost of providing extra housing management staff time needed for people with special needs.

Special Needs Capital Grant encourages more commercial and voluntary organisations to supply supported accommodation. It contributes to the capital costs of building or renovation, and must provide a planned care or support package to enable people to remain in the community. Projects will be funded up to a maximum 40% of total capital costs.

Applications: Guidance notes and advice are available. Applications can be made throughout the year, except for the HomePoint grant where there is a November deadline.

Scottish Homes commissions research, summaries of which can be found in its *Precis* paper. Its publications list gives details of a variety of free and priced papers and books.

EDUCATION AND INDUSTRY DEPARTMENT

Victoria Quay
Edinburgh EH6 6QQ
Tel: 0131-244 7108

The department's responsibilities include the administration of public education, science and technology, youth and community services, the arts, libraries, museums, galleries, Gaelic Broadcasting, and sports. It sponsors Scottish Enterprise, Highlands and Islands Enterprise and the Scottish Tourist Board.

Childcare Strategy

The Strategy will take a similar form to that in England (see separate entry). No details of funding arrangements were available in autumn 1998. However, voluntary organisations were advised that no direct funding was available and funds would be channelled through local authorities and the Enterprise Networks.

Contact: Peter Willaman, Childcare Division, Mailpoint 33,
Tel: 0131-244 0977

Cultural Organisations Grants

Grant total:	
	£811,800 (1998/99)
	£977,000 (1997/98)
	£722,000 (1996/97)

Core grants are made to Scotland-wide organisations which promote the development or understanding of cultural or scientific topics. Some of these activities must be broadly educational. Priority is given to organisations that are not eligible for funding from other public sources. Grants are split between Gaelic and other cultural organisations.

In 1998/99 five grants totalling £543,800 were given to Gaelic organisations ranging from £20,000 to £253,800 and included:

Comann na Gaidhlig, Gaelic development body (£253,800);
Comhairlie nan Sgoiltean Araich (The Gaelic Playgrounds) (£116,200);
National Gaelic Arts Project (£68,730).

Seven grants to cultural organisations totalled £268,020 ranging from £4,000 to £70,000 and included:

Scottish Youth Theatre (£70,000);
National Youth Orchestra for Scotland (£60,000);
Dictionary of Older Scottish Tongues (£30,000).

Applications: Application forms and guidance notes are available from the above contact. The deadline in 1998 was September 30th.

Contact: Area 1A, Grant enquiries: 0131-244 4160

Powers: Section 23 National Heritage (Scotland) Act 1985

The funding of the arts organisations under this scheme may be transferred to the Scottish Arts Council.

Community Education Grants

Grant total:	£1,217,200 (1998/99)

Grants are available to national voluntary organisations for community education. Organisations have to be 'approved associations' in order to be eligible for grants.

There are three categories of grant:
- Headquarters administration costs;
- National Development Projects, prioritising projects combating substance misuse, initiatives tackling adult literacy and numeracy and new initiatives in youth work;
- Training of staff and national voluntary officers.

Grants were allocated as follows in 1998/99.

	Grants	Amount	% of total grant
Headquarters	40	£970,050	80%
National development	6	£225,800	19%
Training	16	£21,350	1%

Examples of grants:

Workers Education Association (£215,000, Headquarters grant);

Scottish Dyslexia Association (£27,000, Headquarters grant);

YMCA (£3,850, Training grant).

Applications: Applicants should contact the department as early as possible in the year prior to which funding is required. Deadlines for applications are advertised each year.

Contact: Denise Swanson, Area 2A, Tel: 0131-244 0996

Powers: Further Education (Approved Associations) (Scotland) Grant Regulations 1989

Special Schools Grants

Grant total:	£7.76 million (1998/99)
	£6.44 million (1997/98)

Recurrent grants are paid to seven special schools which provide particular elements of special educational provision. The aim of the grant is to cover any deficit in the school's running costs. Non-recurrent grants are also made towards the cost of approved capital expenditure by schools. The maximum grant is normally 60% of the approved cost of the project.

Grants made in 1997/98 included:

Royal Blind School (£1,364,500) (core);

Donaldson's School for the Deaf (£26,300) (capital).

Contact: Dorothy Kemp, Area 2A, Tel: 0131-244 5144

Powers: Special Schools (Scotland) Grant Regulations 1990

Scottish Community Education Council

Grant-in-aid:	£600,000 (1998/99)
	£600,000 (1997/98)

The Scottish Community Education Council is a non-departmental public body Funded by the Education & Industry Department which promotes and develops community education. It does *not* provide grant aid but gives information, advice, training and development support.

Scottish Arts Council

12 Manor Place, Edinburgh EH3 7DD

Tel: 0131-240 2443/4; Fax: 0131-225 9833

Contact: Brian Mclaren, Tel: 0131-226 6051

Grant-in-aid:	**£27,097,000 (1997/98)**

The Scottish Arts Council is one of the principal channels of public funding for the arts in Scotland. It is responsible to and financed by the Scottish Office. Current priorities are education; the indigenous arts of Scotland; the encouragement of international collaborations; artistic innovation; greater access to the arts; and improved marketing.

Major arts organisations are funded on an ongoing revenue basis and their work is assessed each year. About 70% of the council's budget is dispersed in continuing revenue funding and three year funding to major national organisations, including performing arts companies, arts centres and festivals. Three year funding is also given to a number of other key activities. These totalled £18,022,400 in 1997/98.

In addition, project funding is available to individual artists and arts organisations.

Applications: Guidelines with full details are available from the relevant department or from the Help Desk: 0131-240 2443/4. Most schemes have precise closing dates.

Scottish Museums Council

County House, 20-22 Torphichen Street, Edinburgh ED3 8JB

Tel: 0131-229 7465; Fax: 0131-229 2728

Contact: Fiona Wilson

Grant total:	**£228,600 (budgeted 1998/99)**
	£265,000 (1997/98)
	£289,000 (1996/97)

The Scottish Museums Council is an independent body with charitable status funded principally by the Scottish Office Education Department. The council's main aim is to improve the quality of local museum provision in Scotland.

Membership is open to local authorities, independent museums and galleries, historic houses – in fact to any museum, gallery or similar body in Scotland.

The council represents the interests of local museums in Scotland, and all members can benefit from the council's advisory, training and information services. Members eligible for grant-aid have access to a wide range of financial assistance schemes (revenue funding is not provided). To qualify for financial assistance, a museum's constitution or trust deed must be approved by the Scottish Museums Council. There are further detailed provisions about what is expected from trustees and staff.

Exclusions: Revenue funding; purchase of objects for collections; work funded through insurance claims.

Applications: Obtain full details about the grant schemes available. Grant applications should be discussed with council staff at an early stage. Further details on criteria for grant-making under each of the headings listed above is available from the Finance Manager. (NB Minimum application value – £200 from any member with an annual budget over £20,000.)

Sportsmatch

**The Scottish Sports Council, Caledonia House,
South Gyle, Edinburgh EH12 9DQ**

Tel: 0131-317 7200; Fax: 0131-317 7202

Contact: Rob Claridge

Grant total:	**£350,000 (1996/97) in 126 projects**

See Sportsmatch England for details of scheme. The Scottish Sports Council is also a Lottery Distributor.

Local Enterprise Companies (LECs)

LECs are funded by the Education and Industry Department of the Scottish Office.

Highlands and Islands Enterprise Network

Bridge House, 27 Bank Street, Inverness IV1 1QR
Tel: 01463-234171; Fax: 01463-244351

This is the enterprise network with a broad economic, social, training and environmental remit for the *north* of Scotland. Highlands and Islands Enterprise (HIE) at its centre helps oversee and resource as necessary the ten Local Enterprise Companies (LECs) each of which has a board of directors drawn from local businesses and the local community. HIE's central office helps with technical and financial back-up for projects which cross LEC boundaries, are of strategic benefit to the region as a whole, or are beyond a particular LEC's individual resources.

Priority is given in distributing funds to remote areas with long-term problems of population decline, lack of employment opportunities, and poor infrastructure, and areas with low employment prospects.

Network members: Contact headquarters for the addresses of the 10 LECs in the north of Scotland.

Scottish Enterprise National

120 Bothwell Street, Glasgow G2 7JP
Tel: 0141-248 2700; Fax: 0141-221 3217

The Scottish Enterprise network is made up of 13 local enterprise companies (LECs) with their respective subsidiaries, in the *southern* half of Scotland. It delivers a range of business development and training services, along with environmental and regeneration programmes. Its work centres on commercial schemes. Expenditure is split into the following categories: Enterprise; Environment; Youth Training; Adult Training.

A range of grants, business loans, financial/marketing/skills advice is available for businesses and small or new firms. Each LEC operates its own schemes and these need to be contacted for particular details.

Financial assistance may be given in a number of ways: grant, participating grant, loan, equity. Projects are more likely to be successful in obtaining support the smaller the percentage of public funding required, and a loan or some other form of pay back, rather than a direct grant, can be made. Awards have ranged from £6,000 to £1 million.

Network members: Contact headquarters for the addresses of the 13 LECs in southern Scotland.

DEPARTMENT OF HEALTH

St Andrew's House
Edinburgh EH1 3DG
Tel: 0131-556 8400

The department is responsible for public health policy and management of the National Health Service in Scotland.

Health Grants

Grant total:	£1,219,100 (1998/99)
	£1,031,769 (1997/98)

Grants are made to assist national voluntary organisations whose aims are complementary to those that the health services are required by statute to provide. In 1998/99 the following areas were covered:

- addictions (including alcohol, drugs and smoking);
- child health;
- the elderly;
- general illness (including cancer and HIV/AIDS);
- physical disability and mental health.

Support usually takes the form of help with administrative costs of running organisation's headquarters. Specific projects are funded in exceptional cases. The Health Education Board for Scotland may give grants at both the national and local level and is required to liaise closely with the department and the Health Boards to ensure that there is no duplication of effort. Scottish Health Boards may give grants at the local level.

A total of 52 grants were made in 1998/99 ranging from £600 to £155,000 and including:

The Scottish Council on Alcohol (£155,000);

Scottish Development Centre for Mental Health (£98,400);
Disability (£32,400);
National Aids Trust (£22,000);
Age Concern (£15,000);
National Childbirth Trust (£5,000).

Applications: By 1st October for a grant in the next financial year.

Contact: Kathleen Glancy, Tel: 0131-244 2502

Powers: National Health Service (Scotland) Act 1978 Section 16B, as amended

Drugs Challenge Fund

Scotland Against Drugs,
40 Anderston Quay, Glasgow G3 8BX

> **Grant total: £500,000 each year for 1998/01 from the Scottish Office**

The Scottish Drugs Challenge Fund was set up in 1996 and relaunched in 1998. It is managed by the Scotland Against Drugs Campaign Team and funded by the Scottish Office. It tackles the problems of drug misuse in Scotland through partnerships between the public, private and voluntary sectors. Local drugs related organisations should produce bids demonstrating support of at least one third of the project costs from the private sector.

Partnerships should address the following areas in relation to drug misuse:
- changing attitudes;
- modifying behaviour;
- diverting young people away from drugs to healthier activities;
- reducing health risks;
- increasing local community safety;
- local enforcement activities;
- increase community involvement.

Applications: The deadline for the first round applications in 1998 was the end of September for bids of up to three years. The deadline for the second round of applications is June 1999 with a further deadline anticipated in June 2000.

Contacts: Louise Hannigan, Scotland Against Drugs, Tel: 0141-204 3380; George Hall, Scottish Business in the Community, Tel: 0131-220 3001.

Health Education Board for Scotland

Woodburn House, Canaan Lane, Edinburgh EH10 4SG

Grant total:	£264,000 (1998/99)
	£260,000 (1997/98)
	£337,376 (1996/97)

The Health Education Board for Scotland (HEBS) promotes improved health, mainly through the provision of information and training. Its priority health topics are set out in its *Strategic Plan 1997 to 2002* as: coronary heart disease; cancer; stroke; HIV/AIDS/sexual health; dental/oral health; accidents/safety; mental health. It also identifies priority behaviours to change: smoking; healthy eating; physical activity; alcohol misuse; drug misuse. These are translated into programmes centred in six social areas: general public; community; health service; schools; voluntary sector; workplace; special projects.

The voluntary sector programme aims to:
- encourage alliances at all levels;
- identify and help meet training needs of both paid staff and volunteers;
- develop a voluntary sector health promotion strategy and policy;
- assist with the production of health promotion resources.

Voluntary organisations should complement the work and priorities of HEBS and specialist promotion services. Grants are available to voluntary organisations based in, and/or active in Scotland, but funding is only available for HEBS commissioned work or pilot projects where a jointly identified need is addressed by HEBS and the voluntary organisations.

Applications: HEBS either commissions work from voluntary organisations or a joint project proposal is developed where there is a mutually identified need.

It is possible that changes may occur in line with the forthcoming White Paper on improving health in Scotland.

Contact: Graham Howie, Programme Manager, Voluntary Sector
Tel: 0131-536 5500

HOME DEPARTMENT

James Craig Walk (J C W)
Edinburgh EH1 3BA

St Andrew's House (S A H)
Edinburgh EH1 3DG

Tel: 0131-556 8400

The department is responsible for social work policy and law and order, including the Scottish Prisons Service Agency.

Social Work Services Group (J C W)

Ethnic Minority Grant

Grant total: £275,000 (1998/99)
                 £225,000 (1997/98)

This grant is open to national and local voluntary organisations working to reduce racial disadvantage and promote racial equality in Scotland. The scheme is designed to provide initial funding for *new* projects, or funding for extension of the scope or area of current work. Projects should be national or cover the boundaries of one local authority area. Priority is given to projects that:

- address an identified need;
- advance other areas of racial equality;
- assist ethnic minorities to gain access to mainstream services;
- have lasting benefits and are likely to attract other funding in the future;
- involve ethnic minorities in developing and carrying out the project;
- involve volunteers.

Grants of up to £25,000 are awarded for a maximum of two years or in exceptional circumstances for three years. A total of 13 grants were made in 1998/99 ranging from £8,000 to £25,000 including:

Community Service Volunteers, Health Advocacy Project (£25,000);

Cancerlink in Scotland, Cancer Support and the Needs of Asian Women in
Scotland (£18,500);
African & Caribbean Resource Centre (£10,000).

Exclusions: Grants are not given to replace existing funding.

Applications: Forms and guidance notes are available. In 1998 applications were
invited in August for the deadline of November 7th.

Contact: Steven Marwick, Tel: 0131-244 5459

Powers: Appropriation Act

Social Welfare – Section 10 Grants

Grant total:	£5.4 million (1998/99)
	£5.9 million (1997/98)

Voluntary organisations that develop social work services and promote social
welfare in Scotland are assisted.

Priority is given to the following areas:
- addictions (including alcohol and drugs) and the social aspects of AIDS;
- children and families, including under fives and out of school childcare;
- community care, in particular for the elderly, mentally or physically handicapped;
- general voluntary action;
- homelessness;
- offender service.

Project and core funding are available for a maximum of three years, although core
funding is renewable. Some capital grants may be provided. Revenue funding is
given to assist national organisations for their headquarters or ongoing activities.
Grants are also made to support innovative ideas of potential national significance
tested by national or local projects.

A total of 96 grants were made in 1998/99 ranging from £3,500 to £850,000
including;
   Local Volunteering Development (£850,000);
   Scottish Council for Voluntary Organisations (Core, Partnership Project and
   Racial Equality Unit) (£336,500);
   Disability Scotland (£243,200);
   SACRO (HQ) (£215,500);
   Marriage Counselling Scotland (£144,800);

Scottish Users Network (£25,000);
Aids Care Education and Training (£17,000).

Support was also given to Victim Support Scotland, see separate entry.

Applications: Forms and guidelines are available. The deadline was 31 October for
funding in the following financial year in 1998.

Contact: Harry Murray, Tel: 0131-244 5464

Powers: Social Work (Scotland) Act 1968, Section 10 (1)

Social Welfare – Training Grants

Grant total:	**£706,450 (1998/99)**
	£842,000 (1997/98)

Training grants are designed to promote competence in key areas of social work
by enabling national voluntary organisations to provide or secure training for their
paid and voluntary workers. Funding is generally for an initial three year period
(subject to annual review) to enable appropriate training arrangements to be set up
which are then expected to be self sustaining in the longer term.

The focus is on community care of older people; people with a mental illness; people
with disabilities; people with a problem arising from alcohol and drug misuse and
HIV/AIDS; children and families with particular reference to child protection and
work with offenders and their victims.

Grants in 1998/99 ranged from £4,800 to £35,000 and included:
   Volunteer Development Scotland (£35,000);
   Children in Scotland (£28,000);
   Scottish Women's Aid (£25,000);
   Scottish Drugs Forum (£20,700);
   Crossroads (£5,000).

Applications: Application forms and an information pack are available from the
above contact. The deadline for a grant in the financial year 1998/99 was in the
preceding September.

Contact: John Williamson, Tel: 0131-244 5472

Powers: Section 9 of the Social Work (Scotland) Act 1968

Victim Support Schemes

> **Grant total:** £1,505,000 (1998/99)
> £1,500,100 (1997/98) (including HQ funding)

Grant aid is provided towards the appointment of co-ordinators or towards running costs to encourage the growth of local schemes affiliated to the Victim Support Scotland (VSS) schemes. A funding panel, independent of the Scottish Office and VSS determines applications for the grant submitted by local victim support schemes. Grants may only be offered to local schemes which meet certain minimum criteria and which are affiliated to VSS. In 1997/98 there were 77 local schemes in operation.

Applications: Forms are available from Liz May, Victim Support Scotland, 14 Frederick Street, Edinburgh, EH2 2HB, Tel: 0131-225 7779/8233; Fax: 0131-225 8456.

Powers: Social Work (Scotland) Act 1968, Section 10

Millennium Volunteers (J C W)

> **Grant total: £1.5 million to be allocated over three years from 1998, an estimated £400,000 in 1998/99**

The details of the scheme parallel those in England, Wales and Northern Ireland (see separate entries). However, the delivery mechanisms are different in each country. The scheme is administered by a consortium of four organisations in Scotland: Community Service Volunteers Scotland; Scottish Community Education Council; Volunteer Development Scotland; Youthlink Scotland.

Unemployed Voluntary Action Fund

Comely Park House, 80 New Road, Dunfermline, Fife KY12 7EJ

Tel: 01383-620780

Contact: Sandra Carter, Administrator

Grant-in-aid:	**£860,000 (budgeted 1999/2000)**
	£867,600 (1998/99) (including
	administrative cost of the trust)

The Unemployed Voluntary Action Fund is a charitable trust that receives grant-in-aid from the Scottish Office as the Scottish element of the national opportunities for volunteering programme. Priority is given to projects delivered and managed by unemployed people themselves and/or, projects designed to benefit those with special needs in the fields of health, social welfare, community education and development.

Main grants programme
Grant total: £830,000 (1999/2000) including administrative costs

The maximum amount available over a three year period is £31,000 per annum for new schemes. A total of £270,000 was available for new projects in 1999/2000, in addition to second and third year funding of already approved schemes. Grants are made for staff salaries, volunteer expenses and office and training running costs.

A total of 37 grants were made in 1998/99 including new grants to:
  Penumbra – Borders Youth Project (£26,215);
  Deafblind UK – Health Awareness Project, Glasgow (£23,917);
  Dumfries & Galloway Rape Crisis Centre (£22,093);
  Arbroath CAFE Project (£20,799).

Small grants scheme
Grant total: £30,000 (1999/2000)

This grant is available for new organisations piloting projects initially without paid staff. The maximum grant available for a period of up to one year is £5,000.

A total of 14 grants were made in 1997/98 including:
  Smith's Place Group, Edinburgh (£3,500);

Homeaid Caithness (£3,060);
WAVE Radio – Dr Gray's Hospital, Elgin (£1,165).

Exclusions: The main grants programme is not available for established schemes. The small grants scheme is not available for salaries and is a non renewable starter grant. Neither of the schemes can be used to 'top-up' other public funds.

Applications: Guidelines and application forms are available from the above address. Roadshow advice days and a telephone helpline assist promote the applications for general grants for which the deadline is the end of June. Small grants scheme applications are considered throughout the year.

Powers: Appropriation Act

THE WELSH OFFICE

The Welsh Office is the UK government department with responsibility for Wales. All of the Welsh Office Groups and Departments are centrally located at:

> **Crown Buildings, Cathays Park, Cardiff CF1 3NQ**
>
> **Tel: 01222-825111**
> **Fax: enquiries through switchboard**
>
> **Web site: www.cymru.gov.uk**

The Welsh Office is organised into 11 Groups/Departments. This variation in terminology seems idiosyncratic. There are groups *within* departments but, as can be seen below, groups and departments can also hold similar authority. The difference seems to be that departments more closely reflect the responsibilities of parallel departments in England. The groups and departments highlighted below are those where funding of the voluntary sector is covered in this guide.

Economic Development Group

Regional, urban and rural development and regeneration.

Education Department

Culture and the arts, nursery, primary, secondary, further and higher education.

Local Government Group

Responsible for local government, housing and social services.

Transport, Planning & Environment Group

Responsible for transport and the environment.

Other Groups/Departments

Where no funding of the voluntary sector has been identified for this guide:

- Agriculture Department;
- Establishment Group;
- Finance Group;
- Health Department;
- Health Professionals Group;
- Industry and Training Department;
- Legal Group.

Funding of the voluntary sector

The total funding in 1998/99 to voluntary organisations from the Welsh Office is shown in the pie-chart. It splits the total into three sectors, Housing for Wales, the Arts Council of Wales and 'All other grants' ie. programmes open only to the voluntary sector.

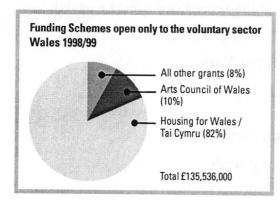

Funding Schemes open only to the voluntary sector Wales 1998/99

All other grants (8%)
Arts Council of Wales (10%)
Housing for Wales / Tai Cymru (82%)

Total £135,536,000

The following graph breaks down the section 'All other grants' in the pie-chart. It shows the different contributing departments and the relative proportions of funding they made available via programmes aimed exclusively at voluntary organisations in 1998/99.

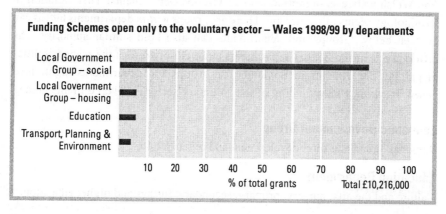

Funding Schemes open only to the voluntary sector – Wales 1998/99 by departments

Local Government Group – social
Local Government Group – housing
Education
Transport, Planning & Environment

10   20   30   40   50   60   70   80   90   100
% of total grants   Total £10,216,000

Notes

The Local Government Group funds housing, social services, which includes health and welfare, and the infrastructure of the voluntary sector.

The Education Department funds youth organisations.

The Transport, Planning and the Environment Group funds of Environment Wales.

Detailed Breakdown of 'All other grants"
Grant Schemes for Voluntary Organisations

£'000

Local Government Group
Housing
Prevention and Alleviation of Homelessness 650
650

Social
Support for Child and Family Services 1,983
Local Voluntary Services Scheme 1,637
Local Mental Health Grants Scheme 1,550
Older People, Disabled People and Carers 1,128
Support for Voluntary Intermediary Services 615
Mental Illness Strategy 549
Volunteering in Wales Fund 530
Mental Handicap Strategy 370
Combating Drugs and Alcohol Misuse 237
8,599

Education Department
National Voluntary Youth Organisations 361
361

Transport, Planning and Environment Group
Environment Wales 406
406

Health Department
Health Promotion Wales 200
200
TOTAL 10,216

The Future

The National Assembly for Wales will take over most of the responsibilities and functions of the Secretary of State for Wales in May 1999. The Welsh Office (probably renamed) will serve the National Assembly for Wales. The White Paper on the National Assembly for Wales, *A Voice for Wales,* sets out the powers and structures with scope for further transfers of power in future years. Under the Assembly Wales will remain an integral part of the United Kingdom, sharing a common legal system with England. Parliament will continue to pass new primary legislation for Wales as well as retaining responsibility for subjects which are handled on a common basis throughout the United Kingdom – including *taxation, defence, foreign affairs, social security* and *broadcasting.* Changes to the Assembly's budget will be determined in the same way as the present Welsh Office's budget, by a formula linked to Wales' population.

There will be a separate Housing Department from the end of 1998 with responsibility taken over from the Local Government Group. Housing for Wales / Tai Cymru will be incorporated as part of this department. Changes are also anticipated in the organisation of Health in Wales, as part of this Health Promotion Wales will be incorporated into the Welsh Assembly.

Contents

ECONOMIC DEVELOPMENT GROUP

The Economic Development Group is made up of three divisions:

- European Affairs Division;
- Regional Development Division, which sponsors the Wales Tourist Board and the Welsh Development Agency;
- Urban & Rural Development Division, responsible for urban policy and for co-ordination of rural policy. It operates the Strategic Development Scheme and the Welsh Capital Challenge.

Urban and Rural Development Division

The Strategic Development Scheme (SDS)

Grant total:	£38 million annually

The Strategic Development Scheme supports projects and local strategies which promote economic, environmental and social development and which benefit areas of social need.

In 1998/99, about £27 million of SDS resources were delegated to the unitary authorities. The local authorities are solely responsible for determining successful new bids, provided they meet SDS criteria set by Ministers. Within these criteria individual authorities set their own priorities.

Local authorities are required to allocate a minimum of 20% of their SDS funding to voluntary sector projects. In 1998/99, funding included £604,000 to the Groundwork Trusts for project work and a contribution towards their core costs through existing SDS funding commitments. They are also able to put forward bids to the relevant local authorities for delegated SDS resources for project funding.

Exclusions: Party political and purely religious activities are *not* eligible, although religious institutions may initiate and participate in projects that contribute to the aims of the scheme.

Applications: Bids should be submitted to the relevant local authority. Further advice and guidance can be obtained from the Economic Development or Planning Department of your local unitary authority.

Leaflets are also available published by the Wales Council for Voluntary Action, Llys Ifor, Crescent Road, Caerphilly CF83 IXL (01222-855 100).

Powers: Housing Grants, Construction and Regional Regeneration Act 1996

Welsh Capital Challenge

The Capital Challenge aims to support an integrated approach to capital expenditure which benefits disadvantaged urban and rural areas of Wales. Whilst the scheme only supports capital projects, exceptional bids to support short term revenue costs associated with them will be considered.

Local authorities were invited to submit a maximum of one bid in 1998/99. This could have been a single scheme or a tightly focused regeneration strategy comprising a small number of projects. All kinds of projects were eligible as long as their primary aim was to promote regeneration or development and it benefited disadvantaged areas. Bids that had an economic focus and created employment opportunities were favoured. There was no minimum amount devoted to the voluntary sector.

The criteria for the 1999/2000 bidding were expected to be circulated in August and with a deadline in October.

Applications: Voluntary organisations should submit bids to their relevant unitary authority in response to the annual Welsh Office circular. Further advice and guidance can be obtained from the Economic Development or Planning Department at the relevant unitary authority or from the Welsh Office.

Contact: Mrs J Maxwell, Tel: 01222-823136; Fax: 01222-823797

Powers: Housing Grants, Construction and Regional Regeneration Act 1996

Welsh Development Agency

Pearl House, Greyfriars Road, Cardiff CF1 3XX

Contact: Tom Bourne, Environment Director

The Welsh Development Agency (WDA) is the NDPB charged with promoting the economic development of Wales, and enhancing its environment. It does this primarily by attracting new inward investment, and helping indigenous companies to grow.

Grants are given to the public and private sectors for the reclamation of derelict land, urban renewal and environmental improvement. It concentrates on large strategic schemes, but also works in partnership with the Prince's Trust-Bro to grant aid community-based projects which can demonstrate the delivery of sustainable development objectives in selected target areas.

The WDA was about to merge with the Development Board for Rural Wales and the Land Authority for Wales at the time of going to press, to form an enlarged agency covering the whole of Wales.

Applications: Advice and information on the current state of affairs are available from the divisional offices listed below, also contactable via the central switchboard Tel. 0345-775577.

North Wales
Unit 7, St Asaph Business Park, Glascoed Road, St Asaph, Denbighshire LL17 0L3

Mid Wales
Ladywell House, Newtown, Powys

South West Wales
Llys-y-Ddraig, Penllergaer Business Park, Penllergaer, Swansea SA4 1HL

South East Wales
QED Centre, Treforest Estate, Pontypridd CF37 5YR

Wales Tourist Board

Brunel House, 2 Fitzalan Road, Cardiff CF2 1UY

Tel: 01222-475268; Fax: 01222-485031

The Wales Tourist Board makes grants towards tourist development projects. Its priorities for support have been:

- upgrading of existing serviced accommodation;
- development of new accommodation only where it will create additional demand or where a shortage of capacity is identified;
- improved landscaping and the provision of central facilities at holiday parks and groups of self-catering units;
- the improvement of existing visitor attractions and the development of new attractions;
- improvements in the interpretation of our natural and built heritage;
- improvements in the signposting of tourism facilities;
- schemes which help pioneer new methods of managing visitor numbers to help conserve the environment;
- provision for disabled visitors.

Applications: Applicants are advised to contact the Tourist Board for further information and to discuss proposals with Tourist Board staff. Eligible applicants will be sent an application form after completing an Introductory Questionnaire.

EDUCATION DEPARTMENT

The Education Department is made up of the following divisions:

Culture & Recreation Division

Responsibilities: the arts; sport and recreation; museums and libraries; Welsh language matters. Additionally it liaises with the Department for Culture, Media and Sport on broadcasting issues. It provides sponsorship for the following organisations; Arts Council of Wales; Sports Council for Wales; Welsh Language Board; Welsh Books Council.

Further & Higher Education Division

Responsible for further and higher education, adult and lifelong learning as well as youth issues. It sponsors the Further and Higher Education Councils for Wales as well as providing grant aid to the Wales Youth Agency and the Basic Skills Agency.

Schools Administration Division

Responsible for the administration of nursery, primary and secondary schools, including provision for the under fives.

Schools Performance Division

Responsible for educational standards.

Further & Higher Education Division

National Voluntary Youth Organisations

Grant total:	£361,000 (1998/99)

Grants are made to assist national voluntary youth organisations working in Wales to increase the extent and quality of programmes of informal and social education for young people, in the age range 11 to 25 years, with particular emphasis on 13 to

19 year olds. Financial assistance is given towards central costs and projects undertaken by a single organisation or a combination of organisations and agencies with a distinct Welsh dimension. Any *national* voluntary youth organisation which shows that it provides good youth work (as defined by the Youth Work Curriculum Statement for Wales) is eligible to apply. The scheme is administered by the Wales Youth Agency on behalf of the Welsh Office.

Grants do not normally exceed 50% of an organisation's total income and are available for up to three years.

A total of 15 grants were made in 1998/99 ranging between £7,000 and £45,000 including:
  National Council of YMCAs of Wales (£45,000);
  Wales Young Farmers' Clubs (£30,000);
  United Nations Association (Wales) International Youth Service (£25,000);
  Boys Brigade (£11,000).

Applications: Detailed guidance and application forms are available from July onwards from Wayne Warner, Wales Youth Agency, Leslie Court, Lon Y Llyn, Caerphilly CF83 1BQ Tel: 01222-880088; Fax: 01222-880824;
E-mail: wya@msn.com. The deadline for applications is 1 October.

Contact: Russell Dobbins, Tel: 01222-825854

Powers: Sections 11 and 12 of the Education (Grant) Regulations 1990

Out of School Childcare Grant

Grant total:	£900,000 (1998/99)
	£300,000 (1997/98)
	£300,000 (1996/97)

Out of School Childcare or Kid's Clubs cater for 4 to 12 year olds offering play and care outside school hours to enable parents to work or study. The majority of clubs are run by voluntary organisations. Start up grants are available from Training and Enterprise Councils for up to 12 months or up to 30 months in an agreed 'area of deprivation'.

Applications: Applications should be made through Training and Enterprise Councils.

Training and Enterprise Councils:
Trish Hopkins, Gwent TEC, Tel: 01633-678200
Jane Taylor, Mid Glamorgan TEC, Tel: 01443-841594
Mary Allanson, North Wales TEC, Tel: 01978-295519

Sue Wood, Powys TEC, Tel: 01686-622494
Lindsay Evans, South Glamorgan TEC, Tel: 01222-261000
Liz Cole, West Wales TEC, Tel: 01792-460355

Contact: Jane Hutt, Chwarae Teg / Fairpla, Tel: 01222-381331

Powers: 1973 Employment and Training Act: section 2.1

Under Fives Initiative

Grant total:	**£232,000 (1998/99)**
	£160,000 (1997/98)
	£150,000 (1996/97)

The Under Fives Initiative has run demonstration projects from 1995. The initiative is sponsored by the Welsh Office but managed by Chwarae Teg / Fairplay. Start up grants are available up to a maximum of £30,000 for day nurseries or childminding networks for children from six weeks old to school age. They are run by voluntary, private or public groups in conjunction with employers. Eligible costs: equipment costs; conversion of premises; initial running costs; marketing; staff training.

A total of nine grants were made in 1997/98 ranging between £11,250 and £30,000 including:

Holywell (£30,000);
First Steps (£29,000);
Gwynedd Community Health (£20,000).

Applications: Apply to Chwarae Teg.

Contact: Jenny Francis, Chwarae Teg, Companies House, Maindy, Cardiff
Tel: 01222-381331

Powers: 1973 Employment and Training Act: Section 2.1

The future of both of these schemes was under review pending the results of the Childcare Strategy Consultation in autumn 1998.

Arts Council of Wales

Museum Place, Cardiff CF1 3NX

Tel: 01222-376500; Fax: 01222-221447

Government grant-in-aid:	**£14,339,000 (1998/99)**
	£14,249,000 (1997/98)

The Arts Council of Wales is the national organisation with specific responsibility for the funding and development of the arts in Wales. Most of its funds come from the Welsh Office but it also receives funds from local authorities, the Crafts Council and other sources.

The council provides regular annual and revenue grants to arts organisations which account for the most of its spending, 78% of its grant total in 1998/99. It also operates a number of schemes which provide grants and other forms of financial support on a one-off basis.

A few schemes are open throughout the year as long as funds last but the majority have closing dates, sometimes only a single one, each year. Potential applicants can obtain this information from *A Guide to Grants from the Arts Council of Wales* produced by the Arts Council for Wales. Contact the relevant department for further details.

In addition it is the distributor of National Lottery arts funds in Wales.

Regional Offices:
North Wales Office
36 Prince's Drive, Colwyn Bay LL29 8LA
Tel: 01492-533440; Fax: 01492-533677
West and Mid Wales Office
6 Gardd Llydaw, Jackson Lane, Carmarthen SA31 1QL
Tel: 01267-234248; Fax: 01267-233084

Welsh Language Board

Market Chambers, 5-7 St Mary Street, Cardiff CF1 2AT

Tel: 01222-224744; Fax: 01222-224577

Government grant-in-aid:	**£5,800,000 (1998/99)**
	£5,800,000 (1997/98)
	£2,000,000 (1996/97)

The board was established under the Welsh Language Act and is funded by the Welsh Office. It aims to increase and facilitate the use of Welsh and makes the following grants to voluntary organisations.

Main Grants Programme

Grant total:	**£2,272,000 (budgeted 1998/99)**
	£2,255,000 (1997/98)
	£651,000 (1996/97)

Grants support existing Mentrau Iaith (language agencies) and other voluntary or private sector organisations that respond to the challenges and objectives set out in the 1996 *A Strategy for the Welsh Language*. The four main challenges are:

- to increase the number of Welsh speakers;
- to provide opportunities to use Welsh;
- to challenge habits of language use;
- to strengthen Welsh as a community language.

The following activities are supported: the production of Welsh language resources; relevant research; information on opportunities to use Welsh; the use of Welsh with Information Technology. Priority is given to national projects.

Core grants contribute towards an organisation's administrative costs and are made only if the promotion and facilitation of the use of Welsh is a central part of an organisation's constitution.

Project grants are made for activities which increase the use of Welsh. Applications can be made for more than one project at a time and should include administration and management costs.

The board contributes no more than 75% of an activity's cost. A total of 48 grants were made in 1998/99 ranging between £2,000 and £607,000 including:

Welsh Books Council (£607,000);

National Eisteddfod of Wales (£347,800);

Mentrau Iaith Myrddin (£80,000);

Welsh for Adults Consortia (£50,000);

Wales Council for Voluntary Action (£40,000);

Wales Pre-School Playgroups Association (£15,000).

Exclusions: The main grants programme does not cover: the production of bilingual material (funded by the *Small Grants Scheme*); staff costs for providing bilingual services; provision of educational materials; attending Welsh for Adults Courses.

Applications: Full guidelines and application forms are available. Applications were invited from the beginning of August with a closing date of 31 October in 1998.

Contact: Huw Onllwyn Jones, Head of Grants Department,
E-mail: huw.jones@bwrdd_yr_iaith.org.uk

Small Grants Scheme

Grant total:	£20,000 (1998/99)
	£20,600 (1997/98)

Grants of up to 50% of the total cost, (to a maximum £500), are made towards the cost of translating, designing and publishing bilingual materials. Priority is given to voluntary or private organisations just beginning to use Welsh and those with extensive public contact. A total of 80 grants were made in 1997/98.

Applications: Full guidelines and application forms are available. Applications are considered at regular intervals.

Contact: Dr Gwenan Llwyd Evans

Powers: Section 3 of the Welsh Language Act 1993

Council of Museums in Wales

The Courtyard, Letty Street, Cathays, Cardiff CF2 4EL

Tel: 01222-225432/228238; Fax: 01222-668516

Contact: Jackie Day

The Council of Museums in Wales is a membership body composed of local authorities and non-nationally funded museums registered with the Museums and Galleries Commission within the Principality. The membership ranges from small museums run by societies through to large municipal institutions and also includes regimental, university and country house museums.

It is established as a charitable, limited company mainly funded by Welsh Office grant-in-aid and based in Cardiff with a second office in North Wales. It fosters the preservation of the Welsh heritage through support of local museums as both a provider and enabler. In the former role it offers professional, management, curatorial, conservation and training advice; training packages; and display services including travelling exhibitions. It also represents its members at local and national level. As an enabler the council administers governmental, subscription and earned income as grant aid for project and challenge-funding to eligible museums (MGC registered).

Applications: The bulk of grant applications are processed together in February/ March for availability early in the incoming financial year, though depending on resources awards continue to be made throughout the period. Projects should be discussed with council officers well in advance of submission.

Sportsmatch

The Sports Council for Wales, Sophia Gardens, Cardiff CF1 9SW

Tel: 01222-300500; Fax: 01222-300600

Grant total:	£270,000 (1998/99)
	£270,000 (1997/98)

Sportsmatch is a Welsh Office initiative administered by the Sports Council for Wales. It is an incentive scheme to encourage commercial sponsorship in grassroots sport by matching successful applications £1 for £1. Awards range from £500 to £15,000. Any not-for-profit distributing sports organisation operating mainly in Wales may apply, including sports clubs and voluntary youth organisations.

To be eligible for support an activity should: be in the government approved list of eligible activities (for safety reasons some sports have to be affiliated to the recognised governing body of sport); benefit grass-roots sport; consist of a revenue project or an essential capital equipment project.

Exclusions: Capital projects; professional sport; international or major national events; tobacco sponsorship; alcohol sponsorship if the majority of participants are under 18 years of age; conferences; corporate hospitality; individual sportsmen and women.

Applications: Guidance notes and application forms are available. Each application must consist of one sponsor to the minimum of £500. The panel meets six times a year.

Contact: Victoria Ward, Sportsmatch Scheme Manager
Helen Gilbert, Sportsmatch Scheme Administrator

Health Promotion Wales

Ffynnon-Las, Ty Glas Avenue, Llanishen, Cardiff CF4 5DZ

Tel: 01222-752222; Fax: 01222-756000
Web site: http://www.hpw.org.uk

Grant total:	**£200,000 (1998/99)**
	£201,000 (1997/98)

Health Promotion Wales (HPW), a former non-departmental public body, is to be incorporated into the Welsh Assembly from April 1999. Its address will remain the same for the foreseeable future, as will its grant scheme that was established to run for three years from 1998.

The grant scheme supports *national* voluntary organisations which contribute to general health promotion and complement the work of health authorities and HPW. Priority is given to projects that address:
- inequalities in health;
- health in deprived areas of Wales;
- health of hard to reach groups;
- rural and urban deprivation.

Funding is given for a maximum of three years. Funding takes the form of core, project and 'other' grants. In 1997/98:

Core grants totalling £73,000 to four organisations included:
Ash in Wales (£40,000);
Family Planning Association (£20,000);

Project grants totalling £109,000 to four organisations included:
St John's Breath of Life (£38,000);
West Glamorgan County Voluntary Service (£32,000);

'Other grants' totalling £17,900 in seven grants included:
Europe Against Cancer (£6,000);
British Fluoridation Society (£2,000).

Exclusions: Mainstream research. Local projects are only funded in exceptional circumstances.

Applications: Detailed notes for guidance and application forms are available from Heath Promotion Wales. The deadline for applications in 1998 was 30 September.

Contact: Sue Wood, Project Officer, Tel: 01222 -681270

Powers: Section 64 of the Health Services and Public Health Act 1968

LOCAL GOVERNMENT GROUP

The Local Government Group is made up of the following divisions:

Housing Division

Responsible for allocation of resources to local authorities and housing associations, refurbishment and special needs housing as well as sponsorship of Housing for Wales / Tai Cymru.

Local Government Policy and Finance Division

Social Services Inspectorate Wales

Social Services Policy Division

Responsible for the funding and promotion of voluntary sector activity and volunteering. It covers policy for vulnerable people including children and those with mental health problems.

Housing Division

Home Improvement Agencies (Care & Repair Ltd)

Grant total:	£976,000 (1998/99)
	£976,000 (1997/98)

Revenue funding supports home improvement/care & repair agencies which help elderly and disabled people to claim home improvement and disabled facilities grants from local authorities. The focus is on improving housing stock, maintaining the health of residents, care in the community and aiding older and disabled people to stay in their homes and live independently. This is achieved through advice, financial assistance, administrative help, technical assistance, monitoring and support for repair and adaptation of properties. Schemes are funded at 50% of their running costs for the first year and 35% in following years. Care and Repair Cymru is the national coordinating body for individual home improvement agencies.

A total of 25 grants were made in 1998/99 ranging from £14,220 to £187,170 and including:
Care and Repair Cymru (£187,170);
Cardiff Staying Put (£60,790);
Merthyr (£28,670);
Ynys Mon (£23,980).

Applications: Forms are issued to the coordinating body, Care and Repair Cymru, and should be returned to the Welsh Office by 31st October.

Care and Repair Cymru, National Office
Norbury House, Norbury Road, Fairwater, Cardiff CF5 3AS
Tel: 01222-576286; Fax: 01222-576283

Care and Repair Cymru, North Wales Office
1 Lon Pobty, Bangor, Gwynedd LL57 1HR
Tel: 01248-371528; Fax: 01248-371528

Contact: Carole Stevenson, Executive Officer, Housing Division
Tel: 01222-825111

Powers: Section 169 (6) of the Local Government and Housing Act 1989

Prevention & Alleviation of Homelessness

Performance & Resources Unit, Branch B Housing Division

Grant total:	**£650,000 (1998/99)**
	£650,000 (1997/98)
	£600,000 (1996/97)

Revenue support for voluntary organisations to alleviate homelessness is available to:
- assist homeless or potentially homeless people, particularly those for whom local authorities are not required to secure housing under the 1996 Act;
- provide specialist advice, support and/or accommodation not readily available elsewhere.

Approximately £300,000 in 1998/99 was allocated to support national voluntary homeless organisations. The remainder went to voluntary organisations working on locally-based projects.

Applications: Bids must be submitted through the local authority, who are also required to provide a 25% contribution towards the cost of the project. Local authorities are invited to submit co-ordinated bids in consultation with voluntary sector organisations working in their area.

Contact: Helen Arthur, Tel: 01222-823729
J E Westlake, Tel: 01222-825510

Powers: Section 180, Housing Act 1996

Housing for Wales /
Tai Cymru

25-30 Lambourne Crescent, Llanishen, Cardiff, CF4 5ZJ

Tel: 01222-741500

Housing for Wales / Tai Cymru's role of funding and regulating registered social landlords was taken over by the Welsh Office Housing Division from 1 January 1999. Local authorities will also have an enhanced role in social housing allocation.

Levels of funding were undecided at time of going to press although grant total for Housing for Wales / Tai Cymru at £112.7 million in 1996/97 may provide an indication.

SOCIAL SERVICES

Social Services Policy Division (1)

Older People or People with Physical/Sensory Disabilities and their Carers

> **Grant total:** £1,128,000 (1998/99)
> £1,141,000 (1997/98)

Grants are made to support the activity of voluntary organisations working at the all Wales level in support of people with physical and/or sensory disabilities, older people and their carers. Support is given to providing and promoting the development of services to these groups. Priority is given to:

- organisations which target different groups and whose activities are complementary in supporting the needs of older people, people with different disabilities and their carers;
- organisations that provide flexible, cost effective services, information and support.

Grants are usually awarded on a three year basis. A total of 14 grants were made in 1998/99 ranging between £3,900 and £270,100, including;

Disability Wales (£270,1000);
Age Concern Cymru (£234,800);
Carers National Association (£112,100);
Arts Disability Wales (£40,600).

Applications: Detailed notes for guidance and application forms are available. The deadline for applications in 1998 was November.

Contact: Ms L Edwards, Older People and Carers. Tel: 01222-823423
Jenny McKinlay, Physical or Sensory Disability. Tel: 01222-823357

Powers: Section 64, Health Services and Public Health Act 1968

Section 28B, National Health Service Act 1977

Support for Child & Family Services

Grant total:	**£2.8 million (1998/99)**
	£2.8 million (1997/98)

71% to the voluntary sector in 1998/99

Core and project grants, consistent with family support services and provisions of the Children Act 1989 are made to promote the welfare of children in need and their families.

Core grants are made for a period of three years to national voluntary organisations providing services to children and their families. Additions to the list of core funded bodies are made only in exceptional circumstances. A total of 15 core grants were made in 1998/99 ranging from £5,360 to £182,350 and include:

Children in Wales (£182,350);

Wales Pre School Playgroups Association (£170,000);

British Agencies for Adoption & Fostering (Wales Centre) (£81,780).

Project grants are made for a period of three years at up to 75% of costs. Organisations may then reapply for tapering funding of 50% for two more years. The voluntary sector received about 55% of the grant total in 1998/99. Emphasis is placed on collaboration between local authorities and voluntary organisations and consistency with local children's services plans. In 1998/99 priority was given to the following areas:

- family support services for disabled children;
- services which provide independent representation and advocacy for children looked after by local authorities.

A total of 71 grants, totalling £1,434,800, were made in 1998/99 ranging between £1,350 and £132,300. Those to voluntary organisations included:

NACRO, Community Alternatives to Secure Accommodation Project (£68,000);

Cardigan Women's Aid, Childworker (£15,600);

The Children's Society, Torfaen Advocacy in Child Protection (£11,800);

Powys Victim Support, Child Witness Project (£4,500).

Holiday Playschemes: Limited support is also given to holiday projects for children in need. A total of 13 grants were made totalling £46,200 in 1998/99.

Support for Children Under Eight: County voluntary councils and others operating the Under Eights Small Grants Scheme may apply for a grant. A total of 17 grants were made in 1998/99 totalling £81,590.

Applications: Guidance notes and application forms are available from the contact above. Applications may be made by local social services authorities or voluntary organisations. The deadline in 1998 was 30 January.

Contact: Vivian Martin, Tel: 01222-823676

Powers: Sections 28B (1) and (2) of the National Health Service Act 1977

Social Services Policy Division (2)

Mental Handicap Strategy – National Voluntary Organisations

Grant total:	£370,000 (1998/99)
	£369,000 (1997/98)

Grants are made to national voluntary organisations offering help and support services to individuals with a mental handicap, and their carers, in Wales. Responsibility for the planning and delivery of services for people with learning difficulties under the strategy lies with the relevant local authority which receives the bulk of funding from the Welsh Office. Voluntary organisations also play an active part in meeting and assessing local needs.

Priorities include:
■ encouraging joint statutory and voluntary sector participation;
■ developing a clear voice for the voluntary sector on policy and planning;
■ encouraging the involvement of service users;
■ promoting good practice.

Funding contributes mainly to the core costs of organisations and modest project funds. Six grants were made in 1998/99:
The Standing Conference of Voluntary Organisations for People with a Learning Disability in Wales (SCOVO) (£163,300);
MENCAP (£88,900);
National Autistic Society (£40,400);
People First Wales (£36,000);
Downs Syndrome Association (£20,600);
All Wales Forum of Parents and Carers (£20,200).

Applications: Organisations seeking support should contact the relevant social services department. Exceptionally a voluntary organisation may be funded directly by the Welsh Office, if its proposal could not be appropriately funded by one or more social services departments. Application forms were available in mid September for a completion deadline of 30th November in 1998.

Powers: Section 28B, National Health Service Act 1977 as amended by Section 1, Health Services and Social Security Adjudications Act 1983

Mental Illness Strategy – National Voluntary Organisations

Grant total:	**£549,000 (1998/99)**
	£543,000 (1997/98)

Grants are available to national voluntary organisations which offer help and support services to individuals with mental illness and their carers in Wales. The strategy promotes joint planning between health authorities, social services departments, voluntary agencies, users and carers of local and community-based services that avoid unnecessary reliance on institutional care. Funding contributes mainly to the core costs of organisations and modest project funds.

Eight grants were made in 1998/99:
 MIND Cymru (formerly Wales MIND) (£190,500);
 National Schizophrenia fellowship (NSF) (£164,700);
 Alzheimer's Disease Society (ADS) (£48,100);
 Manic Depression Fellowship (£39,500);
 All Wales User Network (US Network) (£34,200);
 Cruse Bereavement Care (£31,400);
 The Samaritans (£20,500);
 Depression Alliance (£20,200).

Applications: In 1998, application forms were sent to prospective applicants by 15th September with a deadline of 30th November.

Contact: Rowland Jones, Tel: 01222-823628
David Tutton, Tel: 01222-823405

Powers: Section 28B, National Health Service Act 1977, as amended by Section 1 of the Health Services and Social Security Adjudications Act 1983

Social Services Policy Division (3)

Combating Drugs & Alcohol Misuse

Grant total:	**£237,100 (1998/99)**
	£239,900 (1997/98)

Funding is available for projects that provide:
- a range of services to combat drug and alcohol misuse at a national level;
- treatment and rehabilitation in residential facilities.

Grants for local projects such as counselling, drop-in or advice centres catering for drug and alcohol misusers are generally funded by the relevant health authority. But those voluntary organisations which provide services for the whole of Wales or which provide treatment and rehabilitation services in residential facilities may receive financial assistance from the Welsh Office.

The following six grants were approved in 1998/99:
Youthlink Wales (£70,300);
Rhoserchan (£45,000);
CAIS (£43,300);
Dyfrig House (£32,500);
Cardiff Housing Link (£25,000);
Brynawel House (£21,000).

Applications: To health authorities for locally based schemes and to the Welsh Office for all Wales developments and residential provision. The deadline for applications is in the autumn.

Contact: Mrs K M Phillips, Mr D Robinson, Tel: 01222-825512

NB: This scheme is under review.

Powers: Section 64, Health Services and Public Health Act 1968. Section 28B National Health Service Act 1977

Voluntary Sector Branch

Support for Voluntary Intermediary Services

Grant total:	£615,000 (1998/99)
	£630,000 (1997/98)

This scheme allocates funds to voluntary organisations covering the whole of Wales of a 'generalist' or 'intermediary' nature. Grant aid is provided primarily in order to make an overall contribution to the efficiency and effectiveness of more specialised voluntary bodies, through activities such as: working up and managing projects; providing training; offering technical advice; support with monitoring and evaluation; identifying and planning for organisations' needs.

Organisations are funded to:
- support other voluntary organisations;
- encourage co-operation and collaboration between voluntary organisations;
- encourage effective liaison and partnerships between voluntary sector organisations, statutory agencies and the private sector;
- support and promote good practice in volunteering;
- develop and support new initiatives to meet previously unmet needs;
- assist local communities by encouraging participation in development;
- enhance the internal managerial capability of intermediary services.

Funding mainly takes the form of core grants with a small proportion of project grants. The maximum period for a project grant is three years. Capital grants for land, buildings or movable assets are only considered in exceptional circumstances. However, a small capital grant for movable assets (to a maximum of £5,000) may be considered as part of a core or project grant application.

Grants given in 1997/98:
    Wales Council for Voluntary Action (£420,000);
    Community Enterprise Wales (£51,500);
    Community Service Volunteers (£33,500);
    CSV Retired and Senior Volunteers Programme (£25,000);
    Student Community Action Wales (£25,000);
    Business in the Community Wales (£20,000);
    Welsh Black Voluntary Sector Network (£20,000);
    WCVA Media Project (£20,000).

Applications: Detailed guidance notes and applications forms can be obtained from the above contact. The deadline is 30th September.

See also separate entries for: Local Voluntary Service Schemes and Volunteering in Wales, funded by Voluntary Sector Branch and administered by WCVA.

Contact: Wayne Cowley, Tel: 01222-823092

Powers: Section 26, Development of Rural Wales Act 1976

Millennium Volunteers

A consortium managed by *Wales Council for Voluntary Action*, the *Council for Wales of Voluntary Youth Services* and the *Wales Youth Agency* is planned but details were undecided at the time of going to press.

Contact: Karin Phillips, Tel: 01222-825512

Wales Council for Voluntary Action (WCVA)

Llys Ifor, Cresent Road, Caerphilly CF83 1XL

Tel: 01222-855100; Fax: 01222-855101

The following grants are administered by Wales Council for Voluntary Action on behalf of the Welsh Office.

Local Mental Health Grants Scheme

> **Grant total:**   **£1.55 million (1998/99)**
>   **£1.45 million (1997/98)**

The scheme has two elements:

Local development service – ensures an effective development service throughout Wales for local voluntary organisations, user groups and family and carer groups concerned with mental health issues. A total of nine grants were made in 1998/99 ranging from £15,000 to £107,160 including:
   UNLLAIS (£107,160);
   Vale Council for Voluntary Services (£60,534);
   Powys Agency for Mental Health (£47,695).

Local mental health services – supports voluntary sector initiatives that enable people experiencing mental health problems and their carers to live as independent and fulfilled lives in the community as possible. A total of 39 grants were made in 1998/99 ranging from £1,743 to £192,949, with the majority between £20, 000 and £40,000. Grants included:
   Newport Mind (£192,949);
   Gofal Housing Trust (£43,507);
   Age Concern Gwent (£21,990);
   Advance Advocacy Service for Brighter Futures Project (£21,379);
   Delyn Women's Aid (£20,000);
   Mental Health Users Forum, North Wales (£5,425).

Grants may be available for up to 100% of core, service delivery, project and capital costs.

Applications: Detailed information and advice are available. Application forms were issued in July for the deadline of 31 October in 1998.

Contact: Cath Lindley, Mental Health Grants Officer, WCVA

Powers: Section 28B of the National Health Service Scheme Act 1977

Local Voluntary Services Scheme

Grant total:	£1,637,000 (1998/99)
	£1,615,000 (1997/98)

Funds are made available to local voluntary councils to help assure an effective, independent support structure for voluntary organisations in each Welsh unitary authority. Grants are primarily towards core costs or project grant or, in exceptional circumstances, capital grant.

The scheme supports local voluntary councils which:
- provide a range of support services to help the development and effectiveness of voluntary and community action;
- identify the views of a broad range of local voluntary groups and represent them to decision makers;
- assist in voluntary sector initiatives which meet previously unmet needs and enhance community participation;
- assist in the provision of an effective volunteering support service.

In 1997/98 grants to 16 new voluntary councils totalled £1,210,500. They ranged between £59,600 and £105,600, with an additional £404,495 to the two existing voluntary councils.

Applications: Application forms and guidance notes are available. The closing date for applications was 30th October for a grant in the next financial year in 1998.

Contact: Phil Jarrold, Head of Funding Services, WCVA

Powers: Section 26 of the Development of Rural Wales Act 1976

Volunteering in Wales Fund

> **Grant total:**   £127,930 (first quarter of 1998/99)
> £400,000 (1997/98)
> £404,000 (1996/97)

This grant is open to registered charitable organisations that promote volunteering in the health and social welfare fields, especially where the unemployed are involved. Grants are made for general volunteering projects and to volunteer bureaux.

General awards are offered up to a maximum of £25,000. The focus is on:
- supporting projects whose aims are mainly achieved by the use of volunteers;
- supporting agencies whose primary purpose is the recruitment and placing of volunteers;
- encouraging good practice in volunteering;
- encouraging agencies/projects in areas where volunteering is under-developed.

Grants are made to local bodies, Wales-wide bodies and UK bodies working in Wales. In the first quarter of 1998/99 these ranged from £3,000 to £10,000 and included:
Swansea Drugs Project (£10,000);
After Adoption Wales (£8,660);
Student Community Action Wales (£3,500).

Volunteer bureaux are supported which: increase the local knowledge of volunteering; provide support to enable people to volunteer; distribute information and advice; represent volunteers' interests; match volunteers with suitable opportunities. New services can receive level funding for up to three years, with possible funnelling of funds for a further two years. A total of seven volunteer bureaux were supported in the first quarter of 1998/99. The funding ranged between £1,300 and £15,280 and included:
Pembrokeshire Association of Voluntary Services (£15,280);
Presteigne and Norton Community Support (£7,500).

Exclusions: Projects eligible for funding from other public sources. The purchase or refurbishment of buildings. The purchase of motor vehicles, their repair and upkeep.

Applications: Application forms, advice and guidance notes are available from the above contact. Applications for the support and development of volunteer bureaux should be made on a separate form. The VIWF committee meets quarterly to consider applications.

Contact: Stan Salter, WCVA

Powers: Section 26, Development of Rural Wales Act 1976

TRANSPORT, PLANNING AND ENVIRONMENT GROUP

The group comprises:
- Environment Division, including sponsorship of the Countryside Council for Wales and joint sponsorship of the Environment Agency;
- Estates Division;
- Planning Division;
- Transport Policy Division, responsible for transport infrastructure projects;
- Cadw: Executive Agency.

Transport Policy Division (3)

Rural Community Transport Initiative

Grant total:	£250,000 (1998/99)

This initiative forms part of the extra funding for rural transport in the 1998 budget. Details were not known at the time of going to press.

Rural Transport Innovation Grant

Government funding:	£125,000 (1998/99)
	£100,000 (1997/98)
	£2,000 (1996/97)

Grants are available towards the capital costs of providing new or improved public services in rural areas with less than 10,000 population. Grant is not restricted to any particular type of public transport but the scheme must have a wide measure of support, and not compete significantly with an existing service.

Grant is available towards:

- appointment of a Rural Transport Officer;
- community transport vehicles for specific groups such as the elderly, disabled or young people;
- construction of and improvements to waiting-points and bus shelters where this will help to establish a new service or enhance an existing service;
- continuation of an existing or establishing a new transport service;
- conversion of any community vehicle serving rural areas whether or not it has been previously grant assisted;
- conversion of vehicles which have already received rural transport innovation grant assistance towards meeting Disabled Persons transport Advisory Committee standards;
- up to three year revenue funding where necessary to establish a service;
- voluntary car-sharing schemes run by properly constituted organisations.

Any individual, business, organisation or Community Council may apply. The rate of grant is normally up to 50% of the capital costs, though in exceptional circumstances a higher rate may be awarded. There is no minimum or maximum grant size.

Applications: Guidance notes and application forms are available.

Contact: Mrs C Swidenbank, Tel: 01222-826516

Powers: Section 108 of the Transport Act 1985

Welsh Historic Monuments – CADW

Crown Building, Cathays Park, Cardiff CF1 3NQ

Tel: 01222-825363; Fax: 01222-826375

Contact: Keith Jones

Grant total:	£4,499,000 (1998/99)
	£4,272,000 (1997/98)
	£4,338,000 (1996/97)

Cadw is an executive agency of the Welsh office and performs a service very similar to that of English Heritage and Historic Scotland. Grants are made to:

- historic buildings, for repair-restoration;
- conservation areas, for external work only;
- civic initiatives (heritage) grants;
- archaeological trusts, for rescue archaeology.

Archaeological grants are made to only four trusts; Clwyd-Powys, Dyfed, Glamorgan-Gwent and Gwynedd Archaeological Trusts.

The civic initiatives (heritage) grant is of particular interest to civic societies or other local voluntary groups. It covers a range of activities and priority is given to those which increase awareness of the built heritage and promote its appreciation eg. exhibitions, publications. Grants can be up to 50% of the eligible costs with a maximum of £2,000 and a minimum of £150. Applicants are expected to raise the remainder themselves and *not* from other public sources.

Other schemes have particular guidelines for grant rates but they can vary as every application is treated on its merits.

Exclusions: Applications will not be considered for projects that have already started or been completed.

Applications: Obtain a copy of *Historic buildings grants and conservation area grants* and check for other useful advice leaflets. The grant case officers will be able to answer most general queries. Technical details should be discussed with a member of the architectural staff. Grants are made on the advice of the Historic Buildings Council for Wales and independent panel which meets five times a year to consider applications. In the case of civic societies a copy of the application should be sent to the Civic Trust for Wales.

Powers: Ancient Monuments and Archaeological Areas Act 1979
Section 304, Town and Country Planning Act 1990
Section 26, Development of Rural Wales Act 1976

Countryside Council for Wales

Plas Penhros, Fford Penrhos, Bangor, Gwynedd LL57 2LQ

Tel: 01248-385500; Fax: 01248-355782

Contact: Ruth Taylor

Grant-in-aid:	about £3 million annually to 2000

The Countryside Council for Wales (CCW) is accountable to the Welsh Office which provides its annual grant in aid. It is the national wildlife conservation authority and the government's statutory advisor on "sustaining natural beauty, wildlife, and the opportunity for outdoor enjoyment in Wales and its inshore waters". Grants are made towards programmes and projects meeting its objectives.

The council's booklet *Priorities for Grant Aid 1997-2000* highlights its four themes for grant. The proportion of grant is given in brackets.
- Landscape – to conserve the natural beauty and amenity of Wales (17%);
- Biodiversity – to conserve the quality and richness of wildlife and habitats (30%);
- Access and enjoyment – to provide, improve and sustain opportunities and facilities for public assess to, and enjoyment of the countryside (33%);
- Understanding – to promote understanding of environmental issues (20%).

Obviously many programmes will integrate all these priorities into their operations: conserved woodland benefits both the landscape and wildlife habitats, encourages owners to allow greater public access and increases enjoyment and greater understanding of the countryside.

Levels of grant are discretionary but do not exceed 50% of the eligible costs of any one scheme. Grants cannot be offered in retrospect and payment will not be made where a project has started prior to the CCW issuing a formal offer of grant and its acceptance by the applicant.

A selection of grants made to voluntary sector organisations in 1996/97 follows to illustrate the range (with the first five the largest made in that year):

   National Trust, for management work in designated areas (North £60,255; South £38,559);

BTCV, for management work in non-designated areas (£42,500);
North Wales Wildlife Trust, for partnership programme (£37,450);
RSPB, for management work in designated areas (£30,262);
Council for the Protection of Rural Wales, for partnership programme (£27,250);
Wales Young Farmers' Club, rural life project (£12,500);
Association of Welsh Wildlife Trusts, otter project (£7,456);
Mammal Society, for information project (£4,000);
Shell Better Britain Campaign (£7,650);
Field Studies Council, for training (£3,356);
RSNC, for lowland grassland booklet (£1,200);
Botanical Society of British Isles, for co-ordination of plant recording (£1,046);
Marine Conservation Society, for advisory service (£896);
Black Environmental Network, partnership programme (£416).

Applications: Applicants are encouraged to consult CCW officers at their nearest office (see list below) at an early stage in the formulation of their project. Whilst applications can be submitted at any time, it is better for them to be received as early as possible before the planned start of a project. Funding programmes are negotiated in the autumn and are expected to be submitted by the January before the start of the next financial year.

Regional Offices:
Abergavenny Tel: 01873-857938; Fax: 01873-854753
Aberyswyth Tel: 01970-828551; Fax: 01970-828314
Bala Tel: 01678-521226; Fax: 01678-520534
Bangor Tel: 01248-373100; Fax: 01248-370734
Cardiff Tel: 01222-772400; Fax: 01222-772412
Dolgellau Tel: 01341-423750; Fax: 01341-423739
Fishguard Tel: 01348-874602; Fax: 01348-873936
Newtown Tel: 01686-626799; Fax: 01686-629556
Stackpole Tel: 01646-661368; Fax: 01646-661368
Swansea Tel: 01792-771949/895; Fax: 01792-771981
Llandeilo Tel: 01558-822111; Fax: 01558-823467
Llandrindod Wells Tel: 01597-824661; Fax: 01597-825734
Martin's Haven Tel: 01646-636736; Fax: 01646-636744
Mold Tel: 01352-754000; Fax: 01352-752346

Environment Wales

c/o The Prince's Trust – Bro, 4th Floor, Empire House,
Mount Stuart Square, Cardiff CF1 6DN

Tel: 01222-471121; Fax: 01222-482086

Contact: Siân Phipps, Coordinator

Grant total:	£406,000 (1998/99)
	£368,000 (1997/98)

Environment Wales (EW) is a partnership initiative between the Welsh Office and the voluntary sector. It receives annual grant-in-aid (£664,000 in 1998/99) to contribute to sustainable development by supporting voluntary action which protects and improves the environment. It operates through a team of Development Officers based with the seven core partners in the initiative: BTCV (Wales); Wales Groundwork Cymru; CSV Wales; Keep Wales Tidy; the Welsh Wildlife Trusts; the RSPB; and the National Trust. The Coordinator and Administrator are based with The Prince's Trust-Bro.

Projects need to be registered with the initiative to be eligible for funding. Contact the Coordinator. There are three grant funds:
- Management Grant Fund towards the cost of project staff – (£179,690) in 25 awards (1997/98);
- Project Grant fund towards the costs of project materials – (£170,255) in 60 awards (1997/98);
- Training Support Grant for staff and volunteers attending training courses, etc. – (£8,200) in 49 awards (1997/98).

Additional support is given for which pre-registration is not a requirement:
- Pre-Project Grants – £15,300 in 7 awards (1997/98);
- Start-Up Grants – £4,950 in 5 awards (1997/98).

Management funding may be agreed for up to six years in which case level funding is given for three years, followed by three years in which the grant is tapered. Renewal bids are needed every year for Management awards.

In 1997/98 grants included:
  West Wales Sea Watch Centre for a Centre Manager (£10,000);
  Fforestwr for woodland skills training for the unemployed (7,550);
  Lake Vyrnwy for hedgerow and dry stone wall restoration (£4,100);
  Kilvy Community Woodland for a sculpture trail (£3,000);
  Abergavenny Cycling Project to promote cycling in the town (£2,230);
  Fairwater Community garden (£1,500).

Applications: The coordinator will be pleased to respond to inquiries from projects applying for registration or grant. A detailed Information Pack is available including criteria and general conditions of grant. Applicants are encouraged to discuss their ideas at an early stage with their allocated development officer. However, applicants should also accept that the award of registered status is not a guarantee that funding will be available. Project Funding is available throughout the year. Management grants for project staff are invited in August with a deadline of the first week in November for grants starting in the following April.

If funds are being given by another organisation funded by the Welsh Office eg. Countryside Council for Wales, Welsh Development Agency, Wales Tourist Board, Prince's Trust-Bro, funds from EW and the other funders should not exceed 50%. However, up to 75% of eligible costs can be given when Environment Wales is the only grant-maker funded by the Welsh Office. All grants must be spent in the financial year in which they are made. Any underspend will be returned to the Welsh Office and lost to the voluntary sector. The Grants Committee meets monthly on average. Applications can be made at any time (apart from Management Grant Fund) but those made earlier in the financial year are more likely to be successful. Funds are often completely allocated by December.

THE NORTHERN IRELAND OFFICE

Stormont Castle, Belfast BT4 3ST

Tel: 01232-520700; Fax: 01232-528478

Web site: www.gov.nio

The Northern Ireland Office (NIO) is the UK government department with responsibility for Northern Ireland. The Secretary of State for Northern Ireland is directly responsible for political and constitutional matters, law and order, policing and criminal justice policy and community relations as well as broad economic questions. The NIO is distinct from the six Northern Ireland departments. However, during 'direct rule' these departments are subject to the direction of the Secretary of State.

The six Northern Ireland departments are listed below with their main responsibilities:

Agriculture

Economic Development

- training and employment
- industry
- enterprise
- tourism

Education

- arts
- youth
- nursery through to further education

Environment

- housing
- transport
- urban regeneration
- environmental protection

Finance and Personnel

- European Union funding
- funding through the Central Community Relations Unit

Health and Social Services

Funding of the voluntary sector

The total funding in 1998/99 to voluntary organisations from the Northern Ireland Office is shown in the pie-chart. It splits this total into three sectors, the Housing Association Branch, the Arts Council of Northern Ireland and 'All other grants' i.e. programmes open only to the voluntary sector.

The graph breaks down the section 'All other grants' in the pie-chart. It shows the different contributing departments and the relative proportions of funding they made available via programmes aimed exclusively at voluntary organisations in 1998/99.

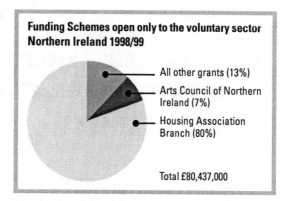

Funding Schemes open only to the voluntary sector Northern Ireland 1998/99

All other grants (13%)
Arts Council of Northern Ireland (7%)
Housing Association Branch (80%)

Total £80,437,000

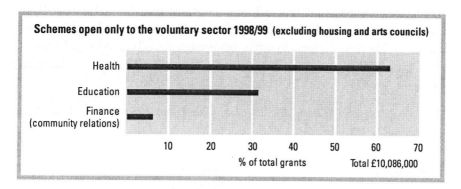

Schemes open only to the voluntary sector 1998/99 (excluding housing and arts councils)

Health
Education
Finance (community relations)

10   20   30   40   50   60   70
% of total grants   Total £10,086,000

Notes

The Health Department funding covers health, social welfare and volunteering.

The Education Department funding covers cultural projects, youth organisations and community relations.

The Finance and Personnel Department funding covers community relations and reconciliation.

**Detailed Breakdown of 'All other grants'
Funding Schemes for the Voluntary Sector**

	£'000	
Department of Health		
Health & Personal Services	5,567	
Community Volunteering Scheme	816	
		6,383
Department of Education		
Youth Council for Northern Ireland	1,487	
Community Relations Branch	805	
Cultural Traditions Programme	580	
Youth Service Branch	267	
		3,139
Department of Finance and Personnel		
Central Community Relations Unit	558	
		558
Department of Economic Development		
NI2000	6	
		6
TOTAL		**10,086**

Other key funding sources

Large tranches of funding in Northern Ireland are available from the European Union through the Special Programme for Peace and Reconciliation. Matching funding comes from the Northern Ireland departments with the total programme worth approximately £275 million. The largest element of the package is Sub-programme 4: Social Inclusion intended to fund projects by voluntary and community groups. The sub-programmes are operated by both departments and voluntary bodies.

Northern Ireland Agreement

The Good Friday Agreement of May 1998 was followed by the formation of a Northern Ireland Assembly in June. At the time of going to press departmental structures and arrangements were being reviewed.

Contents

DEPARTMENT OF AGRICULTURE FOR NORTHERN IRELAND (DANI)

Dundonald House,
Upper Newtownards Road,
Belfast BT4 3SB
Tel: 01232-520100; Fax: 01232-525015

The Department of Agriculture for Northern Ireland (DANI) is responsible for agriculture, forestry, fishing industries and rural development. In addition it is an agent for MAFF in the administration of UK-wide schemes in Northern Ireland and applies EU agricultural policy.

Rural Development Division

The Rural Development Strategy 1994/99 aimed to 'stimulate economic and social revitalisation of the most disadvantaged rural areas of Northern Ireland through partnership between the public, private and voluntary sectors'. Rural Development strategies work through:

- The department's Rural Development Division;
- Rural Development Council for Northern Ireland (see separate entry).

The Rural Development Division strategies fall into the following categories:

Area Based Strategies
Disadvantaged rural areas are targeted through partnerships to draw up strategies identifying and responding to local needs. These aim to provide a framework for socio-economic development and support the provision of essential infrastructure for rural economic growth.

Support is available for private, co-operative and community proposals for:
- business/enterprise development;
- off-farm diversification;
- rural business innovation exploiting local skills and products;
- specific training and skills development;
- environmental improvements/conservation;
- provision of local services;
- basic infrastructural provision.

Community-Based Regeneration Projects

Complementing the area based strategies community based projects include:
- development of local enterprise;
- provision of workspace units;
- farm diversification;
- rural tourism;
- improvements of the business environment;
- human resource development;
- teleworking using advanced telecommunications and information technology;
- environmental improvement.

Contact: Stephen Hogg, Tel: 01232-524880; Fax: 01232-524776

The funding of the regeneration projects listed above comes from the European programmes listed below, which are then matched by government.

Interreg II

Funding: **£1.08 million (1998/99)**
£291,000 (1997/98)

Support is available to community-based initiatives for regeneration of the local economy especially those on a cross-border basis. It develops local area action plans for joint cross-border co-operative economic action.

Funding is normally for up to 50% of the project costs. However, in exceptional circumstances, funding up to 75% of the project cost may be approved.

Applications: Applications from INTERREG Development Office, Unit 22, Armagh Business Centre Ltd, 2 Loughgall Road, Armagh or Department of Finance and Personnel, European Division (check address as Department of Finance and Personnel scheduled to move premises).

Contact: Catherine Coll, Executive Officer I, Tel: 01232-524887

LEADER II
(Liaison Entre Actions de Developpement de L'Economie Rurale)

Funding: £3.07 million (1998/99)
£2.565 million (1997/98)
(match funding 65% from European
sources, 35% from DANI)

Addressing rural problems through innovative solutions within a specific geographical area or sector of the economy. Funding is available for up to 50% of project costs to a maximum of about £50,000.

Applications: Apply to LEADER Local Action Groups. A list is available from the contact.

Contact: Eugene Cranney, Executive Officer, Tel: 01232-524885

Pesca

Funding: £500,000 (1998/99)
£55,000 (1997/98)

Support is available for socio-economic regeneration of fishing ports by:
■ stimulating new, alternative employment-creating activities;
■ conversion from fishing to other activities;
■ retaining and vocational guidance for workers;
■ restructuring within the industry.

Funding is available for up to 75% of project costs with no maximum funding for community groups.

Applications: Applications to Newry and Mourne Enterprise Agency, Win Industrial Estate, Canal Quay, Newry.

Contact: Rural Area Co-ordinator South, Tel: 01693-251288

Spard
(Sub-Programme for Agriculture: Rural Development)

Funding: £5.79 million (1998/99)
£4.784 million (1997/98) (50% from
European funds, 50% from DANI)

SPARD aims to revitalise the wider rural economy through:
■ capacity building of rural communities;
■ implementation of Strategic Area Plans;

■ development of regeneration projects by Community Groups.

It provides between 50 and 70% of total project costs but up to 100% of training project costs. The maximum grant is about £350,000.

Applications: *Projects:* No deadline set. *Area-Based Strategies:* Contact Strategy Managers for deadlines of individual strategies (listing from contact).

Contact: Paul Moore, Staff Officer, Tel: 01232-524880; Fax: 01232-524776

DANI Regional Offices
Counties Antrim and Londonderry
Rural Area Co-ordinator North, Unit 17, Tower Centre, Ballymena BT43 6AB
Tel: 01266-632199
Counties Armagh and Down
Rural Area Co-ordinator South, Holt's Building, Cecil Street, Newry BT35 6AH
Tel: 01693-251288
Counties Fermanagh and Tyrone
Rural Area Co-ordinator West, Inishkeen House, Killyhevlin,
Enniskillen BT74 4EJ
Tel: 01365-343144

Forest Service

Grant total for private planting: £800,000 (1997/98)

To encourage the establishment of woodland the Northern Ireland Department of Agriculture offers two national grant schemes, both administered by the Forest Service and part funded by the European Community. The schemes are open to all including the voluntary sector although most applications came from farmers and other landlords.

Woodland Grant Scheme (WGS)
Three types of grant are given as follows.

Establishment Grants to create woodland and restock existing woodland after felling or windblow, by planting or natural regeneration. These include:
■ *Enclosed land supplement* for new planting on land previously enclosed and improved for agricultural purposes;
■ *Natural regeneration*, a discretionary payment on completion of approved work to encourage natural regeneration;

■ *Community woodland supplement,* for those planting new woodlands close to towns and cities which can be used for informal public recreation.

Annual Management Grants help towards the cost of management work in special woodlands of high environmental potential. At least one of three criteria must be met: safeguarding or enhancing the existing special environmental value; bringing the site up to minimum Forest Service environmental standards; maintaining or creating public access to woodlands.

Special Grants include:

■ *Livestock exclusion,* an annual premium in Disadvantaged Areas to farmers to promote natural regeneration of woods by positive management;

■ *Woodland Improvement grant,* a discretionary payment towards work in existing woodlands needing one-off remedial measures.

Farm Woodland Premium Scheme (FWPS)

Encourages the establishment of new woodland to enhance the environment and as a productive alternative land use. Applicants must first be accepted under the Woodland Grant Scheme.

Applications: Full details are given in an information booklet accompanying the application forms obtainable from the District Forest Offices and County Agriculture Offices. Applications can be made for the WGS or for both the WGS and the FWPS but *not* the FWPS alone. The deadline for applications is 31st December.

Forest Service:
Antrim District - Balymena
Tel: 01266-662888; Fax: 01266-662877
Down/Armagh District - Castlewellan
Tel: 013967-71144; Fax: 013967-71762
Fermanagh District - Enniskillen
Tel: 01365-325004; Fax: 01365-324753
Londonderry District - Limavady
Tel: 015047-62547; Fax: 01504-68075
Tyrone District - Omagh
Tel: 01662-251020; Fax: 01662-253440

County Agricultural Offices:
Armagh Tel: 01861-524979
Ballymena Tel: 01266-662800
Coleraine Tel: 01265-41000
Downpatrick Tel: 01396-618249
Enniskillen Tel: 01365-325004
Omagh Tel: 01662-251020

Contact: Brian O'Hara, Tel: 01232-520100; Fax: 01232-524570

Rural Development Council for Northern Ireland

17 Loy Street, Cookstown, Co. Tyrone BT80 89Z

Tel: 01648-766 980; Fax: 01648-766922

Contact: Esmé Charles

The RDC can grant-aid disadvantaged rural communities who want to become involved in the economic and social development of their area. It is particularly interested in assisting with the costs of identifying, appraising, planning and running projects which will create employment. Training in technical and managerial skills is also eligible. Small grants are also available to help communities include a wider range of people in their activities and get them working effectively as a group.

Most of the grant budget is disbursed *in the communities targeted for assistance* on the recommendation of the three Project Managers following local consultation. Groups in communities not targeted in this way may also receive support if they are: established as a community group; located in a disadvantaged rural area; representative of their community; a not-for-profit organisation. Funding is only available for up to a maximum of 80% of a project's costs.

Exclusions: Capital costs involved in project start-up.

Applications: Obtain guidelines on grant-aid for full details. Advice and guidance will initially be given by the Regional Project Managers. Applications are sent to the main office in Cookstown. Decisions for grants of less than £5,000 will be made by staff. Larger grants are decided at a full council meeting.

DEPARTMENT OF ECONOMIC DEVELOPMENT (DED)

**Netherleigh, Massey Avenue,
Belfast BT4 3SX
Tel: 01232-529900; Fax: 01232-529551**

The responsibilities of the Department of Economic Development include consumer protection; energy matters; and equality and health and safety at work. A number of other responsibilities are enacted through the following executive agencies:

Industrial Development Board

Promotes a larger home industry and inward investment;

Local Enterprise Development Unit

Promotes enterprise and small businesses;

Northern Ireland Tourist Board

Develops tourism (see entry below);

Training and Employment Agency

Training and employment issues (see entry below);

Industrial Research and Technology Unit

Technology transfer and research.

In addition it funds the following non-departmental bodies relevant to this guide: Equal Opportunities Commission for Northern Ireland and NI2000.

Training and Employment Agency

Adelaide House, 39-49 Adelaide Street, Belfast BT2 8FD

Tel: 01232-257777; Fax: 01232-257778

Action for Community Employment

Grant total:	**£22,222,000 (1998/99)**
	£29,822,000 (1997/98) (99% to
	voluntary organisations)

Action for Community Employment (ACE) provides temporary employment with training of up to one year for long term unemployed adults in projects of community benefit. ACE is open to people between the ages of 25 and 64 who have been unemployed for 12 out of the last 15 months. Special conditions apply to those who are disabled. The scheme aims to improve the worker's performance and enhance their prospects of obtaining a permanent job through structured training. The majority (99%) of projects are sponsored by voluntary organisations with the remainder provided by District Councils.

The sponsors receive a maximum grant of £93 a week for each ACE employee of which £11 may be allocated towards overheads and running costs. For every 20 persons employed an additional core worker grant of between £11,937 and £19,185 per annum for management, supervision and training is available.

Projects must fit the following criteria:
- all relevant employers and trade unions interested must be consulted;
- not put existing jobs at risk;
- not take the place of work that would normally be voluntary;
- pay should be at the local rate for the job;
- private gain must be minimal;
- provide community benefits.

The types of projects funded include: building; community service; environmental improvements; exhibitions; repair work/decoration; youth work. In 1998/99 the projected number of ACE placements was 3,900, compared to 4,193 in 1997/98.

In operation since 1981, it has been reviewed to compliment the New Deal for the over 25s and will take a revised form from April 1st 1999.

Applications: Applications must be made through Training and Employment Agency offices.

Contact: Michael Brennan, Tel: 01232-257565; Fax: 01232-257544

Powers: Employment and Training Act (Northern Ireland) 1950 as amended by the Employment and Training (Amendment)(NI) Order 1988

Disablement Advisory Service

Grant total:	£4.86 million (1998/99)
	£4.79 million (1997/98) (34% to
	the voluntary sector)

A number of advisory services and programmes are funded to help disabled people to get into and stay in work. A range of practical assistance, comprehensive information and an assessment service for both disabled people and their employers in the public, private and voluntary sectors is provided.

Financial assistance is available under the following programmes:

Employment Support
Grant total: £3.9 million (1998/99)
£3.5 million (1997/98)

This programme gives those who cannot reach standard output levels at work because of their disability the opportunity to work in jobs earning full pay rates. Three organisations are grant aided each year, with the following amounts in 1997/98:
   Ulster Sheltered Employment Limited (£2,641,000);
   Disability Action (£729,000);
   Industrial Therapy Organisation (£152,000).

Access to Work (NI)
Grant total: £310,000 (1998/99)
£270,000 (1997/98)

This programme is available to disabled people who are unemployed, employed or self-employed and who are facing difficulties obtaining or retaining work because of their disability. Depending on circumstances, assistance can be up to 100% of costs although in most cases the employer will be expected to make a contribution.

Job Introduction Scheme
Grant total: £650,000 (1998/99)
            £1,020,000 (1997/98)

This scheme is aimed at encouraging employers to offer a job introduction to a disabled person on a trial basis. A contribution is made towards the cost of wages during the trial period.

In addition, match funding is provided for a wide range of organisations, mostly in the voluntary sector, participating in EU funded programmes.

Contact: Mairead Mageean, Tel: 01232-257465; Fax: 01232-257468

Jobskills Programme

Grant total:	£61,625,000 (budgeted 1998/99)
	£72,135,000 (1997/98)
	£72,989,000 (1996/97)

The Jobskills Programme trains young people towards National Vocational Qualifications (NVQs) with the aim of increasing their employability. Trainees are issued with a Training Credit indicating the funding available and specifying the occupational area and level of training to be followed. They then have freedom to choose a suitable training organisation. Training is available to:
■ unemployed 16 and 17 year-olds who are guaranteed a training place;
■ disabled people up to the age of 22;
■ those aged up to 24 if following Modern Apprenticeship whilst in employment.

The voluntary sector receives 17% of the funding total shown above.

Different NVQ levels are available in the following programmes: *Access*, level 1 NVQ for young people with special needs who are not ready for level 2 training; *Mainstream*, primarily level 2 NVQ; *Modern Apprenticeship* level 3 NVQ for those who train while employed.

Training Organisations may be community-based, private sector organisations, further education colleges or Training and Employment Agency Training Centres. Funding levels depend on the occupational area and NVQ level being followed. In *Jobskills Mainstream* there are four funding bands with net weekly training fees to Training Organisations ranging between £25 and £36. *Young Access* trainees with special needs are funded an enhanced weekly training fee of £67 for the first year, whilst those with disabilities can be funded at the enhanced rate for up to three years.

Incentive payments of 30% for the Mainstream and 20% for the Access schemes are made to Training Organisations' trainees on achievement of targeted training outcomes.

Applications: Organisations can be involved as a main Training Organisation or as a Training Partner. Contracts in respect of main Training Organisations are awarded by the Training and Employment Agency's regional managers (see below). Training Organisations may award sub contracts to training partners. Existing contracts expire in March 1999 with the recontracting process currently under review. Training Organisations must be capable of managing training plans of up to three years duration.

Regional Managers:
Belfast
D Wheeler, Tel: 01232-252289
South-East
W Boyd, Tel: 018206-62149
West
D Shields, Tel: 018687-22525

Contact: Tom Arthur, Deputy Principal, Tel: 01232-257512; Fax; 01232-257544

Powers: Employment & Training (NI) Act 1950, amended by the Industrial Relations (NI)Order 1987, further amended by the Employment & Training (Amendment) (NI) Order 1988

Equal Opportunities Commission for Northern Ireland

Chamber of Commerce House,
22 Great Victoria Street, Belfast BT2 7BA

Tel: 01232-242752; Fax: 01232-331047
E-mail: info@eocni.org.uk
Web site: http://www.eocni.org.uk

Contact: Irene Kingston, Deputy Director of Communications

> **Grant total:**   **£91,860 (1998/99)**
>   **£67,300 (1997/98)**

The Equal Opportunities Commission for Northern Ireland is an independent public body which challenges sex discrimination. It promotes equality in employment, legislation and the provision of goods and services. It gives equality and research grants. It receives annual grant-in-aid from the Department of Economic Development (£1.5 million in 1997/98).

Equality grants cover the following categories: arts projects; awareness, raising the profile of women; education of rights under equality legislation; practical projects.

Research grants focus on the following employment issues: education & training; reconciliation of work & family; employment practices; women's economic independence; public awareness of equality; legislative reforms. Research applications can be made by women's and community groups as well as established researchers.

The breakdown of funding was as follows:

	1998/99	1997/98
Equality grants	£3,820	£2,700
Research grants	£88,040	£64,600

Applications: See *Grants for Equality* and *Grants for Research* leaflets. Deadlines for research grants in 1998 were 15th January, 15th April and 15th October. Write to the Director, Investigation and Research. There is no deadline for equality grants applications. Write to the Director, Equality and Information.

Powers: Article 55 of the Sex Discrimination (NI) Order 1976

Northern Ireland Tourist Board

St Anne's Court, 59 North Street, Belfast BT1 1NB

Tel: 01232-231 221; Fax: 01232-240960
E-mail: general.enquiries.nitb@nics.gov.uk

Contact: Bob McMillen, Development Manager

> **Government grant-in-aid: £13.9 million (1998/99)**

The Northern Ireland Tourist Board is a non-departmental public body promoting the tourist industry. It provides the following grant from governmental funding as well as others from EU funds.

Tourism Development Scheme

> **Grant total:** **£4.7 million (1998/99)**
> **£4.7 million (1997/98)**

This scheme offers funding for projects including accommodation, activity and special interest holiday facilities, or enhancement of natural/cultural tourism. Projects should increase employment, fill market gaps by spreading the benefits of tourism across Northern Ireland and extend the season. Special priority is given to projects in disadvantaged areas.

A total of 14 grants were made in 1997/98 of which two were to voluntary organisations:
    Silverbrook Mills (£49,200);
    Royal Society for the Protection of Birds (£16,600).

Up to 30% of the eligible total project costs can be met if the project is part of the private sector. Higher levels of assistance are available to the public / voluntary sector. All funding is discretionary and calculated on a case by case basis. Offers are the minimum necessary to allow the project to proceed.

Applications: Applications forms are available.

Powers: Tourism (Northern Ireland) Order 1992

NI2000

**Nore Villa, 16 Knockbracken Health Care Park,
Saintfield Road, Belfast BT8 8SG**

**Tel: 01232-403 779; Fax: 01232-403780
E-mail: ni2000@dnet.co.uk
Web site: http://www.aaranet.co.uk/ni2000/**

Contact: Brendan McSherry

Grant total:	£5,500 (1998/99)
	£5,000 (1997/98)
	£3,850 (1996/97)

NI2000 is a charity funded predominantly from government sources to encourage and help groups and individuals to carry out projects which benefit the environment and the local community. It is a partnership of councils, government, business and voluntary organisations. In 1997/98 it received government funding of £57,000. The Training & Employment Agency provided 65% and the remainder came from the Environment & Heritage Service, of the Department of Environment.

NI2000 is funded primarily to help job creation and environmental work by voluntary groups, it also promotes and encourages more environmentally sustainable waste management, especially recycling. It provides advice and guidance, and a networking service with other groups, as well as small start-up grants up to a maximum of £500. Work eligible for a grant must:

- involve a specific practical environmental activity;
- involve Action for Community Employment, Community Work Programme, environmental Task Force or volunteer labour;
- demonstrate community and environmental benefit.

A total of 18 grants were made in 1998/99 ranging between £200 and £500 including:

Creggan Education and Research Ltd (£500);
Desertmartin Development Association (£400);
National Trust / Voluntary Services Belfast (£250);
St Pius X Conservation Group (Magherafelt) (£200).

Exclusions: Purchase of land or buildings.

Applications: For further information and help with completing the application form contact the Project Officer at the address above.

DEPARTMENT OF EDUCATION FOR NORTHERN IRELAND (DENI)

Rathgael House, Balloo Road, Bangor BT19 7PR

Tel: 01247-279279; Fax: 01247-279100
E-mail: deni@nics.gov.uk
Web site: http://www.deni.gov.uk

The department deals with legislative and financial control of education from nursery through to the further and higher levels. Education is administered centrally through the department and regionally through the five Education and Library Boards. In addition to mainstream and special needs education the department is responsible for: sport and recreation; youth services; arts and culture; development of community relations between schools.

Community Relations Branch

Community Relations Core Funding Scheme

> **Grant total:**   £805,000 (1998/99)
>   £800,000 (1997/98)

This fund supports voluntary and non-profit making organisations to improve community relations among young people, up to the age of 25. The focus is on activities which contribute to the "promotion of mutual understanding, respect for difference and tolerance of diversity". Within this, preference is given to organisations which support the development of programmes which:

- work through formal and informal education;
- enable issues of social, cultural, religious and political identity to be addressed;
- increase the confidence and capacity of teachers and other practitioners working with young people;
- encourage greater commitment, ownership and infrastructure within the education system.

Funding is offered for no more than three years for salary and running costs. It can cover up to 100% of total project costs.

A total of 20 grants were awarded in 1997/98 ranging from £9,000 to £85,000 including:

Speedwell Project (£85,000);
Churches Peace Education Programme (£60,000);
Northern Ireland Children's Holiday Scheme (£51,000);
Council for Education in World Citizenship (£24,000).

Exclusions: General appeals for assistance towards core funding.

Applications: Application forms and guidance notes are available. There are two deadlines in 1998: 31st January for funding from 1 April, and 31 May for funding from 1 September.

Cultural Traditions Programme

Grant total:	£580,000 (1998/99)
	£603,000 (1997/98)
	£709,000 (1996/97)

Cultural traditions projects are supported that help young people appreciate their common cultural heritage and gain respect for cultural diversity.

A total of seven grants were made in 1997/98 ranging from £30,000 to £250,000 including:

Arts Council NI (£250,000);
National Trust (£85,000);
Ulster Folk & Transport Museum (£53,000).

NB New funding criteria are to be introduced in 1999.

Contact: Susan Carnson, Tel: 01247-279748; Fax: 01247-279100

Youth Service Branch

Capital grants

Grant total:	£567,000 (1998/99)
	£170,000 (1997/98)

Grants are made as capital funding for voluntary groups and to cover training courses for youth workers. Clubs must be registered with their local Education and Library Boards. They must also own or hold long term leases on their buildings.

Most minor works are approved to help clubs comply with health, fire and safety regulations and are for a specific project. Grant-aid usually covers 75% of approved expenditure. Major works grants are discretionary and only cover one or two groups.

In 1997/98 the only major works grant of £100,000 was to Hazelbank Youth Wing. Five minor works grants were made:

St John Bosco Youth Club, Newry – replacement roof (£38,000);
Bosco Youth Club, Cookstown – renovation of premises (£15,500);
Strabane Scout Hall – Flooring (£7,300);

The Guide Association – refurbishment of kitchen (£7,000);
Patrician Youth Centre – fire alarm centre (£1,700).

In 1998/99 grants were split between 88% to major works, schemes costing over £100,000 and 12% minor works, schemes costing under £100,000.

Applications: Application forms and guidance notes forms are available from the above contact. The deadline for minor grant applications in 1998 was March 31. There is no formal application process for major works grants.

Contact: Alex Fergie, Tel: 01247-279365; Fax: 01247-279248

Education & Library Boards

```
Grant total:      £2 million (1997/98)
```

Schools Community Relations Programme
(formerly The Cross Community Contact Scheme)

Grants are available to schools, youth and community groups registered with the Education & Library Board delivering curriculum-based programmes to young people. Programmes should bring together young people from across the community through creative, sporting or enterprise schemes. Small grants may also be made for preparation work by groups at the pre-project stage.

The grant was split in the following proportions in 1997/98:

Schools	£1,210,000 (62%)
Youth	£632,000 (32%)
Youth Council	£115,000 (6%)

The regional Education & Library Boards vary in their allocation of this funding (see below).

Belfast Education & Library Board
Youth Service Branch, 40 Academy Street, Belfast BT1 2NQ
Tel: 01232-564000

Priority is given to groups working with adolescents providing a regular programme of social, educational and physical activities. For groups employing paid staff up to 100% of salaries and 75% of their running costs are covered. Other groups may receive occasional grants of up to 75% of their running costs.

Contact: Barry Mullholland, Education Officer (Youth), Tel: 01232-564000

South Eastern Education & Library Board

Block Three, Dundonald Complex, Grahamsbridge Road, Dundonald BT16 OHS

Assistance is given towards the cost of equipment, premises and salaries.

Contact: Hans Martin, Education Officer, Tel: 01232-381188; Fax: 01232-410176

North Eastern Education & Library Board

Youth Service Branch, County Hall, 182 Galgorm Road, Ballymena, Co. Antrim BT42 1HN

Grants range between £300 and £40,000 towards building maintenance, running costs and 100% of staff salaries. Average grants are between £300 and £400. Assistance is also given towards approved training of staff and cross-community activities. An Annual Camp Scheme offers assistance of up to £200 towards overnight stay costs of up to four nights, as part of an overall programme. It is also given for youth exchange activities. An information pack is available from the above address.

Contact: Gilbert Bell, Youth Welfare Adviser, Tel: 01266-662271

Southern Education & Library Board

Youth Service Branch, 3 Charlemont Place, The Mall, Co. Armagh BT61 9AX, Tel: 01861-512200; Fax: 01861-512491

Grants for purpose-built and long lease *full-time youth clubs* are available for 100% of heat, light and maintenance and 75% of insurance costs; 90% or 100% grants are available for full and part-time workers and specialist instructors; 75% grants are available for full-time caretakers, ancillary staff, equipment, transport and telephone rental; 50% is available for hire of facilities. *Part-time clubs* can receive 75% for heat, light and maintenance as well as the same levels of funding for other categories as full time clubs. Grants are also available for annual camps, exchanges and purchase of equipment.

Contact: Gregory Butler, Youth Adviser; Tel: 01861-512281

Western Education & Library Board
Youth Service Branch, Headquarters Office, 1 Hospital Road, Omargh,
Co. Tyrone BT79 0AW, Tel: 01662-411411; Fax: 01662-411403

Grants range from £150 to several thousand pounds are made to registered youth
clubs towards their running costs. Project and travel grants are also available.
Priority is given to the 10-20 year-old range. New groups are considered for
registration in February and November of each year.

Contact: W F Haugh, Senior Youth Officer, Tel: 01662-411486

Exclusions: Headquarters, governing bodies or umbrella bodies are *not* supported.

Applications: Information packs are available from the appropriate Education &
Library Board, to which applications should also be made.

Millennium Volunteers

Northern Ireland Volunteer Development Agency,
Annsgate House, 70 / 74 Ann Street, Belfast BT1 4EH

Tel: 01232-236100; Fax: 01232-237570

Contact: Paul Murray

The Northern Ireland Volunteer Development Agency is administering the
Millennium Volunteers scheme in Northern Ireland. At the time of going to press
£700,000 had been allocated over three years to cover administration of the scheme
and grants. The programme will follow the same form as in England, Wales and
Scotland (see main England entry for details), although the national guidelines for
contracting arrangements will allow for some local determination.

Arts Council of Northern Ireland

MacNeice House, 77 Malone House, Belfast BT9 6AQ

Tel: 01232-385200; Fax: 01232-661715

Contact: Damian Smyth, Public Affairs Officer, Tel: 01232-385204

Government grant-in-aid:	£6.67 million (1998/99)
	£6.67 million (1997/98)
	£6.85 million (1996/97)

The Arts Council of Northern Ireland is a registered charity and company limited by guarantee which receives an annual grant from the Northern Ireland Office through the Arts and Museums Branch of the Department of Education. Major institutions operating all the year round and implementing an artistic and financial policy agreed with the council receive renewable annual grants. These grants which form the major part of the council's funding are negotiated each year. The deadline for applications falls in October. Other applications for more than £5,000 are generally submitted in the January before the new financial year. In addition, awards of £5,000 and less are allocated.

Applications: Obtain full details about grant programmes from the art form departments. Stress is placed on the need for forward planning in applications. For example applications for events in July to October should reach the Arts Council in April.

The Arts Council is a Lottery distributor.

Northern Ireland Museums Council

66 Donegal Pass, Belfast BT1 1BU

Tel: 01232-550215; Fax: 01232-550216
E-mail: museums.council@nimc.org.uk

Contact: Aiden Walsh

Grant total:	£72,300 (1998/99)
	£53,590 (1997/98)
	£65,040 (1996/97)

The Northern Ireland Museums Council is a non-departmental public body which channels central government support to local, non-centrally funded museums. It receives about 90% of its core grant from the Department of Education Northern Ireland (DENI). It provides advice and information; training; grant-aid; support for the care of collections; and advocacy for museums. Grant-aid is usually provided at 50% of the total project costs, although a higher percentage can be awarded where a group of museums will benefit.

The following schemes give project grants:Collections Care; Use of Collections; Feasibility grants; Specimen Purchase grants; Training & Travel grants.

Exclusions: Only members of NIMC are normally eligible for grants. However, feasibility may be awarded to unregistered museums and bodies considering the establishment of museums.

Applications: Forms and guidance notes are sent out two or three times a year by NIMC to its members.

Youth Council for Northern Ireland

Forestview, Purdy's Lane, Belfast BT8 4TA

Tel: 01232-643882; Fax: 01232-643874
E-mail: ycouncil@demon.co.uk

Contact: Frank Murphy, Professional Adviser

Grant total:	**£1,486,700 (1998/99)**
	£1,486,700 (1997/98)

The Youth Council for Northern Ireland was established in 1989. It advises on the development of youth services, encourages cross-community activity, the provision of facilities and co-ordinates the efficient use of resources. It receives annual grant-in-aid of over £2 million, predominantly from the Department of Education with a small contribution (2%) from the Department of the Environment.

Grants are made to voluntary organisations providing Northern Ireland-wide services exclusively to 5 to 25 year-olds. Organisations should be politically unaligned and have provided programmes for children and young people for at least three years.

Grants ranged from £1,420 to £230,000 in 1998/99 including:
   Youth Action Northern Ireland (£230,000);
   Youth Link NI (£104,700);
   Northern Ireland Youth Forum (£75,900);
   Boys Brigade (£84,800);
   International Voluntary Service (£31,700).

Applications: Application forms and guidance notes are available.

NB The grant process was reviewed in 1998 with a new funding regime coming in to operation on 1 April 1999.

ABSA Northern Ireland

The Pairing Scheme, Association for Business Sponsorship of the Arts (ABSA) Northern Ireland

**PO Box 496, Danesfort, 120 Malone Road, Belfast BT9 5GL
Tel: 01232-664 736; Fax: 01232-664 500**

The Northern Ireland Pairing Scheme operates independently from that covering England, Scotland and Wales (see separate entry). It is funded by the Department of Education for Northern Ireland.

DEPARTMENT OF THE ENVIRONMENT (NORTHERN IRELAND)

Clarence Court, 10-18 Adelaide Street,
Belfast BT2 8GB

Tel: 01232-540540; Fax: 01232-540021
Web site: http://www.nics.gov.uk

The main responsibilities of the Department of the Environment (Northern Ireland) are housing, transport and urban regeneration. However, the majority of its functions are carried out by 'next steps' agencies, which include: planning; environmental protection; water service and roads.

Housing Division

Housing Associations Branch

Grant total: £64.7 million (1998/99)
                  £54.5 million (1997/98)

The branch deals with the promotion, registration and control of the 42 registered housing associations in Northern Ireland. Their main activities are:
- providing purpose-built accommodation for those with special needs;
- provision of accommodation for general use, eg. families;
- revitalising communities through urban and rural regeneration;
- providing housing by equity sharing through the Northern Ireland Co-ownership Housing Association (NICHA).

To qualify for financial assistance all development proposals must:

- have the support of the Northern Ireland Housing Executive on the grounds of housing needs; and
- comply to the department's standards of design and cost, as set out in the *Housing Association Guide*.

All new registered housing association rental projects are financed using a fixed percentage grant from the department, with the remaining cost (where appropriate) being met by a private loan. Running costs including loan repayment, management, maintenance and repair costs are met by rents set by the association. Registered housing associations may enter into agreements with other voluntary bodies whereby the day-to-day management of projects are devolved to a voluntary body. The department does not, however, grant-aid these voluntary bodies.

Grants made in 1997/98 included the following:

    BIH Housing Association Ltd. (£6.8 million);

    North & West Housing Association Ltd. (£6.8 million);

    Fold Housing Association (£6.4 million);

    Oaklee Housing Association Ltd. (£5.4 million).

Policy changes: Housing Policy in Northern Ireland was under review in 1998 with legislative changes expected in 2000/2001. For further information please contact the branch.

Further advice and information about housing associations may be obtained from Northern Ireland Federation of Housing Associations, Carlisle Memorial Centre, 88 Clifton Street, Belfast BT13 1AB, Tel: 01232-230446.

Contact: William Graham, Principal, Room 3-06, Tel: 01232-540611; Fax: 01232-540604

Powers: Part II of the Housing (Northern Ireland) Order 1992

Housing Management Branch

Grant total:	£413,800 (1998/99)

The Housing Management Branch funded the following voluntary organisations in 1998/99 which provide housing advice and promotion:

    Housing Rights Service (£221,000);

    Northern Ireland Tenants Action Project (£188,000);

    Housing Organisations and Mobility Exchange Services (£4,800).

Although the grant-aid powers do not limit funding to the above bodies, any requests for funding of new projects is unlikely to be available due to budgetary constraints.

Contact: George Davidson, Tel: 01232-541165; Fax: 01232-541153

Powers: Article 156A of the Northern Ireland Housing Order 1981, inserted by Article 88 of the Housing Order (NI) 1983

Urban Regeneration Branch

Brookmount Buildings, 42 Fountain Street, Belfast BT1 5EE

Tel: 01232-547801; Fax: 01232-251944

The branch links responsibilities with schemes run from the Belfast and Londonderry Development Offices. It focuses on particular areas and is not Northern Ireland-wide. Support is given to regeneration and environmental improvement work which may also be carried out by planning offices in divisional offices. The department is amalgamating all the schemes.

Belfast Regeneration Office

Grant total:	£18 million (1998/99)
	£21.5 million (1997/98)

The Belfast Regeneration Office (BRO) is the amalgamation of Making Belfast Work (MBW) and the Belfast Development Office. BRO focuses on the most disadvantaged areas of Belfast, although exact funding details were not available in autumn 1998 as the release of a joint strategy and official amalgamation was not expected until spring 1999. Projects funded under MBW were in the following categories: capacity building; crime reduction; economic development; education; environment; health and social welfare. Special emphasis has been given to improving employment opportunities and quality of life for residents through community, private and government initiatives.

Funds were targeted through government departments and agencies and the MBW teams. In 1998/99 the MBW teams received £4.5 million (25% of total funding) directly. The remaining £13.3 million was split between the following departments and agencies: Training and Employment Agency; Department of the Environment; Department of Education; Department of Health & Social Services; Local Enterprise

Development Unit; Northern Ireland Office; Department of Economic Development; Industrial Development Board.

The teams can access further funds via bids to departments and agencies although cuts in funding were made in both 1997/98 and in 1998/99. As an indication, a total of 96 grants were made in 1996/97 ranging from £5,000 to £3 million including the following:

    MBW Teams, locally based teams (£3,000,000);
    HALT (£98,000);
    Schoolgirl Pregnancy Project (£32,000);
    Shop-Front Addiction (£32,000);
    Recycle Workshop (£31,000);
    Speech & Language Therapy Skill Mix Project (£23,000).

There were four Making Belfast Work Teams in 1998 which focused on particular areas:

East Team
First Floor, 257-261 Woodstock Road, Belfast BT6 8PQ
Tel: 01232-456822; Fax: 01232-456814

Greater West Team
Twin Spires, 115 Northumberland Street, Belfast BT13 2JF
Tel: 01232-244535; Fax: 01232-321699

North Team
North City Business Centre, 2 Duncairn Gardens, Belfast BT15 2GG
Tel: 01232-744022; Fax: 01232-744042

South Team
South Belfast Economic Resource Centre, 1-5 Coyles Place, Belfast BT7 1EL
Tel: 01232-240117; Fax: 01232-239348

Applications: Forms can be obtained and applications made through local MBW Teams.

Contact: George Mackey, Director, Tel: 01232-251455; Fax: 01232-547800

Powers: Social Need (NI) Order 1986

Urban Development Grant (UDG)

Grant total:	£3.5 million (1998/99)
	£7 million (1997/98)
30% for new build and 50% for refurbishment	

The UDG aims to promote job creation, inward investment and environmental improvement by the development of vacant, derelict or underused land and buildings. UDG was available during 1998 within priority areas of Belfast and Londonderry.

However, it is possible for the grant scheme to respond to urgent needs outside these priority areas.

Grants are usually given to cover a funding gap or shortfall between the cost of the development and value on completion. Applications are assessed against criteria which include provisions regarding direct benefit to deprived areas as well as environmental benefits. The minimum grant size is £100,000.

Applications: Application forms and additional information can be obtained from:

Regional Offices:
Belfast Development Office based at the Belfast address (Tel: 01232-251928; Fax: 01232-251976);
Londonderry Development Office, Orchard House, 40 Foyle Street, Londonderry BT48 8AT (Tel: 01504-319900; Fax: 01504-319700).

Contacts: Brendan McConville; Tel: 01232-251927; Paul McLoughlin, Tel: 01232-251967

Regional Development Office

Londonderry House, 21 Chichester Street, Belfast BT1 4JB

Tel: 01232-252500; Fax: 01232-252721

Funding total: £3 million, Department of the Environment, £3 million, International Fund for Ireland (1998/99)

Community Economic Regeneration Schemes (CERS)
Community Regeneration & Improvement Special Projects (CRISP)

CRISP and CERS form a package of funding which helps community and voluntary groups to regenerate areas that do not attract private sector investment. Groups should be established as limited companies.

CERS target towns with a population of over 10,000. They focus on areas of disadvantage to stimulate economic activity; provide retail and industrial facilities; reduce unemployment; and improve the environment. Funding is given for up to 80% of capital costs. The schemes give grants to community groups where there is:

- a clear need for an economic activity;
- reluctance by the private sector to invest;
- cross-community group ownership of facilities;
- an economically viable project.

CRISP targets disadvantaged small towns and villages with populations of under 10,000. It offers funding to community groups (up to 80%) and commercial property owners (up to 30%) mainly for refurbishment of derelict town centre property and improvements of public spaces. Priorities are to:

- stimulate local activity;
- develop partnerships of statutory/private and community sectors;
- improve business confidence to increase private investment;
- enhance the quality of public spaces and property in target areas;
- capacity building for community projects;
- involve the community in regeneration projects.

A total of eight projects were approved in 1997/98 ranging from £250,000 to £1,700,000 including:

Derrylin & District Development Association, workspace & service sites (£625,200);

Armoy Community Development, shops, community facilities & flats (£625,000);

Pomeroy Community Projects, for 'spruce-up' (£250,000).

CRISP & CERS fund up to 80% of the capital costs and some very limited revenue costs for up to two years.

Applications: Department of Environment and International Fund for Ireland officials help community organisations to identify projects and put forward applications.

Contact: Cliff Thompson, Tel: 01232-252721; Gary Gray, Tel: 01232-252711; E-mail: gary.gray.doe@nics.dove.uk

Powers: Social Need (Northern Ireland) Order 1986

Londonderry Regeneration Initiative

Londonderry Development Office, Orchard House, 40 Foyle Street, Londonderry BT48 6AT

Grant total:	£2.704 million (1998/99)
	£2.704 million (1997/98)

The Londonderry Regeneration Initiative was established in 1995. It is funded by the Department of the Environment (£1 million) with the remainder from the Western Health & Social Services Board, Western Education & Library Board, Local Enterprise Development Unit and the Training & Employment Agency. It supports the following:

- changing conditions in the designated disadvantaged areas of the City;
- equipping communities to respond to problems;

- encouraging partnerships between voluntary, community, private and public sectors;
- generating sustainable economic activity and employment;
- improving community health;
- complementing projects initiated by other regeneration agencies or funds.

Projects are given preference if they are innovative and multi agency, involve partnerships and encourage volunteering. Whilst areas of most disadvantage are targeted, the Initiative is flexible and also covers disadvantaged 'communities of interest' such as elderly people. Projects in less disadvantaged areas are considered on merit. Grants given in 1997/98 included:

Rosemount Primary School (£162,000);

Access to Business Information Project (£60,000);

BYTES Project (£50,000);

Partnership Carewest (£37,000);

Parent and Toddler Association (£24,000).

Applications: Applications can be made at any time with forms available from the above address. Refusal rates for grants are very low at only about 1%.

Contact: Ken Strong, Deputy Londonderry Development Officer,
Tel: 01504-319900; Fax: 01504-319700

Powers: Social Need (NI) Order 1986

Northern Ireland Environment & Heritage Service

**HQ & Corporate Affairs, Commonwealth House,
35 Castle Street, Belfast BT1 1GU**

**Tel: 01232-251477; Fax: 01232-546660
E-mail: ehs@nics.gov.uk**

The service was established as a 'next steps' executive agency of the Department of the Environment (NI) in 1996. This means that it concentrates on day to day operational responsibilities and on supporting work practices whilst policy and legislation remain with the department. The service is an adviser to the Heritage Lottery Fund and the EC LIFE programme.

Its three main areas of work are carried out in separately located offices.

Natural Heritage

> **Grant total:**   **£1,100,000 (1998/99)**
> **£1,314,000 (1997/98)**

Grants to voluntary bodies are made through the following schemes:

	1998/99	1997/98
Conservation grants (NGOs)	£370,000	£370,000
Access to countryside (NGOs)	£14,000	£14,000

The service sees its primary role as encouraging district councils and easing public access to the countryside. It also provides *grants to voluntary conservation organisations* for a wide range of initiatives: core funding, staff funding for specific projects, surveys, conferences and general interpretation with a conservation benefit. Grants are usually 50% of approved expenditure. Its priorities for grants are:

- action for biodiversity;
- community involvement;
- educational value;
- opportunities for increased enjoyment for the countryside.

Access grants to the countryside are paid to district councils for works on public rights of way and long distance routes. Grants can also be paid to other bodies where their scheme has endorsement from the district council. The service is also responsible for the administration of EC grants.

Since the early 1990s a *Schools Conservation Project Scheme* (maximum grant £500) has also been provided for schemes involving pupils and more recently grants to farmers to try to revive corncrake numbers under the *Corncrake Protection Scheme.*

Contact: Dr John Faulkner, Director of Natural Heritage
General enquiries: 01232-546530.

Built Heritage

> **Grant total:**   **£1,836,000 (1998/99)**
> **£2,218,000 (1997/98)**

Historic Buildings Grant is available towards repair and maintenance of 'certain eligible items which constitute the historic fabric of the building'. Generally, new works are not grant aided even if carried out in a sympathetic manner but grant may be paid when approved alterations replace previous inappropriate works. Grants towards professional consultancy fees (up to 75%) are also given. Although there is no statutory grading of listed buildings in Northern Ireland, rates of grant vary according to an internal grading system within the service.

Grants in 1998/99 were allocated in the following categories:
Private grants   £870,000
Local authority   £150,000
Historic churches   £288,000
Conservation Area   £528,000

Recent grants have included:
St Mark's Church, Belfast (£236,000);
Royal Belfast Academical Institution, Belfast (£14,830).

The grant system was under review and details were not available at time of going to print.

Contact: Dr Ann Hamlin, Director of Built Heritage, 5-33 Hill Street, Belfast BT1 2LA, Tel: 01232-235000; Fax: 01232-543111; E-mail: hmb.ehs@nics.gov.uk
General enquiries: 01232-543061.

Applications: Further information and grant application forms are available. Contact each of the main offices for the location of the relevant regional office. Further advice and support is available at this level.

Northern Ireland Housing Executive

The Housing Centre, 2 Adelaide Street, Belfast BT2 8PB

Tel: 01232-240 588; Fax: 01232-318008

Contact: Roy Cassidy, Development Divison, Grants Section

The Housing Executive (HE) aims to improve housing conditions throughout Northern Ireland. It assesses housing requirements, develops strategies to influence the housing market and targets programmes at areas of greatest need. HE's main grants programme is directed at the private sector with a total of £42 million available through the home improvements grant programme to owner occupiers, landlords, long leaseholders or tenants in 1998/99. However, the following grants were made to voluntary organisations in 1998/99:

FOLD Housing Trust and Shelter to provide assistance and advice to elderly or disabled grant applicants.

HE has been nominated as the energy conservation authority for Northern Ireland. A budget of £2.8 million in 1998/99 is available in grants to help those on benefits or over 60 years of age with draught proofing or loft insulation.

Powers: Housing (NI) Order 1992

Department of Finance & Personnel for Northern Ireland

The department's responsibilities include managing EC Structural Funds and the International Fund for Ireland. It also provides funding through the Central Community Relations Unit which in turn funds the Community Relations Council.

Central Community Relations Unit

20-24 Donegall Street, Belfast BT1 2GP

Tel: 01232-544524; Fax: 01232-544500

Grant total:	£5,530,000 (1998/99)
	£5,327,000 (1997/98)

The Central Community Relations Unit was established in 1987 and formulates and reviews government policies to address issues of equality and to improve community relations. The unit is only a small scale direct provider with the majority of its grants being administered by the Northern Ireland Community Relations Council which was awarded £2,500,000 in 1997/98 (see separate entry).

The following grants are made directly from the Unit:

Cultural Traditions
Grant total: £407,000 (1996/97)

Grants are made to support Irish language initiatives. A total of 9 grants were made in 1996/97 ranging from £196,800 to £2,800 including:
  Queen's University Belfast, Origins of Place Names Project (£196,800);
  Ultach Trust (£92,000);
  Lá (£25,250);
  European Bureau for Lesser Used Languages (NI Committee) (£7,600).

Community Reconciliation Bodies
Grant total: £251,000 (1996/97)

Preference for both the above grants is given to proposals that:
- develop cross-community contact;
- explore and increase understanding of cultural heritage and diversity;
- provide facilities accessible to all sectors of the community;
- increase knowledge about community division and effective interventions;
- provide employment opportunities especially in the arts and sports.

Grants are given for up to 90% of salary and 75% of other costs.

Contact: D Ritchie, Principal Officer, Tel: 01232-544511

Powers: Departments (Transfer of Functions) Order Northern Ireland 1990

Northern Ireland Community Relations Council

6 Murray Street, Belfast BT1 6DN

Tel: 01232-439953; Fax: 01232-235208
E-mail: info@community-relations.org.uk
Web site: http://dspace.dial.pipex.com/town/estate/yo13

Contact: Ray Mullen, Director of Communications

Grant total:	**£1,795,000 (1998/99)**

The Northern Ireland Community Relations Council was established in January 1990 as a charitable company. It aims to 'challenge sectarian divisions, promote cross-community contact and respect for cultural diversity'. It supports a wide range of groups involved in bringing about increased understanding and contact between Protestants and Catholic communities. Most of its funding comes from the Central Community Relations Unit of the Northern Ireland Department of Finance and Personnel, the remainder from the European Union.

The following grants are available:

Core-funding grant scheme
Grant total: £1.2 million (1998/99)

Core funding over three years is given to organisations of strategic importance in community relations or cultural traditions. Grants range from £5,000 to £180,000 a year with the majority in the £30,000 to £70,000 range. A total of 39 grants were awarded in 1997/98 including:

Comhchoiste Na Gaelige Aontroim Thuaidh – Irish language network;
Counteract, trade union anti-intimidation unit;
Foyle Women's Information Group;
N.Ireland Mixed Marriage Association;
Prison Arts Forum.

Deadline: 31st December for funding in the next year.

Contact: Michelle Cherry, Project Officer

Development Grant Scheme
Grant total: £30,000 (1998/99)

This scheme aims to improve community relations work through support to management, staff training, development plans and evaluation. Grants of up to £3,000 cover the costs of professional consultants, facilitators, administration and meeting costs.

Deadline: The committee meets every six weeks.

Contact: Elaine Rowan, Programme Director

Development Support Grant Scheme
Grant total: £25,000 (1998/99)

Grants are given to help groups with community relations objectives in applying for capital funding from the European Union's regional Development Fund (PSEP).

This may include a community relations audit, developing skills and fundraising strategies. Up to 75% of preliminary work costs are covered, to a maximum of £3,000.

Contact: Will Glendinning, Chief Executive

Inter-Community Grant Scheme
Grant total: £235,000 (1998/99)

Small grants (up to a maximum of £6,000) are given as seeding grants and to specific projects which aim to increase contact and understanding between people of different religions, political and ethnic traditions.

A total of 194 grants were awarded (mostly for up to £1,500) were made in 1997/98 including:
    Churches in Co-operation;
    Derry Family Project;
    Enniskillen Together;
    Indian Community Centre;
    Windsor Women's Centre.

Exclusions: Running costs and capital expenditure.

Deadline: The committee meets every six weeks.

Contact: Elaine Rowan, Programme Director

Cultural Diversity Grants
Grant total: £125,000 (1998/99)

These grants of up to £6,000 aim to encourage cultural confidence and an appreciation of diversity through a variety of forms from music and story-telling to history and literature. Projects **must** involve at least one of the following: "Expression; Education; Exploration; Encounter and Debate" and should not, however, be "exclusive or triumphalist".

A total of 101 grants were awarded in 1997/98. Previous grants included:
    Conradh na Gaeilge, towards the Celtic Festival of Samhain;
    Multi-Cultural Resource Centre, for their Food & Arts Festival;
    Sole Purpose Productions, for a touring play about marching;
    Tartaraghan Boys Brigade, for an exhibition on the horrors of WW1.

Most awards are for below £3,500.

Deadline: The committee meets five times a year. Applications for grants under £1,500 can be considered at any time.

Contact: Malcolm Scott, Project Officer

Other small grant schemes include: Media grants; Publication grants; Fellowships.

The Council also has responsibility for administering part of the European Union's Special Support Programme for Peace and Reconciliation in Northern Ireland. This is a major programme. For more information contact Mark Adair, Programme Director.

Applications: Forms, guidance notes and information are available from the Community Relations Information Centre, 21 College Square East, Belfast BT1 6DE, Tel: 01232-311881; Fax: 01232-244364.

DEPARTMENT OF HEALTH AND SOCIAL SERVICES (DHSS NI)

**Castle Buildings (C B),
Stormont, Belfast BT4 3PP**

Tel: 01232-520780; Fax: 01232-522799

**Dundonald House (D H),
Upper Newtownards Road,
Belfast BT4 3SF**

Tel: 01232-520500; Fax: 01232-524972

The department is responsible for: Health and Social Services; Social Security and Child Maintenance.

Voluntary Activity Development Branch (C B)

Grant total:	£5,566,700 (1997/98)
	£5,825,000 (1996/97)

Grants are made to voluntary organisations that provide similar services to any of the health or personal social services. Support is given to regional organisations whose services help the Department of Health and Social Services to further its

policy objectives as set out in the *Regional Strategy for Health and Social Wellbeing 1997-2002* and *Well into 2000*. These are:
- promoting health and social wellbeing;
- targeting health and social need;
- improving care in the community;
- improving acute care.

Core grants
Grant total: £4,660,800 (1997/98)
£4,720,900 (1996/97)

Grants are made towards: central organisational administration; training, information and other support to local groups; development work; representation; involving volunteers. Grants rarely exceed 75% of the estimated costs.

A total of 86 grants were made in 1997/98, ranging between £1,670 and £359,400, including:
    NI Council for Voluntary Action (£359,400);
    NI Pre-school Playgroup Association (£190,000);
    Disability Action (£119,440);
    Praxis (£64,100);
    Family Planning Association (NI) (£24,960);
    Belfast Unemployed Resource Centre (£19,680);
    British Fluoridation Society (£2,047).

Grants may be offered for a period of up to three years.

Exclusions: Core grants do not cover administration costs included in the price of contracted services.

Project grants
Grant total: £891,900 (1997/98)
£1,014,460 (1996/97)

Grants are made to projects that test innovative ideas or services, and reflect a clear need. Grants cover a maximum of 75% of the project's costs.

A total of 71 grants were made in 1997/98 ranging between £360 and £172,000 including:
    NI Volunteer Development Agency (£172,000);
    United Response (£39,250);
    Scottish Community Development Centre (£25,000);
    Away from Home and Safe (£10,500);
    Home-Start UK (£4,160);

National Lottery Research (£2,900);
Traveller Movement (NI) (£1,250).

Capital grants
Grant total: **£163,000 (1998/99)**
                 £14,000 (1997/98)
                 £89,600 (1996/97)

Capital grants are rarely made and do not normally exceed 50% of the costs except for the following: innovative projects; children's and young person's homes where grant is normally 75%; where there are anticipated savings to the statutory services.

Only one grant was made in 1997/98 compared to seven in 1996/97.
Harmony Community Trust (£14,000).

Applications: In 1998 the deadline for application was November. Guidance notes and separate application forms for revenue and capital grants, can be obtained from the Staff Officer at the above address, Tel: 01232-520505 direct line.

Contact: S T P Wilson, Tel: 01232-520780; Fax: 01232-522799

Powers: Children (NI) Order 1995 amended the Health and Personal Social Services (NI) Order 1972 to include services under the Children Order in the definition of personal social services

Child Care Strategy (C B)

The National Childcare Strategy has, as its name implies, the same objectives throughout the UK although its administration will vary between countries. In autumn 1998 it was understood that funding would derive from the DHSS, DENI and T & E Agency, but no further details were available.

Contact: Maureen Boyd, Tel: 01232-525051; Fax: 01232-524196

Community Volunteering Scheme

**Northern Ireland Volunteer Development Agency,
Annsgate House, 70-74 Ann Street, Belfast BT1 4EH**

Grant total:	£818,900 (1998/99)
	£810,000 (1997/98)
	£820,700 (1996/97)

The Community Volunteering Scheme is administered by the Northern Ireland Volunteer Development Agency (NIVDA) for the Voluntary Activity Development Branch of the DHSS. Grants are available to voluntary organisations that create volunteering opportunities primarily, but not exclusively, for the unemployed of all ages. Activities should be of community benefit and include: school clubs; befriending schemes; respite care; meals on wheels; environmental projects.

A total of 33 grants were made in 1998/99 ranging between £7,000 and £58,600 including:
  Voluntary Service Belfast (£58,600);
  NIACRO (£52,000);
  Conservation Volunteers NI (£50,100);
  Belfast Women's Aid (£21,300).

In addition, Managing Agency Grants are made to organisations which then provide small grants to locally based groups. A total of five grants were made in 1998/99 ranging between £7,000 and £60,900 including:
  Churches Voluntary Work Bureau (£60,900);
  Voluntary Service Belfast (£42,000);
  Newry Volunteer Bureau (£7,000).

Applications: At the time of going to press applications were invited between September and November, although applicants should check with the Agency as this may change. Application forms and guidance notes are available from NIVDA.

Contact: Paul Murray, Tel: 01232-236100

NB At the time of going to press a review was being undertaken the outcome of which *may* radically alter the scheme.

NORTHERN IRELAND OFFICE

Criminal Justice Service Division

Massey House, Stoney Road, Belfast BT4 3FX

Tel: 01232-527349; Fax: 01232-527359

> **Grant total:**   **£1,417,000 (1998/99)**

The division grant aids three voluntary organisations in the criminal justice field that meet its statutory objectives. Grants are reviewed every three years.

In 1998/99 grants were made to:
  Victim Support (NI) (£667,000);
  Northern Ireland Association for the Care and Resettlement of Offenders (NIACRO) (£447,000);
  EXTERN (£303,000).

Contacts: Mary Paterson – Victim Support; Tina Gambell – NIACRO, EXTERN; Tel: 01232-527612

Appendix 1

Other Key Funding Sources

Contents
The National Lottery
   Lottery Board Addresses
   New Opportunities Fund
   National Endowment for Science, Technology & the Arts (NESTA)
ENTRUST- Landfill Tax Credit Scheme

National Lottery Board Addresses

Arts Council of England
14 Great Peter Street, London SW1P 3NQ
Tel: 0171-312 0123; Fax: 0171-973 6590; Web site: www.artscouncil.org.uk

Scottish Arts Council
12 Manor Place, Edinburgh EH3 7DD
Tel: 0131-226 6051; Fax: 0131-225 9883; Web site: www.sac.org.uk

Arts Council of Wales
9 Museum Place, Cardiff CF1 3NX
Tel: 01222-376 500; Fax: 01222-221 447

Arts Council of Northern Ireland
MacNeice House, 77 Malone Road, Belfast BT9 6AQ
Tel: 01232-667 000; Fax: 01232-664 766

English Sports Council
16 Upper Woburn Place, London WC1 0QP
Tel: 0345-649 649; Fax: 0171-273 1768; Web site: www.english.sports.gov.uk

Scottish Sports Council
Caledonian House, South Gyle, Edinburgh EH12 9DQ
Tel: 0131-339 9000; Fax: 0131-317 7202

Sports Council for Wales
Sophia Gardens, Cardiff, South Glamorgan CF1 9SW
Tel: 01222-300 500; Fax: 01222-300 600

Sports Council for Northern Ireland
House of Sport, Upper Malone Road, Belfast BT9 5LA
Tel: 01232-382 222; Fax: 01232-383 822; Web site: www.sportscouncil-ni.org.uk

United Kingdom Sports Council
Walkden House, 3-10 Melton Street, London NW1 2EB
Tel: 0171-380 8000; Fax: 0171-380 8010

Heritage Lottery Fund
7 Holbein Place, London SW1W 8NR
Tel: 0171-591 6000; Fax: 0171-591 6001

Millennium Commission
Portland House, Stag Place, London SW1E 5EZ
Tel: 0171-880 2001; Fax: 0171-880 2000; Web site: www.millenium.gov

National Lottery Charities Board
St Vincent House, 16 Suffolk Street, London SW1Y 4NL
Tel: 0171-747 5300; Fax: 0171-747 5214; Web site: www.nlcb.org.uk

New Opportunities Fund

Dacre House, Dacre Street, London SW1H 0DH

Tel: 0171-222 3084; Fax: 0171-222 3085
E-mail: new.opportunities.fund.@dial.pipex.com

Contact: Stephen Dunmore, Acting Chief Executive

The New Opportunities Fund (NOF) was set up as a NDPB in July 1998. It was created along with the National Endowment for Science, Technology and the Arts (NESTA) as a sixth good cause from the Wednesday Lottery. It is responsible for distributing grants for health, education and environment initiatives determined by government.

Total UK funding for the next five years for NOF's first three initiatives (which do not include the environment) was announced in spring 1998:

Healthy Living Centres	£300 million
Out of school activities	£400 million
of which	
▪ Learning activities	£180 million
▪ Childcare	£200 million
▪ Integrated childcare/learning	£20 million

Information & Communications Technology	£300 million
of which	

- Teacher training   £230 million
- Librarian training   £20 million
- Content creation   £50 million

Resources will be allocated between England, Scotland, Wales and Northern Ireland "on a basis appropriate to each of the different initiatives".

The support to healthy living centres and out of school activities will be distributed on the basis of population size and weighted by deprivation factors.

The NOF board intends to consult on its draft bidding guidance for the three initiatives in autumn 1998 and start to inviting bids in early 1999.

In addition the government confirmed in autumn 1998 that the fund will receive *one third of all Lottery revenue allocated to good causes* **after 2001.**

Other new initiatives were also then announced:

Green Spaces and Sustainable Communities – grants to help communities to understand, improve and care for their natural and living environment.

Cancer Prevention, Detection, Treatment and Care – to build on local fundraising and help individuals and families to cope with the impact of cancer.

Community Access to Lifelong Learning – a step-change to bring adults to lifelong learning including IT learning centres for the University of Industry.

 # National Endowment for Science, Technology and the Arts (NESTA)

1st Floor, Gainsborough House, 34 Throgmorton Street, London EC2N 2ER

Tel: 0171-861 9670; Fax: 0171-861 9675

Contact: Jeremy Newton, Chief Executive

NESTA was announced with the People's Lottery White Paper (in summer 1997) and set up as a trust independent from government with a one-off endowment of £200 million in July 1998. Grants of around £10 million a year are expected to be made from the interest on its investments.

It will have three objectives:

- helping talented individuals to develop their full potential in the creative industries, science and technology;
- helping to turn creativity and ideas into products or services which are effectively protected;
- contributing to the advancement of public education about, and awareness and appreciation of, the creative industries, science and technology and new art forms and their contribution to the quality of life.

(UK) ENTRUST
(re Landfill Tax Credit Scheme)

Central Office, Suite 2, 5th Floor, Acre House, 2 Town Square, Sale, Cheshire M33 7WZ

Tel: 0161-610 1219; Fax: 0161-972 0055

Contact: Dr Richard Sills, Chief Executive

Landfill Tax contributions: £85 million (from January 1997 to mid July 1998), contrasting with £9 million in September 1997. The dramatic rise was caused by the end of the Landfill Tax year (which runs from end September to beginning March)

In 1996 the first green tax, the Landfill Tax, was introduced on waste disposal in landfill sites in the UK with the expectation that the industry will reassess and reduce waste and its associated problems. HM Customs & Excise will collect the tax at variable rates depending on the type of waste.

An ingenious additional notion means that up to 20% of landfill operators' tax liability may be diverted to environmental organisations. The idea is related to the need for companies to improve their environmental image and local relations. Companies get no direct cash benefit. Instead they are invited to support approved environmental organisations with the lure that for every £1 they so donate, £10 will be released from their tax liability up to a maximum credit of 20% of their annual liability.

ENTRUST is not a supplier of funds. Funding can only be obtained from a landfill operator who should be approached directly by an environmental body. However, environmental organisations have to meet criteria laid down in the Landfill Tax Regulations and be approved by ENTRUST the 'Regulator of Environmental Bodies under the Landfill Regulations' which is set up as a separate company limited by guarantee.

Approved work under this scheme includes:
- land reclamation for economic, social or environmental use;
- measures for pollution reduction;
- research into sustainable waste management;
- education on waste issues;
- provision of amenity facilities in the vicinity of a landfill site;
- reclamation and creation of wildlife habitats;
- restoration of buildings of architectural and heritage interest in the vicinity of a landfill site;
- provision of financial, administration and other services to environmental bodies.

'Vicinity' is being interpreted loosely, at about a 10 miles radius.

Once enrolled, environmental organisations, which must be non-profit distributing bodies, can spend the contributions they receive from landfill site operators on approved activities, including their running costs and the fees payable to the regulatory body (£100 in 1997). It is again emphasised that environmental bodies have to find their own landfill operator.

By mid July 1998, 871 approved organisations had been enrolled with, and 3,335 projects been approved by ENTRUST. Examples of approved work have included:

RSNC from ARC to expand its co-ordinatory work throughout the country by setting up and running a grant scheme for environmental projects (£3.5 million);

Environmental Council from Biffa Waste Services for 'Conservers at Work' - information programmes and events called Reduce, Reuse, Recycle in the Workplace to encourage employees to take initiatives (£25,000).

ENTRUST provides a list of recipients, but without information of the size of the funding involved. Organisations which have received funding include:
North West Environment Trust, for a landfill odour control study;
Kentish Stour Countryside Project, for improving public rights of way;
Global Balance Trust, for unused plant recycling;
Cory Environment Trust, Thurrock, for improvements to Grays Town Wharf;
The Wise Group Ltd, for environmental story telling challenge;
Somerton Community Association for green play areas.

Applications: A detailed application form is available from the above address including a supplementary one asking for information about all the associated trading partnerships.

Two information leaflets are available setting out the conditions.

A northern office was being set up in Glasgow at the end of 1997.

Landfill Tax Help Desk, HM Customs & Excise, Dobson House, Regent Centre, Gosforth, Newcastle-Upon-Tyne NE3 3PF; Helpline 0645-128484 (local call rate); Fax: 0145-129595.

Appendix 2

Better Regulation Taskforce – Access to Government Funding for the Voluntary Sector

The Taskforce published this report in July 1998. Its *Executive Summary* is reproduced since its findings point to key problems and possible solutions for the voluntary sector in its funding relationships with government departments.

The Better Regulation Task Force assessed the regulatory framework for government funding of the voluntary sector against its principles of good regulation: transparency, accountability, targeting, consistency and proportionality. An analysis of central government funding frameworks was carried out with the help of departments and in consultation with the sector. Recommendations are made to the central government. We urge departments to reflect these in their plans to implement the Government's Compact with the voluntary sector. We believe that many of our recommendations are equally valid in relation to Non-Departmental Public Bodies (NDPBs), Training and Enterprise Councils and local authorities in their respective roles as funders (not least by the rules imposed on them by central government), and to EU funding.

Whilst organisations in receipt of public funds must be accountable, meeting minimum standards of financial viability, this needs to be balanced against the other principles of good regulation. An overemphasis on accountability appears to be impacting particularly disproportionally on medium-sized voluntary organisations, stifling innovation and development, and on those working with certain vulnerable groups such as drug prevention. Ethnic minority voluntary sector groups, by virtue of their relative newness, may also be at a disadvantage in accessing funding.

This report seeks to promote a 'virtuous circle of funding' by highlighting good practice and making recommendations for improvements.

Recommendations for improving proportionality and targeting:

Funding rules should not concentrate on projects, nor prescribe purely output-related funding, but allow for capacity building within organisations.

Funding rules should allow risks to be balanced against wider policy objectives, and auditing requirements made proportionate to the risks involved.

Matching funding requirements should be prescriptive, but should be made proportionate to the size of the applicant organisation or project, and should allow matching to include the value of volunteer time, or help in kind.

Rules should allow co-operation in funding bids between groups serving particular client groups, or sharing an expertise across different organisations.

Recommendations for improving consistency:

Departments should work towards creating and using a single application form.

Departments should adopt more consistent payout terms. Subject to the organisations to meet a minimum standard of financial viability, we call for a presumption in favour of payment quarterly in advance. Funders should justify any alternative arrangements against the principles of good regulation, and agree them with the organisation concerned.

Departments should adopt a consistent approach to record-keeping requirements, for instance a standard length of time that management records need to be kept.

Departments should introduce standard thresholds below which there should be simplified accounting and audit requirements.

Recommendations for improving transparency:

A detailed, comprehensive, cross-departmental directory of grants should be made available on the Internet, together with a details of the criteria for access, the timetable for application and any support available for applicants.

Local authorities should co-operate in a similar exercise.

Funders should build more tie into funding cycles to allow networking organisations to play a part in disseminating information.

Funders should use a more transparent bidding process. This should publishing how much money is in the "pot" and giving feedback on failed applicants.

Departments should co-operate in adjusting the timing of grant applications to allow for better phasing of funding.

Good practice guides to support the Compact should be developed, and produced in formats which can apply equally to local authorities, NDPBs and to EU funding.

Appendix 3

How research for this guide was carried out

1. Contacts with officers handling grant programmes were made first by telephone then followed up by letter. The spoken introduction was very useful (except in a few notable cases) to ensure the appropriate officers were approached, to stimulate some interest in the work and to speed up the response rate. These contacts were found via:

- delegated Voluntary Sector Liaison Officers in each department and in Welsh, Scottish offices and Northern Ireland offices, supplied a list of contacts (not always current);
- divisional managers, unit heads, team leaders of policy areas where programmes were believed to occur and later on if certain areas of avtivity seemed under represented;
- finance officers in certain departments, particularly in Health and Home, where related work for the National Audit Office and the Regulatory Taskforce had been carried out;
- departmental information officers;
- major voluntary organisations with wide departmental funding.

2. Mailing of a brief pro forma/questionnaire; draft entries compiled and copy checked by respondents.

3. Publications used included: previous DSC guide; the 1994/95 Parliamentary Question; Welsh and Scottish Office guides to voluntary sector funding; DETR guide to voluntary sector funding; Civil Service Yearbook; Vachers; annual reports of agencies.

4. Web sites, particularly to check re Comprehensive Spending Review announcements.

Appendix 4

Using the Web

Up to date information on government policy and funding can be found on the Internet with some sites even containing downloadable application forms. Most central government departments and many non-departmental public bodies have a Web site. Although the quality of information and regularity of updates does vary, many contain recent press releases, transcripts of speeches and consultation papers.

Most government sites are linked, allowing the user to move easily from one department's site to another by clicking on an icon, instead of having to know the exact address. The following are good starting points and will have links to other sites:

www.open.gov.uk The government information service site provides an index of sites including departments, councils, NHS Trusts and non-departmental public bodies. These can be accessed directly by clicking on the name of the appropriate site.

www.coi.gov.uk The central office of information site for English departmental and non-departmental public bodies' press releases updated daily.

www.scotland.gov.uk The Scottish Office site.

www.cymru.gov.uk The Welsh Office site.

www.nio.gov.uk The Northern Ireland Office site.

If the exact address of a site is not known then it can be searched for by typing in a key word using a number of search facilities. Many sites include a search facility within them which can save surfing time. To return to a site without having to search or enter in the address every time, it can be book-marked and will form a list of favourite sites to click easily into. E-mail contacts for comments or questions are often incorporated in a site.

Most sites are now easy to use even for the Internet novice and can allow access to a wealth of up-to-date information which will only increase in the future.

Appendix 5

Main Guides to Government and the Civil Service

Civil Service Yearbook, now printed annually as a book and CD, most recent edition April 1988. ISBN 011 312 0931
Order from the Stationery Office, PO Box 276, London SW8 5DT
Tel: 0171-873 9090; Fax: 0171-873 8200
Price: £35.00, plus a mail order handling charge of £2.94

Vachers Parliamentary Companion, a reference book of Parliament, Departments of State, Senior civil servants and Public Offices. It is updated quarterly. Subscriptions Vacher Dod Publishing Limited, 113 High Street Berkhamsted, Herts HP4 2DJ (Tel: 01442-8761325; Fax: 01442-876133). Price: A6 – £30.00 pa; A5 – £35.00 pa. Also available from the Stationery Office.

Short Glossary

Non-Departmental Public Bodies – NDPB   This term is now widely used particularly by the Civil Service to cover a great range of governmental bodies, most of which were commonly referred to as 'quangos'. The following formal definition is taken from the Cabinet Office publication, *Public Bodies – 1995*.

"An NDPB is a body which has a role in the process of national government, but is not a government department or part of one, and which accordingly operates to a greater or lesser extent at arm's length from Ministers. NDPBs include:

- Executive agencies: These normally employ staff and have their own budget. In a few cases they exercise administrative or regulatory functions in their own name but are supported by staff supplied by the sponsoring department, e.g. bodies classified as public corporations for public expenditure control and national accounting purposes. The Prison Service is an executive agency of the Home Office.
- Advisory bodies: These are mainly set up by Ministers to advise them and their departments on matters within their sphere of interest. It also includes certain Royal Commissions. Generally, advisory NDPBs do not employ staff or incur expenditure on their own account.
- Tribunals: This group also includes bodies with licensing and appeal functions. It covers only bodies with jurisdiction in a specialised field of law. In general they are serviced by staff from the sponsoring department. There are two types

of tribunal system: standing tribunals which have a permanent membership, and others that are covered from panels so that the actual number of tribunals sitting varies.

- Others: These comprise the boards of visitors to penal establishments in Great Britain, and boards of visitors and visiting committees in Northern Ireland."

QUANGO A semi-public government financed administrative body whose members are appointed by the government; Qu(asi) A(utonomous) (N)on-(G)overnmental (O)rganisation

Other funding jargon

Many of the following terms are not found in contemporary English dictionaries but are common usage in any number of funding programme documents, funding reports and spoken exchanges between officers. The meaning of the words is often slightly skewed from its customary usage which leads to considerable lack of 'transparency' of understanding for the newcomer to these verbal games.

Every walk of life develops its own forms of jargon, sometimes as a convenient shorthand but more often just as a way of seeming one of the club or someone 'in the know'. Its effect can be to deter the newcomer and make them feel unconfident and ignorant. For instance the United Nations documents were the worst for wilful obscurity and 'complexifying' was the term used to signify that something was being clarified! Don't be hoodwinked or put off by words you don't understand, it's no failing. Just ask Can you explain in other words, please?

Added value/Additionality – activities supported by funding which are additional, more, over and above, those directly funded.

Benchmarks – a criterion by which to measure something; reference point.

Capacity building – assisting organisations to develop their resources, both human and physical, to be better able to meet their aims.

Complementarity – activities funded under different grant-aid programmes must complement each other and not duplicate provision, neither should they represent a divergent policy.

Exit strategy – not how to get out, but a plan, made in the early stage of developing a funded project, which sets out how the work will carry on after the start up funding has come to an end.

Leverage – strategic advantage; power or influence; the increased potential ability to raise money – the confidence that success with one funding source generates within other sources which are considering whether to fund.

Match funding – additional funding from separate funding sources to make up the total funding needed; sometimes, but not always, infers that the contributions are equal or 'match' in size.

Non-statutory grants – grants from sources other than government ie. charitable trusts and companies.

Outcomes / Outputs / Outturns – all refer to the results of a project; 'outcomes' is used in a more general sense whilst 'outputs' and 'outturns' are used about the measurable, quantifiable achievements of a project - the results of the 'inputs'. They are commonly used in manufacturing industries.

Pathfinder projects – recent jargon for pilot schemes to test approaches.

Pump-priming – support to a new initiative to get it going; long term funding to be secured elsewhere.

Targets – outputs agreed at the beginning of a grant or funding cycle which need to be met to qualify for further funding – the profile of groups identified as being in need.

Transparency – openness with information.

Subject Index

All the separate funding entries in the guide are listed in this index: each grant programme, individual grant or special initiative. The countries covered by the funding are shown in the bracketed abbreviations where 'E' is England, 'S' is Scotland, 'W' is Wales, 'NI' is Northern Ireland, and 'UK' is the United Kingdom.

The terms 'the disadvantaged' and 'social exclusion' are not included in the index. As broad umbrella terms they include most of the reasons for voluntary activity and the health, personal services and social welfare funding programmes are aimed at these concerns.

Alphabetical Index

UK and England

Scotland

342

Wales

Northern Ireland

More titles
from the DSC...

Major Trust Guides

A GUIDE TO THE MAJOR TRUSTS VOL.1 1999/2000

Luke FitzHerbert, Dominic Addison & Faisel Rahman

This, our flagship guide and biennial best-seller, gives the most detailed information on grant-making trusts anywhere in print. Volume 1 covers the top 300 UK trusts, which between them give over £1,000 million a year. Each entry provides recent grant information, contact details, exclusions, and applications advice. Many include independent and critical comment from our expert research team – up to six pages of information where necessary. Also included is a diary of trustee meetings so that applicants can target their applications successfully.

In short – this is *the* definitive guide to major charitable trust money.

"My admiration for this hardy publication continues to grow. It is the Good Trust Guide of trust directories; informative, campaigning, opinionated and well written." (Growthpoint)

"Essential for anyone contemplating a major fundraising campaign." (Museums Journal).

A4, c.296 pages, 7th edition, 1999.
ISBN 1 900360 38 1.........**£19.95**

A GUIDE TO THE MAJOR TRUSTS VOL.2 1997/98

Paul Brown & John Smyth

Volume 2 covers a further 700 trusts, each with a potential to make grants of at least £50,000. Together they cover £125 million – an increase of £30 million on the previous edition. Around 150 trusts are new to the Guide and 50 appear in print for the first time. Each entry gives a characteristically clear description of trusts' grant-making policies and practices. The guide provides full regional and subject indices for both volumes and also includes listings of Councils for Voluntary Service and Charities Information Bureaux. As the companion to Volume 1, this best-selling title completes the guide no charity can afford to be without.

"...concise and informative, giving the latest available essential details." (ACTAF)

A4, 302 pages, 3rd edition, 1997. ISBN 1 900360 13 6............**£18.95**

CD-ROM

THE CD-ROM TRUSTS GUIDE

Software development by FunderFinder

The definitive guide to major charitable trust-giving on an easy-to-use CD-ROM. Includes *A Guide to the Major Trusts Volumes 1 and 2*, as well as all four in our *Guides to Local Trusts* series.

This upgraded version includes a new facility for printing out trust information.

The CD-ROM combines all the valuable details for which our trust guides have become famous, together with a fast system for searching by geography and by trust interests. Users will be able to fill in their own notes for each entry and create a mail merge file with the fruits of their search.

The CD-ROM Trusts Guide is your quick and simple key to around £1 billion from over 2,500 trusts – at the affordable price that is DSC's hallmark. (Runs on Windows 3.1 or higher.)

THE CD-ROM
Trusts Guide

DIRECTORY OF SOCIAL CHANGE
Software development by FunderFinder

Single CD-ROM
£98.00 plus VAT = **£115.15**

SPECIAL OFFER For only **£10.00** plus £2.50 p&p, we will upgrade your existing CD to this new version. Simply return the first edition and tick the box on the order form.

Please note that this offer expires December 1998.

"...a confident and easy to use tool which can be mastered by even the most established technophobe."
Charity Magazine
on *The CD-ROM Trusts Guide*

Local Trusts Guides

A GUIDE TO LOCAL TRUSTS IN THE NORTH OF ENGLAND
Dave Casson

Are you looking for local trusts to support your organisation's activities in the North of England? Are you restricted to raising money locally? If so, this regional guide to the 'hidden' trust money is essential. With over 650 trusts – nearly half of which have never appeared in print before – it uncovers £32 million for the North of England. A must for any fundraiser.

A4, 206 pages, 1st edition, 1996.
ISBN 1 900360 03 9 ...... **£16.95**

A GUIDE TO LOCAL TRUSTS IN THE MIDLANDS
Dave Casson

If your organisation is seeking funds for projects in the Midlands, this local trust guide should be your first port of call. It lists over 500 charitable trusts – more than a third of those for the very first time – making it your key to £22 million for the Midlands.

A4, 174 pages, 1st edition, 1996.
ISBN 1 900360 04 7 ...... **£16.95**

A GUIDE TO LOCAL TRUSTS IN THE SOUTH OF ENGLAND
Dave Casson

Uncover more than 700 charitable trusts that support activities in the South of England – excluding London. This grant guide will help you access £35 million in charitable money for the South East and South West – more than a third of which has never before been detailed.

A4, 224 pages, 1st edition, 1996.
ISBN 1 900360 05 5 ...... **£16.95**

A GUIDE TO LOCAL TRUSTS IN LONDON
Karina Holly

A must for any fundraiser looking for charitable money to fund activities in Greater London. This title details around 270 trusts which concentrate their grant giving on organisations working in this area. Around a third of the entries appear in print for the very first time, and between them the trusts represent £40 million in grant money for London.

A4, 124 pages, 1st edition, 1996.
ISBN 1 900360 12 8 ...... **£14.95**

Company Giving

THE GUIDE TO UK COMPANY GIVING CD-ROM

Available in Spring 99

"Contains all the background information you need to target appropriate companies...an excellent source of advice."

Charity Talk

THE GUIDE TO UK COMPANY GIVING 1998

John Smyth, Paul Brown & Dave Casson

An essential Guide for all those seeking to raise money or other forms of support from companies. This title covers the key companies in greater depth than ever before.

It profiles over 550 companies who between them support charities to the tune of £300 million a year, including a massive £200 million in cash donations.

Each entry in the guide provides:

- contact details
- nature of company business
- financial statistics
- examples of typical grants
- areas or subjects not considered
- advice for applicants

It gives information on employee involvement and company charitable trusts, and provides a classification by company activity, within sector comparisons, and a subsidiaries index.

This title amalgamates two of our most successful books – *The Major Companies Guide* and *A Guide to Company Giving*.

A4, 368 pages, 1st edition, 1998.
ISBN 1 900360 23 3.........**£25.00**

"An invaluable book which will be an essential guide to all fundraisers working in the Corporate and Trust sectors."

Macmillan Cancer Relief

Journals

Who **is** this man?

TRUST MONITOR
Edited by Karina Holly

Packed with information on new and newly identified trusts, policy changes in the top 400 trusts, facts, figures and features. The only way to keep fully up-to-date with trust news and information. Published three times a year in March, July and November.

"I can honestly say that we have received a great deal of income from new trusts which have been highlighted in the various issues of Trust Monitor - sums which far exceed the cost of these superb publications. In fact, some of these trusts have become regular supporters. Trust Monitor is certainly value for money; no trust fundraiser can afford to be without it."
(The Mental Health Foundation)

ISSN 1369-4405 .... **£30.00** a year
SEE BELOW FOR SPECIAL OFFER

"Corporate Citizen is an invaluable tool and a key information source for all corporate fundraisers. None of us would be without it."
Cororate Fundraisers' Network

CORPORATE CITIZEN
Edited by Alison Benjamin

Employee volunteering, gifts in kind, and cause related marketing are some of the growing areas of corporate support as companies look for ways to develop staff and enhance their brand image and reputation. Packed full of news, comment and case studies on the latest developments in corporate community investment, this magazine keeps you up to date with the trends. It also produces the annual Corporate Citizen top 100 corporate donors to charity, the top 50 corporate fundraising charities and uncovers newly identified sources of corporate support. Published three times a year in January, May and September.

"After reading the magazine for the very first time I approached four of the new companies listed and had a remarkable response with a 50 per cent strike rate. "
(Association for International Cancer Research)

ISSN 1353-0100
£30 a year for voluntary groups
£55 for others

SPECIAL OFFER
to Voluntary Groups

Subscribe to both **Trust Monitor** and **Corporate Citizen** for the special price of **£50.**

Guides for Individuals

A GUIDE TO GRANTS FOR INDIVIDUALS IN NEED 1998/99
Sarah Harland

A new edition of one of our biggest sellers, this guide contains details of over 2,100 charities concerned with individual poverty, together giving a yearly total of £150 million. Many sources are listed for the first time. Any advice or charity worker, social worker or individual who has used this guide in the past will be able to vouch for its effectiveness as a reference tool.

"Invaluable for social workers, advisory agencies and individuals seeking to help anyone in need."
(Adviser Reviews)

A4, 352 pages, 6th edition, Autumn 1998.
ISBN 1 900360 32 2 ... **£18.95**

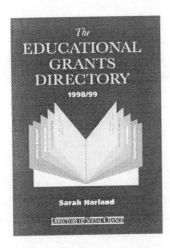

THE EDUCATIONAL GRANTS DIRECTORY 1998/99
Sarah Harland

The most comprehensive listing of educational charities which support children and students in need *up to first degree level*. This popular guide – now in a new edition – lists local charities and national and general sources of funds which give over £37 million in total in educational grants to individuals. An invaluable aid for teachers, education welfare officers, social workers and advisory agencies.

"An astonishing variety of sources of funding."
(Times Educational Supplement)

A4, 240 pages, 5th edition, Autumn 1998.
ISBN 1 900360 31 4 ... **£18.95**

"Very clear and easy to use. They have proved invaluable as a means for us to access funds for individuals." Sefton CVS